BOEING

Metamorphosis

LAUNCHING THE 737 AND 747,
1965–1969

John Fredrickson and John Andrew

SCHIFFER MILITARY

4880 Lower Valley Road   Atglen, PA 19310

Designed by Justin Watkinson
Cover design by Ashley Millhouse
Front and rear endsheet images courtesy of Francis Zera

Type set in Le Havre/Minion Pro/Univers LT Std

ISBN: 978-0-7643-6162-3
Printed in India

Published by Schiffer Publishing, Ltd.
4880 Lower Valley Road
Atglen, PA 19310
Phone: (610) 593-1777; Fax: (610) 593-2002
E-mail: Info@schifferbooks.com
Web: www.schifferbooks.com

For our complete selection of fine books on this and related subjects, please visit our website at www.schifferbooks.com. You may also write for a free catalog.

Schiffer Publishing's titles are available at special discounts for bulk purchases for sales promotions or premiums. Special editions, including personalized covers, corporate imprints, and excerpts, can be created in large quantities for special needs. For more information, contact the publisher.

We are always looking for people to write books on new and related subjects. If you have an idea for a book, please contact us at proposals@schifferbooks.com.

Contents

This view of the Renton waterfront factory is dated July 2019. The 737 final assembly buildings are where production support people work in offices adjoining the three automobile-style moving production lines. *Francis Zera Photo*

Acknowledgments

Reliance on Cold War weapons contracts awarded by a fickle Pentagon and then funded by an uncertain Congress was becoming problematic. Boeing was uniquely able to escape the dilemma during the 1960s by shifting its primary revenue source to commercial airliners. The result was good both for employees and shareholders—increased sales accompanied by greater stability.

With a passion for aviation history fueled by thirty-six years at Boeing between 1975 and 2011, author John Fredrickson was receptive to a collaborative effort with an insider who was a player during the metamorphosis of Boeing between 1965 and 1969. Separately, retired Boeing executive John Andrew was on his own quest to document not only his personal family history but also the changes underway at Boeing during that era. Only after retirement was there time to ponder a lifetime spent in the fast lane.

Mr. Andrew, formally educated at Gonzaga University as a civil engineer, hired into the Boeing facilities department in November 1955 after circumstances dictated withdrawal after a year at Harvard Business School. His resume was also rich in relevant blue-collar work experience. Despite the devastating loss of close friends to industrial accidents and the war in Korea, John Andrew became more and more convinced a top-notch education was essential to achieve his personal version of the American dream; therefore, his energies became evermore tightly focused on that goal. Along with his wife, Nancy; their daughter, Kathi; and their infant son, Jack, he took leave of absence, returned to Harvard, graduated with an MBA in 1959, and then opted to settle into a career at Boeing.

John Andrew was named chief of long-range business planning for Boeing Transport Division in 1960. In 1965, at age thirty-four, Mr. Andrew was placed in charge of creating a parts fabrication center at Auburn, expanding Plant II at Seattle, delivering a bigger final assembly building at Renton, and converting a rugged forest into a manufacturing site for wide-body aircraft at Everett.

Hence, a partnership was formed. John Fredrickson found the subject matter fascinating, educational, and historically significant. Fredrickson's role was to edit, organize, and perform research while seeking archival photographs. Their mutual goal was delivering a cohesive view of Boeing's transformation by melding reconstructed dialogue with history, as already documented, and then organizing it into a single volume.

Eric B. Williams, a nephew of John Andrew, is the Andrew family archivist who professionally scanned a large collection of photographs, working papers, and other graphics. Some of them appear within. Also, Jack Morris (of New Mexico) generously provided aircraft profile illustrations. Separately, Jewel L. Andrew was one of several proof readers, and their inputs were invaluable.

Boeing airplanes that depart Renton Airport will make their first landing at nearby Boeing Field. Like any other modern air terminal, the Seattle 737 Delivery Center now has TSA screening and departure gates. Employees demonstrate their pride with their own sticker.

The University of Washington Library (Special Collections) and Boeing Historical Archives graciously granted access to relevant source documents in their files. Unless otherwise identified, photographs and graphics were licensed by Boeing for this project. Copyright for them resides with the Boeing Company; however, other content within this book has not been underwritten, prepared, or approved by Boeing.

There were many bright and accomplished people at Boeing during this period and only a few of them are mentioned. Names, dates, and events are real. Observations are based on personal interactions and are never rendered with malevolent intent. Sadly, most people from this era are no longer with us, and we rue their passing. (Note: Any references in the text to "John," "I," or "me" always refer to Mr. John Andrew.)

Prologue

A brewery succeeds by making the best beer. A restaurant thrives by serving the finest meals. The key to market leadership is consistent high performance over the long haul. The Boeing Company survived as an industry leader for over a century in the exact same manner—by designing and building the finest and most-advanced aerospace products known to mankind.

Earning a modest profit is necessary for economic solvency, but it is the long tradition of advanced engineering, combined with excellence of manufacturing and customer support, that is central to Boeing. The consistent goals have been safety of flight, longer range, heavier payload, and better fuel efficiency per seat mile, along with reduced noise and emissions. Various lines of nontraditional products (ranging from hydrofoils to mass-transit railcars) have been attempted—but never very successfully.

The postwar quest for airliner market share was a dogfight of epic proportions. As with American automobile brands, the number of airplane builders began with many and then shrank to fewer. The worst shakeout was in the Great Depression. Each surviving aircraft builder prospered during World War II; however, the winnowing resumed at a slower pace after the wartime bonanza abruptly ended in August 1945.

A bevy of innovative airliner designs originated in Europe, and some of them penetrated the American market. The list of US builders included Boeing, Convair, Douglas, Fairchild, Lockheed, and Martin. Douglas airliners prevailed in the 1940s and 1950s, with 60 percent of world market share. Boeing tenaciously clawed its way to dominance because of grit, technological advancements (some adapted from military designs), aggressive marketing, and economic solvency bestowed by profitable aerospace and military programs.

Generations of bright men and women ranging from gifted engineers to skilled assemblers have committed themselves to mutual helpfulness, collaboration, and moving the Boeing Company forward during times when competing firms stumbled and then disappeared. An airplane either maintains adequate forward airspeed, or it stalls. As gravity overcomes lift, it will fall to the ground and crash. It is the same for an airplane company. An aerospace company either advances at the leading edge of technology, or it will stall, lose market share, and disappear. The industrial landscape is littered with the wreckage of bygone airplane builders. Once respected brand names including Berliner & Joyce, Atlantic Aircraft, Republic, Vultee, and others are fading from memory.

Boeing Field, May 1959. The Wichita-built B-52D in the foreground was assigned to dangerous low-level flight testing. The second airplane is the first KC-135, named *City of Renton*. The third airplane, a 707-320 Intercontinental, is pulling out of its stall to do fifth-engine testing (every 707 and 747 has a hard point inboard of engine #2 to ferry a spare engine).

In the high-stakes business of aerospace, a bad decision can send a company into a fatal nosedive. Many long-established US airlines suffered the same fate in the wake of the industry deregulation that began in 1977. Like the carcass of a dead animal that dies in the forest, any remnants with economic value (patents, people, plants, or product) make their way into the surviving companies.

The 1960s was a time of metamorphosis within the Boeing Company. Pentagon procurement awards were disappearing because important Air Force contracts were going to competitors. The customer base was shifting from military products to commercial airliners. Internal tensions were rising, thus yielding friction between the aerospace traditionalists and a cadre of gifted upstarts at Renton's Transport Division. A dire need was growing for new or expanded factories, laboratories, and offices to satisfy the surging demand for a family of jet-powered passenger planes.

More than simple airplanes or factories, this is a story of people working under stress. High-stakes business decisions marching toward resolution sometimes go unseen in the clutter of mundane daily events. Documenting the transformation of Boeing invokes a style that commingles aviation history with the attributes of a Harvard case study. The story provides an intimate view of the human drama, intrigue, and decision-making that play out within a Fortune 100 company. The result is a historically accurate account that invites the reader into the action via the masterful use of re-created dialogue.

The modern Boeing Company organizes and manages itself with numbers. Each building, floor, and location within a building is numbered. Models were traditionally assigned a number for internal purposes. Separately, each branch of the military formerly assigned their own designation. For instance, Boeing model 299 became B-17 to the Army Air Corps, while the Navy assigned its own designation. Secretary of Defense Robert McNamara dictated consistent designations starting in 1962.

The meanings of words and their usage shifts with the passage of time. The Army Air Corps became Army Air Forces in 1942. The US Air Force was created in 1947. The military airfield adjoining Fort Lewis was called McChord Field until then, and with a joint-operating agreement with the Army, that name is now restored.

Consistent with other programs, Boeing made an early decision that oversized parts for the 747 would arrive at the factory by rail. A connection was established in 1966 with the Great Northern (GN) Railway—which plied the most northern US transcontinental route between Lake Superior and Puget Sound. GN soon merged to become the Burlington Northern Railroad and was again rebranded as Burlington Northern Santa Fe (or BNSF).

The "Boeing Aero Products Company" of 1916 is now named "The Boeing Company." In 1955, the Renton-based branch was called "Transport Division." It next became "Boeing Commercial Airplane Group" (BCAG), which further evolved into "Boeing Commercial Airplanes" (or BCA). To this day, Group Offices for BCA remains in Renton, Washington—at the site of the former Longacres horse-racing track.

Acronyms, initialisms, slang, and jargon further clutter the lexicon. We strive for the usage that was typical at Boeing in the 1960s; however, words that some readers might find offensive have been changed. These substitutions are footnoted. The phrase "Industrial Age chivalry" was coined as a euphemism for fair dealings and ethical behavior in the aerospace industry.

Our story depicts the Boeing Company as it was over a half century ago. Working conditions and societal expectations evolve with the passage of time. Environmental laws and practices are now more rigorous. The once-ubiquitous workplace use of tobacco products has abated. The term "white collar" was used because office workers dressed more formally than today. Furthermore, an honest assessment of the 1960s Boeing workforce reveals a demographic inconsistent with today's expectations regarding diversity.

Like a hospital delivery ward, various new airplanes were in simultaneous incubation during early 1965. Boeing was bidding on a C-5A cargo plane for the Air Force. Conceptual design work for model 737 and a still-hypothetical 747 was underway. A government subsidized Supersonic Transport (acronym SST) was generating excitement; however, only two of these projects (737 and 747) would survive beyond mockup. But even the dainty 737, teamed with its oversized sibling (the 747), generated demand for labor, engineering, and new factory space unseen since the ramp-up to World War II.

The year 1965 found Boeing Commercial with five million square feet of productive aircraft plant. Under John Andrew's watch, it grew to 22.5 million square feet just five years later. Previous "greenfields" at Auburn, Thompson Site, and Everett had been converted to manufacturing. Renton doubled in size, and Seattle Plant II was absorbed into Boeing Commercial. ("Greenfield" is a euphemism for an undeveloped manufacturing site.)

Now, over a half century later, John Andrew takes personal pride in these massive buildings. They are at the crux of the "critical mass" needed to deliver transport aircraft. The largest factory is at Everett. The roof is 115 feet (or ten stories) above the adjacent ramps, while sheltering over 100 acres from the weather. A parade of airliners destined for the airlines of the world roll out of the cavernous final-assembly bays and into the daylight beyond. A smattering of military variants is included in the mix.

If you visit, bring along a camera to the bluffs overlooking the airports at Renton or Everett. Lucky visitors might capture the excitement of a brand-new, factory-fresh airliner making its first flight.

CHAPTER 1
Mr. Boeing's Company

I was merely desirous of learning to fly.
—*William E. Boeing*

The Boeing Company celebrated its hundred-year anniversary on July 15, 2016. Mr. William E. Boeing's tenure was shorter than typical in an industry where careers routinely span thirty or forty years. Mr. Boeing founded his namesake company at age thirty-five and then abruptly departed the aviation industry at age fifty-three after Congress passed a dubious piece of jurisprudence called the Air Mail Act of 1934.

After a mere eighteen years at the helm, Mr. Boeing left behind a tradition of fair dealings, product excellence, his unique surname, and a short list of handpicked young people whom he had personally hired and then mentored. As the Great Depression gave way to the war years and the Cold War beyond, they became the leaders who skillfully guided the company on an enduring course.

No other member of the Boeing family ever assumed any significant management role within the company. Why did Mr. Boeing take early departure at age fifty-three? Bill Boeing was always tight lipped about such matters. Two theories abound—maybe it was always his plan to retire early. More likely, and in the common vernacular—he got mad and quit.

Let's rewind the story. Mr. William E. Boeing (1881–1956) was born into a wealthy Detroit banking family. His father, Wilhelm Boeing (1846–1890), was a German immigrant who married into money and skillfully grew it with profitable investments in midwestern timber and mining operations. Sadly, Wilhelm succumbed prematurely to influenza while on a business trip. Boeing's mother soon remarried after the untimely passing of her husband, but her primary focus was always the well-being of their son. Steeped in European culture at a Swiss boarding school, Bill Boeing's education continued with three years at Yale University.

William E. Boeing (*right*) launched an unprecedented string of aviation industry acquisitions in 1929. The list included famed engine builder Pratt & Whitney. Founder and lifelong president Frederick Rentschler (*left*) was then a staunch advocate of air-cooled radial engines but later embraced jet engines.

William E. Boeing was born into wealth but suffered the loss of his father at about age nine. The youngster eagerly poses with an impressive pair of salmon at Monterey, California. Salmon fishing in the pristine salt waters of Puget Sound became one of Mr. Boeing's lifelong passions.

William E. "Bill" Boeing was a young man driven to emulate the economic success of his deceased father. The western Washington timberland was deeded to him. A strong nationwide market for new housing in 1903 convinced William the time was right for lumbering, so he bade farewell to Yale and moved west. His mother managed the balance of the family fortune from her distant home.

Mr. Boeing matured into a large and imposing young man with round eyeglasses and mustache, who enjoyed an occasional drink with his evening meal. A scholarly manner, combined with carefully choosing his words, bestowed upon him the demeanor of a professor—especially in the Wild West frontier town of Seattle, where saloons and bawdy houses still catered to a coarse mix of barely literate transient sailors, longshoremen, and loggers. Instead, Boeing spent his leisure hours at the Rainier Club, where the elite citizens of Seattle gathered to socialize, smoke cigars, and talk of high-minded political matters or economic opportunities.

Bill Boeing became immediately and permanently smitten with airplanes while attending a pivotal air show in Los Angeles in 1910. That air show planted a seed that blossomed into eight separate Southern California airplane builders by World War II. Boeing purchased an airplane from legendary airplane builder Glenn L. Martin, who also taught him to fly.

Meanwhile, it was back at the Rainier Club where Bill Boeing found a kindred soul named Conrad Westervelt (1879–1956). Westervelt, another bachelor, was a Navy officer and a graduate of the Naval Academy at Annapolis and had an advanced degree in engineering from the prestigious Massachusetts Institute of Technology (MIT). Tucked away in this remote corner of the country, this cerebral pair debated the finer points of aircraft design and construction.

I think we could build a better one.
—*William E. Boeing*

As recommended by Conrad Westervelt, the first engineer hired by William E. Boeing was an aeronautical engineer named Wong Tsoo (sometimes written Tsu Wong), educated at Massachusetts Institute of Technology (MIT). Wong worked in Seattle but later returned to his native China and enjoyed a successful career there.

Westervelt performed the engineering and Boeing provided workspace, crew, funding, and business oversight. Lacking an airfield, the resulting two floatplanes were dubbed the B&W (for Boeing and Westervelt), flight tested on nearby Lake Union (where a hangar would later be constructed) and ultimately sold to a customer in New Zealand.

In 1910, Ed Heath was a Seattle entrepreneur saddled with the unfortunate combination of weak management skills and undercapitalization. Heath Shipyard built wooden boats at the Oxbow, a tidewater mud wallow on Harbor Island near Seattle's Elliot Bay. Mr. Heath entered into a boatbuilding contract with William E. Boeing to deliver a yacht. Mr. Boeing was then an unassuming recent transplant from the small, rain-sodden logging town of Hoquiam, on the Washington coast; however, William E. Boeing was no country bumpkin, freshly arrived in the big city.

In a demonstration of business savvy backed up by deep pockets, Mr. Boeing soon took custody of not only his pleasure craft, but also the entire boatyard. For ten dollars, and the assumption of Mr. Heath's debts, the shipyard was to become the first Boeing airplane factory—known as Plant I (Roman numeral, pronounced "Plant One") from 1916 to 1970. A

The Heath Boatyard became Boeing Plant 1 and the source of many historic aircraft (including model 314 Clipper and XB-47 Stratojet) until it was abandoned as a cost-cutting move in 1970.

woodworking facility was perfect because the earliest airplanes were wood framed and covered in fabric.

Local women with the dexterity to sew the aviation fabric were needed. The paint-like dope that stiffened the fabric was applied later. The long collaboration between the men and women of Boeing was underway. Spruce wood was highly sought after for early airplane models because it was tough and unlikely to split. Mr. Boeing had abundant spruce trees ready for harvest on his vast timberlands. Eventually, wood veneer (or plywood) came to replace doped cloth.

Milestone: July 15, 1916. William E. Boeing incorporated the Pacific Aero Products Company for $100,000 under the laws of the State of Washington.

Mr. Boeing bought 998 of the 1,000 shares of stock issued with the expectation that Westervelt would join him as business partner. It was not to be. War with Mexico was brewing. As an active-duty naval officer, Westervelt was ordered back to the East Coast, World War I soon intervened, and the two went their separate ways. Westervelt later demonstrated airplane-building acumen by commanding the Navy airplane factory at Philadelphia. Conrad Westervelt ultimately retired from the Navy as a captain.

Milestone: June 1917. Two young engineering graduates from the University of Washington (Seattle) are hired by Mr. Boeing. They are Claire Egtvedt and Philip G. Johnson. In the decades ahead, each will separately assume the presidency of the company.

Mr. Boeing was an inveterate dealmaker. His "deal" with the University of Washington was funding of a wind tunnel in exchange for enhancing the engineering curriculum. Furthermore, William Boeing hired two promising engineers from the graduating class of 1917—Philip G. Johnson (1894–1944) and Clairmont Egtvedt (1892–1975). They were bright local lads born into Scandinavian immigrant heritage who assumed important lifetime leadership roles within the company.

Military contracts kept the infant company busy during World War I, but the postwar era became a rollercoaster. Bill Boeing valued his entire crew and put them to work during the lean times building furniture. Any shortfall was bankrolled from his own pocket. He dabbled with hauling airmail and then passengers starting in 1919. Through a series of complicated events, this moneymaker became United Air Lines (now spelled United Airlines).

Until 1929, William Boeing managed his various business interests from an office at Second and Cherry Streets in downtown Seattle. The cash cow that funded his airplane hobby remained the logging operations in Grays Harbor County. He went to the plant only for important events such as rollouts. Otherwise, management was summoned downtown to attend business meetings.

Bill Boeing later established United Air Lines headquarters in Chicago. In collaboration with his uncle, Boeing worked remotely from Chicago during the period when his late mother's estate was being settled.

Milestone: June 1925. William McPherson Allen (1900–1985) graduated from Harvard Law School, moved to Seattle, and became a staff lawyer with the firm of Donworth, Todd, and Higgins, Mr. Boeing's outside law firm.

Young "Bill" Allen handled the merger paperwork that yielded United Air Lines, and he soon became William E. Boeing's attorney of choice. Mr. Boeing saw potential in the young man from Montana and personally mentored him in all aspects of the aviation business. Bill Allen was rewarded with a seat on the board of directors at the tender age of thirty in 1930.

It was in 1929 that Mr. Boeing got deadly serious about his aviation holdings, a rapidly growing consortium called United Aircraft and Transportation Company. A hobby had been transformed into a source of wealth, status, and prestige. Offices were moved from downtown into Plant I. Boeing went on a buying spree to acquire other successful aviation companies. Soon, the consortium extended nationwide. It included airlines, airframes, airplane engines, and propellers, plus various other parts and components. The dependable Pratt & Whitney air-cooled radial engines became another windfall for the Boeing cartel.

Bill Boeing catered both to civil transport and military markets. His interest in hauling the mail and passengers spawned several models (model 40, model 80, and model 247). Model 247 made its first flight on February 8, 1933. The first modern airliner was a ten-passenger, twin-engine monoplane of all-metal construction. The company had expectations this game-changer would sweep the market. Despite the worldwide Great Depression, Mr. Boeing's holdings were all prospering—primarily because of capable managers. Furthermore, public interest in everything associated with aviation grew in the wake of the 1927 solo nonstop crossing of the Atlantic by Charles Lindbergh.

Claire L. Egtvedt was elected president and general manager of Boeing Airplane Company on August 2, 1933. Philip G. Johnson became president of United Air Lines, while United Aircraft (Pratt & Whitney et al.) was under the capable leadership of Frederick Rentschler (1887–1956). William E. Boeing presided over the business empire of his own creation as chairman of the board. This was a time for self-actualization. Observers hinted that airmail and airline operations were more fascinating to Mr. Boeing than airframes or engines. He sponsored development of cockpit radios and other innovations to make air travel safer. A passion for business kept his creative mind fully occupied.

When needed, a private 125-foot yacht offered diversion. Alternatives included retreat into solitude or—with onboard crew and dining space for ten adults—an opulent place for entertaining visiting dignitaries. Besides business deals, Mr. Boeing harbored two other lifetime passions. Recreation came in the form of salmon fishing from his yacht or flying aboard the latest of his personal airplanes. One of them was a DC-5 from Douglas Aircraft. His personal and very capable pilot, Clayton Scott (1905–2006), was normally at the controls.

Marriage to Bertha came when Bill was age forty. By all reports, it was a happy and enduring relationship. Bertha (1891–1977) came into the marriage with children of her own and bore him a single son named William Boeing Jr. (1922–2015). Boeing junior played no role in any of his father's companies but became a successful real estate developer, noted philanthropist, and driving force behind Seattle's Museum of Flight.

The "New Deal" Becomes a Sour Deal

Newly elected president Franklin D. Roosevelt, his "New Dealers," and like-minded members of congress rolled into Washington, DC, in 1933 with an anti-big-business attitude and "trust busting" in mind. Famous industrialists such as Henry Ford and Alfred P. Sloan of General Motors came to despise Congress, Roosevelt, and his administration because of the Fair Labor Standards Act, National Labor Relations Act, and various other pro-union actions.

The newcomers began to look askance at Bill Boeing's economic juggernaut as a dangerous vertical monopoly. Maybe the refusal to sell modern model 247 airliners to TWA created distrust of the Boeing-run consortium. In any case, it was the prior handling of airmail contracts by Herbert Hoover's Republican administration that certainly roiled the political waters.

It was very early in 1934 when Senate investigator A. B. Patterson provided a list of thirty-eight wide-ranging questions to his companies. Mr. Boeing and his people failed to grasp the magnitude of the threat. North American Aviation, Inc., a competing aviation consortium, received the same interrogatory. Mr. Boeing was subpoenaed to a Senate hearing on February 6, 1934. The hearings began at 10:30 a.m. Unfortunately, C-SPAN was not yet invented to record this Senate hearing. On the basis of the transcript, it would have been riveting viewing as a tag team of progressive senators lead by future Supreme Court justice Hugo Black mercilessly grilled the introverted aviation mogul.

Senator Black was a seasoned prosecuting attorney. His technique was to persuade witnesses that he already had the facts and merely wanted confirmation for the record. Courteous, smiling, and puffing gravely on his cigar, Black set about to refresh their memories during the review, leading them to admissions that enabled him to conclude with damaging summaries of their testimony.

Abiding by the short response deadline, staffers within corporate headquarters did their best with the overly broad questions. A trap had been set. Maybe expecting a friendly reception, Boeing strode into the hearing unrehearsed and ill prepared to handle the grilling he was about to receive. The inquisitors were out to wreak havoc. No personal attorney was in attendance. Nobody could assist William E. Boeing because the venue was without provision for defense counsel who could interrupt or otherwise stall the proceedings. The inquisition dragged on for hours. Apparently, Mr. Boeing had previewed neither the questions nor the responses already in Senator Black's custody. Therefore, caught flatfooted, Bill Boeing frequently backtracked, stammered, and was portrayed as a knave.

The new law, a wrecking ball, was called the Air Mail Act of 1934. It ordered that manufacture of airframes, engines, and operation of airlines be under separate ownership. Mr. Boeing, an introverted but otherwise ultrapatriotic American, took umbrage with the ego-shattering legislation.

Milestone: On September 18, 1934, Mr. William E. Boeing resigned as chairman of the board, sold his stock, and left the airplane business to focus on his other investments.

His formidable aviation portfolio was completely liquidated.

During hard times, personal funds would no longer underwrite unprofitable operations. On September 28, 1934, United Aircraft and Transport Corporation was divided into three companies: United Aircraft Company (engines, propellers, and parts), Boeing Airplane Company (airframes), and United Air Lines. The high-water head count at the Boeing Airplane Company in 1934 was 1,768. As each of the three severed firms grew independently, each of them came to dominate their own marketplace in the decades that followed.

> I am retiring from active service in aircraft manufacturing and air transportation. The many forward projects now in the making will continue to keep me on the sidelines as a keen and interested observer.
>
> —William E. Boeing

William E. Boeing was rich by Depression-era standards; however, even after adjusting for inflation, his net worth was no match for current Seattle-area entrepreneurs, including Howard Schultz (Starbucks), Jeff Bezos (Amazon), and Microsoft founders Bill Gates and Paul Allen (1953–2018).

For its first fifty years, commencing in 1916, only Mr. Boeing or one of his handpicked trio of worthy disciples (Egtvedt, Johnson, and outside attorney William Allen) guided his company from the position of president. Recognizing their full potential, Mr. William E. Boeing had already molded them into professional managers.

Unlike Douglas Aircraft, McDonnell Aircraft, or Ford Motor Company, all obligations to the founding family were completely severed. Boeing executives were unencumbered by nepotism and could act solely as a fiduciary. Each of the trio, in turn, assumed command and steered Mr. Boeing's airplane company on a course ultimately yielding the world's largest aerospace company. Their collective impact on worldwide aviation (both military and civil) was profound.

Of course, the company was buffeted by external factors beyond its control, including wars and the economic morass of the Great Depression. Wood-framed airliners fell from public favor after a 1931 crash of a Fokker F-10 killed noted Notre Dame football legend Knute Rockne and others. The traveling public demanded metal aircraft like the pioneering Ford Tri-motor. A total of 199 were built from 1925 until 1933, when Ford ceased building aircraft (until World War II). Boeing responded in 1933 with the first "modern" airliner, the all-metal, low-wing monoplane, model 247.

Milestones: Notable First Flights	
Boeing 247 airliner	February 8, 1933
Douglas DC-2 airliner	May 11, 1934
Boeing 299 (B-17)	July 28, 1935
Boeing 314 (Pan Am Clipper)	June 7, 1938

A B-47 banks hard right to show off its incredibly clean lines. The white-painted undersurface reflects nuclear flash, while swept wings were first found on German Luftwaffe aircraft designs. Pod-mounted jet engines provide easy access and an increased measure of safety.

CHAPTER 2
Aluminum Overcast

Aeroplanes are your defense.
—William E. Boeing, ca. 1918

Airplanes became obsolete quickly prior to 1935 because of rapidly improving technology. The year 1935 proved to be pivotal, with the emergence of three important new designs that survived long enough to deliver significant wartime utility. At North American Aviation, it

Former automobile industry (Ford followed by General Motors) executive William Knudsen, performing military service as a lieutenant general, is escorted through the B-17 engine shop by Boeing president Philip G. Johnson in the dark days of April 1942. Knudsen was the personal emissary of President Franklin D. Roosevelt.

was the trainer plane that evolved into the AT-6 Texan. At Douglas, it was the DC-3 airliner, and at Boeing, it was model 299, also known as B-17 within the Air Corps.

Douglas Aircraft earned market dominance with the DC-3 (or C-47 Skytrain in military livery, where it excelled as a wartime transport aircraft). The larger Douglas DC-3 demonstrated clear airliner superiority, which truncated the expected lengthy production run of model 247 and prematurely doomed it to the scrap heap. The painful lesson was well remembered by the three future Boeing Company leaders—Philip G. Johnson, Claire Egtvedt, and William M. Allen.

A DC-3 variant designated B-18 Bolo won the 1935 bomber competition at Dayton, Ohio. Air Corps procurement logic became warped during the Great Depression, when

The most expensive US wartime weapons system was the Boeing B-29. Yes, it was even pricier than the Manhattan Project. Four large plants were dedicated to its production: Boeing at Renton, Washington; Martin at Omaha, Nebraska; Bell at Marietta, Georgia; and Boeing at Wichita, Kansas.

lower acquisition and operating costs outscored combat capability. Terrible news arrived from Dayton the afternoon of Wednesday, October 30, 1935. An Army aircrew crashed the only model 299 prototype because of human error (failure to remove the gust locks before flight). Boeing test pilot Les Tower, aboard as an observer, perished in the ensuing fire.

However, some officers within the Air Corps had the wisdom to see the potential of the Flying Fortress in aerial combat. An order for thirteen was placed. This was enough to trigger design refinements, expedite expansion of Plant II, and begin low-rate production. In fact, a preliminary batch of the bombers was in flight to Oahu (Hickam Field) on the fateful Sunday morning of December 7, 1941.

Meanwhile, the Douglas B-18 was later found to be woefully inadequate for wartime aerial combat and was instead consigned to coastal patrol, aircrew training, or light utility transport missions. In the dark days of April 1942, the same Franklin D. Roosevelt administration that had pilloried the founder eight years earlier now mustered the audacity to send an emissary (Lt. Gen. William Knudsen) to Seattle seeking more B-17 bombers—once shunned, but now desperately needed for the two-front global war.

The urgent needs of America at war halted work on airliner production in favor of heavy bombers. The patriotic people of Boeing responded by hiring a workforce consisting of 46 percent females,[1] and cranking up production at Plant II until fifteen to sixteen Flying Fortresses rolled forth daily. Other companies also built B-17s under license. When joined with Consolidated B-24 Liberators, P-51 Mustang escort fighters, and British Lancaster bombers, the wartime formations flying from England were so massive as to be called "aluminum overcast."

Concurrently, a bigger, faster, and deadlier Boeing bomber was in development. Conceived to avenge the attack on Pearl Harbor on December 7, 1941, it became the B-29 Superfortress. Pressurized and with the range to roam the stratosphere of the Pacific theater of operations, aircrews under command of Army Air Forces general Curtis LeMay incinerated Tokyo and other urban population centers on the home islands with firebombs. Japanese civilians paid a terrible price. A separate top-secret unit utilized their own B-29s to deliver two war-ending atomic bombs in August 1945. The cities of Hiroshima and Nagasaki each had their own "ground zero." The world was changed forever even as the towering radiation-spewing mushroom clouds dissipated.

For his role in the airmail contracts, the charismatic Philip G. Johnson took temporary exile in Canada after 1934 but made his way back to Seattle in 1939 to assume the presidency of the airplane company. Wartime was hard not only on the troops but also on the industrialists, who worked endless hours under incredible stress. Johnson died in September 1944 and was replaced a year later by outside attorney William M "Bill" Allen.

Postwar Era: 1946 to 1954

Commencing on September 1, 1945, Bill Allen's tenure was a time of unprecedented growth, innovation, and change. Allen pursued a course that ultimately transformed the Boeing Company, the US Air Force, and international civilian air transportation. Business travel was fostered by the spread of commerce between continents, while leisure travel (global tourism) fueled further economic growth, including theme parks, cruise ships, lodging,

Gen. Jimmy Doolittle, the heroic "Tokyo Raider," chats with interim Boeing president Claire Egtvedt on June 12, 1945. P. G. Johnson, Egtvedt, and Bill Allen were all mentored by William E. Boeing, the founder. These four men, each in turn, presided over Boeing Company operations for the fifty-two years from the firm's founding in 1916 until Bill Allen finally stood aside in 1968.

restaurants, and car rental companies. Except for a divisive labor union strike in 1948, it was an era at Boeing devoid of legal scandal or controversy worthy of headline-grabbing newspaper coverage. Any internal strife was managed and never spilled into public view.

The wartime workforce peaked at 78,400 in 1943.[2] January 1946 found Boeing nearly out of business, with a payroll consisting of 9,506 intrepid survivors of a Great Depression and the rigors of global warfare. Yet, there was very little work for them to do. Working at Boeing was like a rollercoaster ride.

Bill Allen[3] took inventory of the bleak situation. All the prewar designs were woefully obsolete by 1946; however, the most advanced bomber design of the war was the exclusive franchise of Boeing. Allen skillfully exploited the B-29's potential as variations spewed forth. Equipped with better engines, the updated version of the Superfortress was designated B-50.

Aerial refueling arose as a new military mission in response to the Pentagon's embrace of long-range bombing. Both the B-29 and B-50 were modified into aerial tankers. Adding a portly fuselage and flying boom to the aft created the KC-97, thus winning even more military business for Boeing.

The immediate postwar years found the model 377 Stratocruiser being offered to the airlines, but the life cycle of B-29 technology was short. Under Bill Allen's capable leadership, an expanding portfolio of military and aerospace proposals grew into major undertakings. Transports, jet bombers, and various missile projects were all on his agenda.

The world's ultimate bomber of 1944 hit a brick wall in Korea on October 23, 1951. The date became known as "Black Tuesday" after Soviet MiG-15 swept-wing jet fighters pounced upon and then sliced into the formations of B-29 propeller-driven bombers, sending too many of them flaming to the earth below. Piston power was proven obsolete. Henceforth, jet-powered aircraft would be essential for strategic warfare, with Boeing best suited to fill the void.

Curtis LeMay (1906–1990), the stone-faced, cigar-chomping bomber general of World War II fame, was assembling the most fearsome military force ever known to mankind. The Strategic Air Command (or SAC) ultimately consisted of fleets of long-range nuclear bombers, squadrons of tankers to further extend their reach, and a thousand Minuteman ICBMs secure in their hardened underground silos.

Curtis LeMay was the premier World War II bomber general, who later built the Strategic Air Command (SAC). SAC was the beneficiary of three iconic Boeing products: B-52 heavy bomber, KC-135 jet tanker, and Minuteman intercontinental ballistic missiles (ICBMs). The year 2021 finds all three of these systems still on the job.

The preponderance of the ultimate SAC arsenal was provided by Boeing. Throughout the Cold War and beyond, whether acting as prime or subcontractor, Boeing workers and their technology remained at the crux of America's premier military weapons.

It was a long, slow march, but the incremental aircraft innovations of World War II continued into the postwar era. Located within walking distance south of the Boeing headquarters building, the transonic wind tunnel was named for iconic test pilot (killed in the crash of a prototype B-29) Eddie Allen. This wind tunnel still exists and has been an invaluable research tool for nearly eighty years.

Wehrmacht Connection

Henry "Hap" Arnold was the general of Army Air Forces during wartime. Pentagon leadership reacted with alarm when the German Luftwaffe operated Messerschmitt Me 262 jets, which were 100 miles per hour faster than America's best escort fighter. With the war in the Pacific expected to drag on until 1947, and the festering ill will with the Russians, Arnold badly wanted a jet-powered medium bomber. No fewer than six companies were awarded contracts to build a flying prototype. With straight wings and jet engines randomly inserted, all the designs were terrible. Straight wings limited speed, and engines wrapped within the wings (or, even worse, sticking out of the fuselage) complicated access for servicing. Furthermore, the infant jet engines were unreliable, putting the aircraft in peril in event of fire or explosion.

George Schairer was a famed Boeing aerodynamicist who found engineering and wind tunnel data related to swept wings at Völkenrode, a secret Luftwaffe lab, in 1945. He first applied them to the pathfinding B-47.

The full extent of Germany's advances in aerospace technology was not fully appreciated until the end of the war in Europe. About this time, George S. Schairer, then staff engineer for aerodynamics and power plants at Boeing, was a member of Gen. Hap Arnold's original Scientific Advisory Group (SAG), established in November 1944. General Arnold decided to send the SAG to Europe to survey foreign developments.

George Schairer needed time away from work to clear his head. His Seattle bomber-developmental team was frustrated by the laws of physics. Every iteration of the new jet-powered bomber they were working on ran into a brick wall when tested in the wind tunnel. Schairer discussed sweepback with other SAG members while in transit to Germany. By the time the team reached Paris, Schairer was thinking sweepback might be the solution to the vexing dilemma of straight wing, high drag.

A week after arriving in Europe, just about VE-day, the group went to Braunschweig to interrogate German scientists at Luftwaffe chief Hermann Göring's aeronautical research institute (Völkenrode), so well hidden in the forest that it had never been bombed. During the first evening of their stay, Schairer went snooping in the library and discovered experimental evidence that appeared to be very significant. Their suspicions were confirmed when the group interrogated resident experts.

In his excitement, Schairer handwrote a seven-page letter back home to a colleague in Seattle. Schairer was concerned that military censors would intercept the letter, so he did two things: The first page described the pleasant circumstance of his temporary German accommodations, before diving into the meat of the matter. He also marked the envelope as "censored." The ruses worked. The important message was received, the design of future aircraft was refocused, and the original letter remains a prized artifact in the collection of Seattle's Museum of Flight.

Schairer and his team at Boeing reworked the model 450 (Air Force designation B-47) jet bomber drawings to incorporate not only a swept wing but also jet engines mounted in pods hung from pylons attached beneath the wings. Round-the-clock access to the transonic wind tunnel was vital to timely project success. Furthermore, the future of jet aircraft was established! Safety was enhanced because there was now a gap between the engines and wing in case of fire or explosion. Furthermore, inspection, servicing, or change-out of engines became much easier. Henceforth, pod-mounted jet engines attached to swept wings became the de facto worldwide standard for new aircraft designs.

Two prototype XB-47s were fabricated at Plant I and then barged to Plant II for final preflight preparations. Boeing test pilots Robert Robbins and Edward Scott Osler accomplished the maiden flight on December 17, 1947, when they ferried it over the snow-covered Cascade Range of mountains on a fifty-two-minute short hop from Boeing Field eastward to Moses Lake.

Milestone: In 1947, a fundamental concept of modern aircraft design debuted with the XB-47, which featured pod-mounted jet engines attached by pylons to swept wings.

Scott Osler died in a flight test accident on May 11, 1949. The canopy popped open and struck his head. The experimental aircraft survived the freak event unscathed. B-47 flight testing was reorganized and relocated to Wichita, Kansas. As part of the recovery plan, Alvin M. "Tex" Johnston, an experienced test pilot with swagger, was hired by Boeing to fill the void created by the XB-47 fatality.

To get the new design into SAC nuclear service quickly, high-rate production was established at Wichita, and the balance were assembled under license from Boeing by Douglas at Tulsa and Lockheed at Marietta. Production ended with 2,032 units built. The legendary B-52 Stratofortress, akin to a B-47 on steroids, was close behind, with Seattle-based production starting in 1952.

Bill Allen took a flight at Wichita in a B-47 Stratojet and was amazed by the speed, altitude, and lack of vibration. As an aviation visionary, the flight transformed his thinking—especially after the long and agonizingly slow flight back to Seattle aboard a DC-6. "Flight aboard turbine-powered transport aircraft should be readily available to every person," he concluded, but by 1952, Bill Allen became frustrated by the lack of interest either by the military or the airlines in a big transport jet.

Lacking computers, industrial engineers at Wichita lay out their factory for B-47 manufacturing in 1948. The B-47 profile appears modern, even today.

The airlines professed happiness with their old-style, straight-wing, prop planes from Douglas or Lockheed—especially after the jet-powered British de Havilland Comet demonstrated a repeated propensity to break apart at altitude for no apparent reason—thus killing everybody aboard. The culprit was later determined to be metal-fatigue-induced cracks at the square corners of the cabin windows. When at altitude and under pressurization, each instance of structural failure triggered a catastrophic fuselage explosion.

Building eight hundred propeller-driven tankers, designated KC-97, kept the Renton factory busy. A major part of their mission was refueling the B-47 fleet—but the speed differential created a Rube Goldberg situation during every refueling. Often, the tanker entered a shallow dive at 30,000 feet, and then the flying boom was connected to the receiver B-47—which, despite the speed gained in the descent, was close to stalling. If all went well, refueling was complete when passing 25,000 feet.

Air Force leadership was lethargic and seemed oblivious to the obvious: the KC-97 lacked the speed, capacity, and reach to accompany the far-ranging fleets of thirstier B-52s lurking on the horizon. It was Bill Allen who recognized the dire need for something better. The gambling gene within Allen convinced him to set caution aside with a well-calculated $16 million bet (the net worth of the company) on an unproven conceptual design called the model 367-80 (or "Dash 80," using internal Boeing lingo). Allen acted on his intuition, and his hunch was vindicated. The Dash 80 was a prototype aircraft and engineering test article never intended for sale.

With improved engines and a larger fuselage, the investment in B-29 technology saved postwar Boeing from economic insolvency. While commercial airliner sales of model 377 were a paltry fifty-six units, combined military sales were about 1,258 units—enough to stabilize Boeing manufacturing operations.

The cargo-hauling model 367 was designated C-97 by the Air Force. C-97 tooling was used to fabricate the fuselage. There was no other common thread with the B-29 family. The balance of the airplane was fabricated without benefit of production-quality tooling.

The 35-degree swept-wing design was borrowed from the B-47 and B-52 bombers—but stiffer, with dihedral (upward slope) thrown in. Equally important, unlike passing the wing spars above the payload-bearing bomb bay, the wings of a transport aircraft are attached lower, thus allowing concealment of vital structure beneath the aircraft's main deck. On all Boeing models, the center-wing structure is known as section 11. Its great design strength keeps wings and fuselage securely attached, normally for the entire life of the aircraft. Furthermore, not one square inch of space is wasted, because section 11 supplements the wing bladders as a primary fuel tank.

The internal designator of 367-80 was a ruse to maintain secrecy. Anybody overhearing a loose-lipped engineer, boasting in a barroom setting, would tune out the chatter. Machinists and quality assurance inspectors in the back shops would have no inkling about the true purpose of parts or assemblies undergoing fabrication. The area where the unique aircraft took shape was hidden behind temporary partitions to conceal it from prying eyes.

Bill Allen invited Bertha Boeing to christen the Dash 80 at 4:00 p.m. on May 14, 1954. A week later, the landing gear collapsed during taxi tests, and the big jet was returned to the factory. Two very successful models derived from this prototype: model 707 (commercial) and the Air Force KC-135 jet tanker.

Milestone: The Boeing jet transport prototype, dubbed Dash 80, first flew on July 15, 1954. It is now a historic artifact on display within the Smithsonian's Udvar-Hazy hangar at Dulles Airport.

With preliminary testing successfully accomplished, the prototype then demonstrated to the airlines, Air Force, press, and public the awesome potential of a large jet tanker/transport. The strategy worked. On August 5, 1954, the Air Force announced a change of heart. It ordered a "small number" of the Boeing jet tanker/transports. Work on model 717 (Air Force designation KC-135) began on September 1, 1954. A Boeing test pilot predicted, "It will be the best-liked airplane within the Air Force."

Seven being a lucky number, and within the tradition of bygone models 247 and 307, the airliner version would be marketed as the Boeing 707; however, the FAA was caught unprepared. Bureaucratic regulatory alarm bells rang out. The announcement of a US-built jetliner focused attention on the urgent need for a certification process specific to civilian jet transport aircraft. The Federal Aviation Authority (FAA), in full collaboration with the Boeing Company, set about to invent a rigorous methodology, especially in the wake of the vexing losses of British de Havilland Comet airliners.

An elderly Bill Boeing chats with their host, company president Bill Allen, at the Dash 80 rollout. The first flight on July 15, 1954, was from Renton Airport to Boeing Field. "Tex" Johnston (pilot) and "Dix" Loesch were at the controls for the flight of one-hour-and-twenty-four-minute duration.

The goal of flight testing is earning a one-page document called a "type certificate." It is the prerequisite for a new type of airliner entering revenue service. Bearing the signature of the cognizant federal official, it can either be framed, hung on the wall, or filed away.

At least one airframe is sacrificed to destructive testing. The airframe is secured into a structural steel frame attached to railroad track embedded in 3 feet of poured concrete. Then, the wings are bent to breaking by a bevy of powerful hydraulic rams. A typical failure under load might be expressed as 154 percent of design strength. In the wake of the Comet tragedies, fuselage integrity received special attention. For model 707, thousands of pressurization cycles were performed. Heavy steel guillotines sliced into fuselages under full pressurization to demonstrate the rip-stopping capability of the circular structure. Some of the testing was performed underwater in large tanks.

Normally, the remainder of the test fleet consists of four to seven airplanes pulled directly from the production line and then subjected to certification testing. With special instrumentation installed, some of it is accomplished aloft. The regime includes high angle-of-attack maneuvers ending in stalls, wind-up turns, sideslips, step climbs, dives, various asymmetric configurations, shifting the center of gravity, engine-out performance, and many other conditions a typical passenger will never witness. Ground testing includes overheating the brakes (called "refused takeoff," or RTO), water ingestion, overrotations, evacuations, extreme weather, and more. Every test condition is scripted, performed, evaluated, and documented by multiple means, including narrative gleaned from interviews, instrumentation, data charting, and photography.

Mr. Boeing Passes

William E. Boeing enjoyed a long and productive life. Just two days prior to his seventy-fifth birthday, on September 28, 1956, while on a salmon-fishing trip aboard his yacht, the *Taconite*, Bill Boeing succumbed to an apparent heart attack. Taconite is a form of concentrated iron ore.

Mr. Boeing owned a series of personal yachts, each named *Taconite*. In addition to crew quarters, sleeping space for ten passengers was provided in five staterooms. Separately, the Boeing Commercial Airplane (BCA) sales departments operated a Canadian-based yacht christened *Daedalus* for purposes of business entertainment.

It was speculation in timberland and Minnesota iron ore mineral rights that fueled the original Boeing family fortune. The remains of William E. Boeing were cremated, and his ashes were strewn into the briny Canadian waters at the locations where he loved to fish for wild salmon.

The man died, but his legacy lives on.[4] Originally the obscure anglicized surname of an ambitious German immigrant, "Boeing" is now a worldwide brand name. Consisting of only six letters, the name was never an acronym. More importantly, the values instilled by the founder span over a century. Imprinted onto his apprentice, Bill Allen, were the business goals, values, and decision-making skills that played out from 1965 to 1969. These actions created the Boeing Company of today: America's primary builder of large transport aircraft, the nation's largest exporter, a source of advanced weaponry, and other (more peaceful) aerospace products.

CHAPTER 3
B-52 Factory

Hardened by the Depression, yet enjoying the benefit of two caring parents, and too short to make the high school basketball squad—John Andrew instead turned out for the varsity football team. Many of the other adolescent tough guys then living nearby eschewed academic excellence. At a mere 153 pounds, and via pure grit, he claimed a starting position on both the offensive and defensive lines. The other players knew John was a straight-"A" student but ignored it as another instance of hard luck.

John Andrew contracted two life-threatening diseases: rheumatic fever as a teen and a bout with young-adult-onset polio. He caught polio in the mid-1950s, at about the same time Jonah Salk's vaccine came to market. The dreaded virus rendered him seriously weakened for eighteen months while also permanently damaging his vocal cords. Nancy hung with John and nursed him back to health during this difficult period.

Broke, and badly in need of a job, accidentally stumbling upon the Boeing hiring hall in downtown Seattle in November 1955 launched John Andrew on a lifetime career. Like others, he found Boeing to be a place where hard work, tenacity, and dedication were rewarded with mental challenge, a sense of accomplishment, and a modicum of esteem. Mr. John Andrew's story is best shared in his own words.

On the Highway, East of Boise

After a year at Harvard Business School, multiple unfortunate circumstances dictated that I withdraw, at least temporarily. My wife, Nancy, and I were together in the automobile and nearing our goal—Boise, Idaho. Boise was the world headquarters of Morrison-Knudsen (abbreviated M-K), the world's largest construction company. With roots in the West, a background in construction, and a civil engineering degree from Gonzaga University of Spokane, I was well qualified at age twenty-four for a variety of positions.

It was the autumn of 1955 and the weather was getting cooler. The road was straight and fast. I wanted to arrive by noon, apply for work, and start the following day. The letter in my pocket was from my former M-K boss, Whitey Davis, who wrote I'd done excellent work and left the company in good standing.

It was probably naive to think there'd be a job waiting in Boise. At the time, I didn't know what a formal résumé was—even after spending a year at Harvard Business School. Harvard's well-tested approach to résumé writing and job hunting was not addressed in the first year.

A degree in civil engineering from Gonzaga University combined with an eclectic mix of blue-collar jobs perfectly prepared John Andrew for the challenges that awaited him at Boeing. He is seen as a window washer in Spokane. Dangling high above the street merited premium pay. *John Andrew collection*

My enthusiasm about M-K's line of work was palpable—dam building, tunnel driving, and massive reclamation projects that brought flood control, irrigation, and electric power to huge portions of the world; however, I was on my own to storm the walls of the largest construction company, and it was in the only way I'd ever done it. You just show up, ask for a job, and then go to work. I had worked at the Hungry Horse Dam on the Flathead River in Montana and was certain that experience would help me reenter M-K.

The personnel representative briefly listened to my request but seemed uninterested: "We're not hiring young engineers at this time," he said. "We did that last spring when we hired our annual quota."

News accounts had mentioned a big project in America's northernmost territory. "How about work in Alaska?" I countered. As soon as I mentioned Alaska, he became more encouraging, "Yes, there might be an opening there," he said, "You need to go to Seattle and talk to Ole Strandberg." All I had from the long journey was an address and phone number. I needed work fast. We were running out of money. Nancy stayed with family in Montana.

I arrived in Seattle alone and bunked with relatives for the night. The next morning, I met with Ole downtown and was informed that operations in Alaska were shutting down for the winter, but he was eager for me to return in the spring. I continued up Second Avenue absent-mindedly looking in shop windows, trying to plot my next move while slowly strolling about. Within six blocks I stumbled upon a storefront bearing a sign reading, "Arcade Building, Boeing Employment."

I never considered working for Boeing, because so many acquaintances had cycled through ten years before, during World War II. Almost universally, they described Boeing in terms of mass production, mass hiring, and mass layoffs. Boeing was newsworthy, with big bombers in production and a prototype jet transport flying. Anyone with eyes and ears saw the gleam of aluminum overhead and listened to the thunder of military jet bombers and thought "Boeing."

The Boeing Plant II complex as it appeared in 1953. The World War II–era cafeteria is on the right with a curved roof. The headquarters building (numbered 2-24) is to its left. The Union Pacific railroad spur runs parallel with old Highway 99. Annex A is on the top left (southeast) corner.

The permanent nature of the Cold War and its long-term impact on the military-industrial complex had not yet caught the attention of the academics at the Harvard Business School. I had recently studied five hundred cases out of their stable of two thousand current business cases. Not one case involved the huge defense industry. Instead, cases were heavy on automobiles, textiles, railroads, hotels, retail, banking, and Wall Street. Harvard professors prided themselves on their ability to spot trends and predict the future. One of the biggest gorillas of the American economy, aerospace, had been strangely "not present" at the famed business school. This lack of awareness became more evident to me after joining Boeing.

With little understanding of what lay ahead, I joined the crowd of job seekers in the Arcade Building's reception lobby. Their clothing told me nearly all were applying for factory work or clerical jobs. The women looked classier than the men. Attired in a dark-gray suit, white shirt, and narrow red tie, I was well clad for an East Coast professional position. In laid-back Seattle, my clothing was making me stand out. I felt awkward, conspicuous, and out of place.

I spied a stack of blank application forms, picked one up, went to a high counter at the back of the room, and quickly filled it out. When finished, I took my place at the end of a long line. Being the first week of November, the casual conversation among those in line gave me the impression that most of the applicants were loggers, fishermen, or harvest hands hoping to "winter in" at Boeing. Despite my professional attire, I was there for the same reason.

I watched carefully as persons ahead of me handed their application to a female screener standing behind a counter. After two or three quick questions, a shake of her head meant "no jobs today," sending the disappointed person out the door. A nod of her head sent other applicants to seats in a waiting area for further screening. A man ahead of me had bragged about how good he was—at what I couldn't tell. He got a shake of the screener's head and left with a low curse. He added, "I didn't want to work for this tinhorn outfit anyway!"

I handed my application across the counter, not knowing whether it would yield a shake or a nod. The woman looked at my application, hesitated, frowned, and eyed me in puzzlement. I didn't know if she saw a problem with my long list of former employers. I didn't realize that Boeing had long since wrung the Seattle market dry for engineers and scientists. A degreed engineer, walking in off the street, and the word "Harvard" was unusual. Boeing's professional recruitment took place at colleges and universities in other cities where Boeing placed ads in local papers. Recruiters scheduled appointments and accepted applications.

The screener motioned me to follow her to another room, where she handed my application to a secretary who, after inviting me to sit, passed my paperwork to a man in a glass-windowed enclosure behind her desk. His eyes scanned the application for about thirty seconds. He buzzed the secretary, who escorted me in. After a couple of introductory greetings, he asked, "Do you have your birth certificate with you?"

"Yes," I answered.

"Good, that's proof of citizenship. We have a company bus leaving for Plant II [pronounced "Plant Two"] in five minutes. John Gladding will meet you at the main gate and escort you to the Facilities Department for an interview." He handed me a folder containing my application papers, a temporary pass, and a contact sheet—if I missed Gladding.

The bus dropped me at the main gate about 5 miles south of downtown Seattle. I hardly had time to get my bearings and assess the surroundings before I met Gladding, who turned out to be a personnel clerk. He escorted me through a noisy factory filled with almost

2.40 BUILDING

Ⓝ1956

B-52C PRODUCTION   P 17245

This bulletin board display was intended to brief important visitors on the layout of the B-52 final assembly area in Plant II. A parallel assembly line was established at Wichita, Kansas, and then Seattle production ceased.

complete B-52D Stratofortress bombers. The close-up view startled me. Eight jet engines hanging on pylons attached to the long flexible wings made the wing tips droop almost to the concrete floor. It took small outrigger wheels to balance the behemoth.

We proceeded across a busy alleyway to a large one-floor warehouse sided with gray corrugated sheet metal. The warehouse had been converted to office space by hanging row upon row of fluorescent lights from the bare roof deck overhead. The floor was covered with dark asphalt tile. Long corridors of high partitions hid most of the activity. Upon entering, I did not realize that the warehouse housed nearly two thousand white-collar workers.

Gladding led me to a bay where about two hundred human sardines bent over a sea of drafting boards. The horrors I'd heard about Boeing were confirmed instantly. Nevertheless, I was prepared to work in hell, if it meant a paycheck. I interviewed quickly with a man named Kimbrough and another man named Haselwood, who sat at desks in front of the drafting boards. I had no idea about what they did, except something about civil-structural work, dealing with factories and airfields.

Haselwood, a large, middle-aged, balding man who lisped through a mustache, brightened when he noted "Harvard" on my résumé. "I have a masters from Harvard myself—in soils engineering—got it before the war" (Harvard pioneered geotechnical engineering in the 1930s).

After no more than twenty minutes, I was ushered back to Gladding's office. "We evaluated your qualifications," he said, puffing with importance. "You qualify as a junior-B facilities engineer. The rate is $88.00 for a forty-hour week. That's all we can do."

I thought a minute. For tunnel work, I was paid $96.00 for forty-eight hours, including Saturday, which comes to $2.00 per hour. I quickly did the math and realized that Boeing paid $2.20 per hour. More per hour, less per week. I didn't like the $8.00 reduction in take-home pay. "That's less than I was making previously. Can you go a little higher?"

"The salary's right for beginning engineers with no design experience" was the reply.

"Okay, as long as you say that's what Boeing pays others," I concluded.

"I'll escort you back to the bus. They'll sign you up downtown. We need you as soon as they process the paperwork. You'll work in Haselwood's group," said Gladding.

Back in the Arcade Building, I met with the same man who sent me to the Facilities Department. As I signed the formal papers, I asked why he hadn't sent me to interview for aircraft structural design, considering my excellent college grades in structure, or to the financial area, considering my year at the Harvard Business School.

"The Finance Department doesn't pay engineering rates," he said, "and I don't have a requisition from the Aircraft Structures Unit today. Besides, your work experience is a better fit in Facilities."

With more time and less desperation, I'd have argued the point. I felt I was being placed into a second-rate department without consideration of my academic strengths. In any case, my old formula had worked again: show up, ask for a job, and then go to work.

I bunked with relatives in Seattle and made a quick round trip to Montana to pick up my family. Finally, we made it back to Seattle. On Thursday, November 10, 1955, I drove in unfamiliar morning traffic and found my way to Boeing's south parking lot. I walked about a half mile to an orientation meeting for new hires in a small, two-story frame building directly across Highway 99 from Boeing headquarters.

After two hours of orientation, I picked my way through the noisy factory crowded with half-built B-52s and tried not to get lost. I finally found the rollup vehicle door leading to the South Yard and the converted warehouse called Annex A, and gazed across a sea of desks and drafting boards at the backs of men in white shirts. Finding an open aisle, I made my way to the front, where Bob Haselwood sat at his desk. His eyes focused intently on a blueprint. I walked to him. He was oblivious to me and to the bustle of people walking by, and to the din and chatter that seemed to fill the huge area. Then, I stood politely and waited.

"Hey, Bob! Someone wants to see you" came a voice from somewhere.

Haselwood shook his head, as if suddenly wakened. He squinted at me, seemed surprised, and said, "Oh, you're the guy from Harvard. I remember. You were here a week ago. Del Engle will be your lead engineer until we find whether you best fit in overhead handling or in foundations. He'll help you get started."

Engle, in his late twenties, was a large, affable person who immediately put me at ease. He pointed to a vacant drafting table and an empty desk that sat side by side. The location was in the middle of three rows of civil/structural engineers, all with similar workstations. The drafting board was covered with soiled light-green paper that was torn in several places.

Del introduced me to several nearby engineers and said, "I'll help you clean the board and cover it with new layers of paper." Thus began a ritual dear to every design engineer's heart—setting up their own workstation. Del helped me clean the drafting board by removing paper and masking tape.

"How many layers of paper do you want under the vellum?" he asked.

"I have no idea. Why don't you show me what you use?" I responded.

"I like three layers," he replied. "That makes a cushion for the vellum. You can press hard for heavy lines and soft for light lines. Depends on the hardness of the pencil. Every engineer develops his own preference."

"Let's go with three," I said.

Engle walked to a large table that had a 4-foot-wide roll of green paper bolted to it. He carefully cut three 5-foot strips. "Now comes the hard part," he said. "Each layer has to be shrunk as tight as a drum."

Engle laid one layer of paper over my drafting board, trimmed it with scissors, leaving 1-inch margins of bare wood exposed at the top, bottom, and sides. Then he anchored the paper to the board with strips of 2-inch masking tape. "Make sure none of the masking tape interferes with the metal edge on the right side where the T square runs," he cautioned.

"Now comes the touchy part," he continued. "Wet the paper with a damp sponge; if you use too little water, the paper will be loose and wrinkled. If you get it overly wet, it'll shrink too much and pull away from the edges."

Engle wet a sponge at the drinking fountain and expertly applied the correct wetness to the paper, which immediately darkened. "Drying takes thirty or forty minutes. I'll take you to the supply counter. We'll check out everything you need. If you have personal drafting instruments or a drafting machine that attaches to the board, bring them in. If not, Boeing supplies everything."

While the first layer of paper dried, Engle introduced me to the supply counter, where a female clerk issued a T square, two French curves, several pencils, art gum and Pink Pearl–brand erasers, and other office supplies. Shrinking two more layers of paper took the rest of the day. The whistle blew at 4:00 p.m. sharp. I got into line, removed my time card from the "in rack," punched it, and put it in the "out rack." The Boeing Company now owed me $17.60 for my first day.

I began to feel weak as I walked to my car. Upon entering the motel, I collapsed on the bed, relieved to have a job and be able to finally relax. The next few weeks became a blur. Several things happened. The mad dash back and forth cross-country had taken their toll on my normally healthy constitution. My stamina and resilience were shot. I took seriously sick and remained so for three weeks. During this time, a blizzard of epic proportions befell western Washington. Records were set in November 1955 both for snowfall and sustained cold temperatures. Elk hunters found themselves stranded in the nearby mountains.

Our savings were gone. While I was sick, Nancy found work at Boeing as a clerk-typist on the tooling balcony above the factory. She also found and leased an apartment, which got us out of the rented motel room. I tested my ability to drive the day after Thanksgiving by going to Dr. Siverling's office. At the doctor's, I tried to hide my weakness. I smiled, minimized complaints, but could not disguise my weak, raspy voice.

After examining me the doctor said, "You seem a little better. I'm worried about the recurrence of rheumatic fever. I'll give you another shot of penicillin to kill any remaining bacteria that might attack your heart. Your temperature is normal. You don't seem to be contagious. No one else is catching whatever you have. I guess you had a very bad cold that no one else got. I think your voice will improve with time."

"I'd like to go to work as soon as possible," I volunteered.

"Use your judgment. Don't engage in strenuous activity. I'm still worried about your heart" came the response.

When I left the doctor's office, I thought I'd been given the green light to return to work—when I felt ready. I had a huge incentive to declare myself ready on Monday. On Sunday we sealed a deal for my Aunt Jackie to take care of baby Kathi for $3.00 per day, which was pretty much standard in 1955.

Monday was one of the scariest days of my life. I woke to find 2 inches of snow had fallen. I would be taking a chance with my health and maybe my life if I slid into a snowbank and needed to dig out. I dressed and went outside before breakfast. The air was cold, well below freezing. That meant dry snow. Montana winters had taught me that dry snow was drivable. After the snowy side streets, Pacific Highway South was an easy drive. Soon we entered Boeing's south parking lot. Both of us were headed in the same direction. Nancy was going to the tooling balcony of the main factory. I was going to "Annex A," the large converted warehouse 60 feet south of the main factory.

I threw a scarf around my neck, buttoned up my overcoat all the way, put on gloves, and donned a black fur cap with ear flaps suitable for winter in Montana or Siberia. I was determined to stay warm and not overexert myself. The ten-minute walk would take me fifteen. I knew Nancy would patiently walk with me and steady me if I needed help.

We joined a crowd of workers gathered at the traffic light, waiting to cross the main Seattle to Tacoma highway, now called East Marginal Way. When the light changed, the crowd hurried across six lanes and a railroad track, showing their badges to the guard at Boeing's south gate. I walked at half speed. Nancy and I were soon alone in the crosswalk, except for last-minute sprinters, hoping to avoid a long wait in the cold for the light to change again.

Nancy guided me to Annex A, turned, and entered the main factory. I was proud of her, thankful we were a team, thankful she had the courage to move forward and make decisions when I could not.

My attendance card was in the rack near the time clock. It was blank. A new pay period had begun since last I was there. After I punched the clock the black imprint read 7:12, proving I was ready for work before the whistle blew at 7:30. That imprint was my claim to a day of pay, even if they fired me.

I slowly walked through the sea of desks and drafting boards, feeling like a stranger in a foreign land, much more alone than I felt three weeks before. Someone was sitting at my desk, reading the morning newspaper. "This is your desk?" I asked.

He looked up from the newspaper. "Yes." He resumed reading the paper.

My lead engineer, Del Engle, sat at his desk—also reading quietly. He'd been patient and helpful on my first day of work three weeks before. I struggled to speak. Words did not come. I squinted, nodded toward my former drafting station. With a pained expression I whispered hoarsely, "What happened?"

"We ran out of space in the structural group. We thought you quit. You'll have to ask Bob Haselwood what to do."

I shuffled to Bob Haselwood's desk. I was exhausted. His chair was inviting. I thought about sitting in it until he arrived, but then realized it presumptuous to sit at my boss's desk. Instead, I leaned and half-sat on the end of the desk. I was still fifteen minutes early and waited until the shift whistle blew, then waited and waited apprehensively. What could I say about my absence? Could I even talk? Could I form audible whispers with my damaged voice?

Haselwood came in ten minutes late. He saw me, frowned, seemed unsure who I was, then said, "Oh, yeah, you're the guy from Harvard. I thought you quit."

I smiled as innocently as possible. In a raspy whisper I mouthed slowly, "I was sick. I'm well now."

Haselwood, over 6 feet, was a walrus of a man. He towered over me as I sat on his desk. He seemed perplexed. His squint turned to a frown. I sat on his desk as straight as I could and returned a friendly smile. I realized he could not sit there until he disposed of me. I had no idea what to do, nor did I have the energy to apologize or improvise. I waited.

Haselwood turned and walked about 20 feet to Bob Kimbrough's desk. Kimbrough, the senior supervisor of the Architect and Civil Engineering group, was his boss. I continued sitting on the desk. They looked at me. Then they looked down and seemed to counsel in low voices that I could not hear above telephones ringing and the buzz of 200 engineers at work behind me, beginning their day. Again, they glanced furtively at me. Maybe my hoarse whisper troubled Haselwood.

Finally, both men strode to a glass-walled cubicle, which was the office of Bob Braley, unit chief of Plant Engineering. Braley's desk sat at a 45-degree angle to the glass walls of his cubicle. A table was pulled up to the middle of his desk, making the shape of a "T." I learned later that a desk and table set at a 45-degree angle signified importance, or "unit chief." The several hundred workers and subordinate supervisors in the unit all sat in orderly rows and columns.

Although Braley's table had three chairs, both subordinates remained standing. Kimbrough pointed at me. Braley lowered his glasses, cocked his head, and gazed in my direction. I continued a weak but friendly smile and gazed vacantly. I knew I looked professional, dressed in my gray flannel suit and narrow maroon tie, ready for work in an architect-engineering firm.

Haselwood came to me and said, "John, we're concerned about your health. You may be contagious. We don't know what to do. Anybody returning from a long sickness must clear through Boeing Medical. You must get permission from Boeing nurses—and maybe a doctor."

"Where's Boeing Medical?" I whispered as loud as I could.

Haselwood consulted a Boeing telephone directory and captured the numbers: building number, floor number, and door number on a pass authorizing me to go to Medical. Handing me the paper, he said, "Go through the factory. Medical is in the first floor of the old engineering building. The buildings are all connected. If you can't find the way, just ask someone."

I slowly wended my way through a maze of B-52 wings and fuselages on my way to the labyrinth of hallways that composed the 2-25 building. Twenty years prior it housed the engineers who created the legendary B-17 Flying Fortress. The long corridors dead-ended with doors labeled "Authorized Personnel Only." I passed an open door to a photo laboratory that was heavy with the acrid smell of chemicals. Its dark interior was illuminated by dim red lights. The heavier smell of ammonia announced the order desk of a busy blueprint production area. People came and went. I rested on a bench, as if waiting. No one paid attention. After resting, I slowly rose and walked farther, hoping to find another place to sit down.

Finally, I came to a short hallway labeled "Boeing Medical." I pushed through a glass door into a waiting room. A receptionist took my medical pass and motioned me to sit down in an upholstered chair. Two nurses came in, looked at my medical pass, and ushered me into an examining room. They began a series of simple tests: temperature, blood pressure, weight, height, and a cursory examination of throat, eyes, lungs, and heart. I did not reveal my history of rheumatic fever. Unless I mentioned it, my heart murmur would not be readily detected. Five years of clean living and exercise had almost repaired it.

Despite my hoarse voice, I hid my weakened condition as best I could, maintaining a smiling, cheerful demeanor, mentioning key words such as "snow" and "cold," which were on everyone's mind. They did most of the talking about their experiences in the record-breaking Seattle November. I listened and laughed at their stories. They eventually determined that I'd had a simple cold and that the weather made it worse. I nodded my head. It was the fault of the weather, not me.

A pair of industrial nurses, such as this one, deftly handled the case of John Andrew upon his return to work after illness in November 1955.

They decided I was not a danger to others, and signed a permit with one restriction in big print, "NO HEAVY LIFTING," a restriction that remained forever in my Boeing personnel record.

I slowly picked my way through the maze on my return, stopping frequently to rest. I was terribly thirsty and stopped at a drinking fountain, bent over, and sucked cool water that tasted delicious. I tried to swallow, but the water ran out of my nose and back into the basin of the fountain. I hoped nobody saw me do that. To drink water, I had to suck in a small mouthful, raise my head, and allow gravity to help. I felt like a bird. I needed a cup.

Upon returning to work, Haselwood scanned the permit, looked around the area, and spied a vacant drafting board and desk in the middle of the mechanical-engineering group, three rows away from my counterparts in civil engineering. He met briefly with the supervisor of mechanical engineering, and I could then invade alien territory.

Finally, I had a place to sit down. I smiled weakly at my neighbor, who knew neither who I was nor why I was there. I hoarsely whispered, "My name is John." I extended my right hand while straining to make visible the Boeing badge pinned on my left side pocket, hoping he would not ask me to repeat the whisper. The same gesture was repeated with the man on my right, and I settled into a blessed silence among strangers.

Del Engle was still my lead engineer. He had worked in plant engineering for five years and knew the old-timers in all groups. He pushed his way through the mechanical engineers, smiled, and said in an affable tone, "Hey, guys, this is John Andrew. Give him a break. He'll be sitting near me when we have a setup available."

Del surveyed the condition of my drafting board. The covering was torn and dirty, about as bad as the board we had cleaned nearly three weeks before. "Mechanical engineers don't know how to set up a decent drafting board," he said in a loud voice with a laugh, "Looks like you have an afternoon's chore."

I heard laughter and kidding rebuttals from those around. Del's friendly manner had broken the ice. I sat for a moment, still terribly thirsty. After making my way to the men's room, I stopped at the drinking fountain in the hallway. Bending over to sip the cool liquid, drinking was difficult. A cup would be handy.

Back at my desk, I heard the whistle blow for the 11:30 a.m. lunch break. With a loud commotion, about half the crew pulled lunch boxes from their desks. Others got up and headed for the cafeteria, which was in a different quadrant of Annex A.

PEAK PRODUCTION RATE TABLE PLANT II		
AIRCRAFT	AIRCRAFT/ MONTH	YEAR OF PEAK
B-17	362*	1944
B-50	17	1949
C-97 377		1949 47 AIRCRAFT
B-52	10.5	1957
737	14	1968
★ TOTAL FOR ALL PRODUCTION FACILITIES		

Plant II bulletin board posting, ca. 1960s. Peak production rate history is of great interest to factory management and, by extension, all who work or visit there.

I had no lunch box, nor did I wish to join the throng of people jostling and hurrying down a crowded hallway. I felt too weak to brave the crowd—so I sat at my desk, looking at the soiled paper on the drafting board, while pretending to be engaged in something. I was halfway through a terribly difficult day and wondering if I could endure the remaining hours.

Just then, an attractive woman arrived in the bay. All eyes were on her as she strode toward me. Nancy paused, beckoned, and said, "John, let's go to lunch."

B-52 Stratofortress

B-52 production spanned the decade from 1952 until 1962. Eight different versions were built as the stream of engineering improvements were bundled and incorporated into the subsequent variant. Externally visible changes included height of the tail, radar dome, windows, size of the wingtip fuel tanks, nacelles, and tail gun configuration.

The Holy Grail of 1930s aircraft designers was a bomber with 10,000 miles of range that could cross the Atlantic, drop its payload, and return to home base. It was the mighty eight-engine B-52 that first cracked the 10,000-mile distance barrier. Twenty-two years after calculating that a 300-foot wingspan was needed, the Stratofortress did it with a 185-foot span. The greater power of turbine engines allowed the aeronautical engineers to achieve greater wing loadings than was possible using 1930s technology. The B-52 can fly a second and even a third stretch of 10,000 miles—provided the crew endures and aerial refueling is accomplished.

My first job entailed counting cracks in the concrete under the wings of B-52s on the Seattle flight line in November 1955. The first 277 of the type were built in Seattle. The final 467 were assembled in Wichita. Each B-52 needed to pass a fuel leak test. It would be filled to the maximum with jet fuel and then allowed to sit untouched for twenty-four hours. At the end of the test, there should be no evidence of any leaked kerosene; however, a fully loaded B-52 Stratofortress weighs 488,000 pounds. The concrete had been poured when lighter airplanes prevailed. At that weight, the tires could crack the concrete. Yes, a fully loaded B-52 can sink into the pavement. It was my job to count the cracks.

Bob Haselwood was transferred to Renton, and I went along as a staff member. The Renton Boeing factory is located on the south shore of Lake Washington, about 10 miles southeast of Plant II. KC-97 production ceased as the manufacture of KC-135 tankers commenced in 1956. Model 707 was also evolving, thus creating a need for more manufacturing space. My next assignment, a step above counting cracks, would include a role in getting a new factory (numbered 10-50) constructed.

A construction crane is required to lift the hinged vertical stabilizer on an early model B-52 (ca. 1956). The Plant II factory buildings are only twenty years old but already inadequate for assembly of large aircraft. It will be John Andrew's job to size future airplane factories.

CHAPTER 4
Let's Go Fishing

KC-135A Stratotanker

Boeing invented modern in-flight refueling for the Air Force, starting with the flying-boom-equipped KB-29 in the immediate postwar era. With similar wings but a slightly wider fuselage, the KC-135 was derived from the Dash 80. The long-serving tanker also features a flying boom, ten fuel tanks, a large forward cargo door, and a main deck provisioned for seventy-two troops, supported by taut red-fabric sidewall seats. A spare engine, other bulk-loaded cargo, or wounded troops in litters can also be handled on the main deck.

A steady parade of the tankers rolled forth from the Renton factory between 1956 and 1963. While different versions of the venerable B-52 varied greatly, KC-135s tankers were alike as peas in a pod—even as later examples became ad hoc airlifters. Others drifted into "special missions"—code words for the shadowy business of collecting intelligence via electronic wizardry, eavesdropping, aerial photography, gathering radioactive dust downwind of nuclear tests, or other tasks.

The primary mission of the KC-135 fleet remained aerial refueling. For an airliner at takeoff, a third of the gross weight is normally fuel, another third is airframe, and the balance is payload consisting of passengers, baggage, freight, or a combination of these. In contrast, a fully loaded KC-135 at takeoff weighs a tad over 300,000 pounds, and 200,000 pounds of that is jet fuel. Each engine has its own fuel tank with primary and backup pumps. The bulk of the fuel (kerosene, normally grade JP-4) is held beneath the floor, in the body tanks. Up to four separate pumps can be simultaneously engaged to deliver the fuel to large (B-52-sized) receiver aircraft at a maximum rate of 6,000 pounds per minute. Fuel is transferred to jet fighters at a slower pace.

Meanwhile, in contrast to the cookie-cutter consistency of KC-135 production, model 707 configuration became chaotic as the number of permutations grew.

March 1957

Bob Richardson from the plant layout group stopped by my desk to tell me about a fishing trip he was planning for the facilities engineers and planners. "We'll charter at least three boats next July," Richardson said. "That's when the salmon are running at Westport."

"Count me in," I replied. "If the salmon aren't biting, I'll drop my bait to the bottom and catch flounder and ling cod."

The first KC-135 Stratotanker, bearing serial number 55-3118, emerged from the old Renton sawtooth factory on July 8, 1956. The last KC-97 (parked nearer the lakeshore) preceded it. The Dash 80, with an early model B-52 in close trail, approached overhead on a westbound heading.

Richardson scowled at me through oversized horn-rim eyeglasses, "The salmon will hit your bait long before you hit bottom. The only problem is getting your bait through the silvers to the kings. The silvers average 12 pounds, and the kings go at least 30 pounds, with a few 40-pounders in the mix."

Richardson had a reputation for being overenthusiastic, which was fine for fishing, but an irritation to his supervisors when he insisted that something could be done that probably couldn't. However, on this day his smiling face and the peripatetic movements of his medium-sized frame told me he was happy about something besides fishing.

Suddenly he blurted, "I found a place to squeeze in a set of KC-135 body assembly tools. I just got it approved north of the wing line in final assembly. Let's take a walk. I'll show you."

I wondered why this was such a big deal for Richardson. The first KC-135 jet tanker had taken flight from the Renton factory the previous August. More units were quickly following it along an expanded production line.

I hadn't paid much attention to the minutia going on in the cavernous 2-million-square-foot factory where my desk was located. My work for the past year had been keeping track of the design status of the new factory, which was rising across the railroad tracks.

"Okay," I replied, "I'll go with you if you'll go with me to the new factory. I need to deliver the latest blueprints to the inspector."

While we looked at the space north of the wing line, Richardson pointed to the bridge crane above and said, "This place has overhead crane coverage with a 40-foot hook clearance. We need that much clearance to lift the fuselage section out of the jig." (The terms "jig" or "tool" meant the same thing when referring to large body or wing assembly devices.)

"That's how much clearance we have in the new factory," I said.

"Yes," replied Richardson. "The new factory's where all the bodies for the KC-135 and 707 will be built. This place, by the wing line, is only a temporary location for an extra set of tools for the KC-135. We need to have an extra set to maintain production rate on the tanker while we move the existing body shop to the new building. When that move is complete, this extra set of jigs and fixtures will be scrapped. It's a huge waste, but it's the only way to maintain rate."

Before we walked into the new factory, Richardson took me to the existing body shop to show me what a set of body assembly jigs looked like in production. The amount of heavy steel framework required to hold the aluminum body sections in exact tolerance so they would fit when joined together left a lasting impression—as did the two-story platforms and walkways for the riveters and mechanics.

It had been a cold, calm, and clear wintertime night. We grabbed overcoats for protection from the early March bluster and walked about four city blocks to the new factory. Once past the railroad crossing, we entered the construction gate. Our shoes crunched on the hoarfrost clods of dirt. "Paving will take place in about a month, when the threat of frost has passed," I assured my companion.

I was proud to show off the new factory building. It had been eight months since I counted strokes on the pile driver that punched timber-and-steel-combination piles through soil into a layer of gravel 65 feet below. Now the structure was erected, the roof was on, and the siding was completed. We entered the building through a truck-sized opening where a 14-by-20-foot rollup door would soon be installed.

The unfinished building was cold and dimly lit by temporary construction lights. At first glance it appeared deserted. Soon we heard the clang of metal echoing from high above, and the sound of motors grinding in the distance. I proudly said, "This high-bay area has 180,000 square feet. In the distance is a low bay area with another 180,000 square feet."

Pointing upward, I continued, "The upper chord of the truss is 60 feet above the floor. The lower chord is 50 feet. The iron workers you see up there have hung crane rails and are installing bridge and cabs. The hook of each crane will lift 10 tons 40 feet above the floor, just like in the other building."

Richardson began to size up the place and orient himself. He'd been making layouts of the production line of body jigs and fixtures in the new building. This was the first time he or any of his group had been inside the structure. After pacing a short distance from a column, he said, "The body jigs for the KC-135 will go here, and the 707 jigs will go over there."

I thought about the extra set of temporary tools that Richardson said were to be built near the wing line. I asked, "Is there a reason why the extra set of tools can't be built here while we finish the building? They could be ready when the shop moves, and wouldn't need to be scrapped."

Richardson's large glasses magnified the rapid blinking of his eyes as the thought sunk in. He began skipping and shouting, "We'll save a whole bunch of tools! We'll save a whole bunch of tools!" Then he looked crestfallen. "Christ, no one will believe me! My boss will shoot it down like he always does."

As we walked back, I said, "I'm going to tell my management and find out if there is any objection. I'll also ask the contractor. We're almost finished with that part of the building. Why don't you a least suggest it to your supervisor?"

"He'll kill the idea for sure. He never believes me. He'll lock down against it. He'll say not just no, but 'hell no.' He'll tell his boss why it's a bad idea, and the message will go forward that I'm a troublemaker."

That afternoon the idea was relayed to my boss, Bob Haselwood. He agreed that construction was almost done in that part of the high bay, and said, "The 480-volt power is already activated. The overhead lights will be on in about a week. I see no reason why Boeing should not build assembly tools if they don't mind the inconvenience of a construction site. They'll have to walk through mud for a while. The area around the building won't be paved until better weather."

I commented, "The tools use a lot of heavy steel beams and large pipe columns like we do in construction."

"Yeah," agreed Haselwood, "Tooling builds everything so hell-for-stout that they don't run design calculations. They just add another ton of steel and weld on another brace. I doubt that any tool designer has an engineering degree. They just know what works. So do the tool builders when they weld it all together. I'll alert the contractor and see if there's any objection on their part. I'll also clear it with my management."

The next morning, Haselwood returned from a staff meeting and said everyone in Facilities was agreeable that tools could be built before construction was complete; however, Facilities doesn't wish to push the idea because it is outside our scope. (In a demonstration of the cooperation manifested by the Austin Company, henceforth occupying a new factory building while still under construction became a standard practice and would later be key to making schedule on the 747 at Everett.)

An airplane delivery celebration is underway in front of the original Renton sawtooth factories. The cement ramps descending into Lake Washington confirm that the original purpose was seaplanes.

I told this to Richardson. "Damn it!" he exclaimed. "I knew the cost of a complete set of tools could be avoided." He then hesitated, looked me in the eye, and said, "Meet me in the hallway."

In the hallway I observed a half smile and then a smirk of intrigue as he said, "Don't tell a soul what I'm going to do. I'll be fired if my boss finds out. I'll go way above his head. You've got to promise you won't breathe a word." Amused, I nodded my head in assent.

"I'm going to talk to Mr. Charlie Becvar Jr. He's the manager of the Tooling Section in the Manufacturing Department. He's a good guy. He'll listen to reason. In fact, John, I'd like you to go with me to his office and back me up."

In large, complex organizations, low-level persons in service functions are better received by the organizations they serve than by their home departments. In this case, Becvar, an executive over several hundred tool designers and tool builders, had a first-name relationship with Richardson because Richardson, a low-level factory layout draftsman, could use his powerful manikin (small blocks that represent tools, machines, or desks) to allocate valuable factory floor space in turf disputes between neighboring shops.

As we entered the tooling-design area, Richardson strode down the aisle between tool designers bent over drafting boards. Richardson was obviously a welcomed visitor because I heard several remarks: "Hey, Rich, how's fishing?" or "Rich, where are you going on opening day?" Richardson smiled and waved as we continued our march to Charlie Becvar's glass-walled office.

Becvar looked through the glass and saw us speaking with his secretary to gain an audience. We didn't wait long. Through the glass I saw Becvar excuse the person to whom he was talking and wave us in.

Becvar was a man of medium stature, fiftyish, graying at the temples, with glasses that were slightly smaller than Richardson's. He had a kindly expression and a twinkle in his eye that immediately put me at ease. "What's on your mind today, Rich?"

"Don't tell a soul I'm here," began Richardson. "I'm not supposed to talk to you. I'll be fired. It's actually John's idea. Tell Charlie what you have to say, John."

I was dumbfounded. I was expecting to provide no more than silent affirmation to what Richardson would say. My year at Harvard Business School trained me to be ready to speak intelligible words at a moment's notice; however, the dreaded polio disease stood in the way. I looked straight into Becvar's eyes. Silence makes nearly everyone uncomfortable. I sensed it in Becvar's kindly expression as I struggled to speak. I was not uncomfortable, but intensely concentrating. Finally, the words came: "Tools can be built in the new factory now."

Richardson then enthusiastically jumped into the conversation, "Yes, Charlie, John's right. We don't have to build the extra set of KC-135 fuselage tools! We can also build the 707 body tools in place if we start right away."

Becvar studied both of us. He knew Richardson was a college dropout forced to take low-level work by marriage at a young age and the arrival of children. He knew nothing of me but likely assumed I was a greenhorn engineer lacking in practical knowledge and the good sense to avoid marching into executive turf without an invitation.

Neither my appearance, hesitating speech, nor Richardson's overenthusiasm made a whit of difference to Charlie Becvar. He was a down-to-earth Boeing executive with extensive experience during the production surges of World War II and the more recent B-47 and B-52 jet bomber buildups. As a battle-hardened "survivor," he was now entrusted with delivering all tooling required for the new Boeing transports—both commercial and military.

Becvar spoke slowly, "The story I've been told is that the new factory won't be available till September. I'd like to look at what you guys are talking about. Can you take me to the new factory right now?"

"Grab your coat," I said.

Said Richardson, "I can't go along. If anyone sees me walking around with Charlie, I'll be fired."

Becvar and I walked in silence. He seemed preoccupied. I did not realize how stressed upper management was, striving to get production rolling on three brand-new airplanes, the KC-135 military jet tanker, the basic 707-120, and the upgraded 707-320 Intercontinental. All looked similar but had different wings, body diameters, and lengths. We crossed the tracks. The construction guard opened the gate to the area. He knew me well because I had permission to enter the construction area at will. In a sense, Becvar was my guest.

In the fading light of a March afternoon, the empty doorway to the new high bay seemed like the entrance to a cold tomb. A dimly lighted silence inside confirmed the tomb-like aspect. Iron workers ending their shift were quietly gathering personal tools. The place looked just the opposite of a bustling aircraft factory.

Becvar took a few steps on the concrete floor that had been poured two weeks before. He stamped the concrete and muttered, "It's well set up."

"Yup," I said. "It's twenty-eight-day concrete. It'll be at full design strength in two more weeks."

"Good," he said. "We'll start bringing in steel in two weeks." He looked up at the dim outline of a bridge crane. "I hope that crane will be ready to go. Then we won't have to use mobile cherry pickers."

The next morning, I told Bob Haselwood that the tooling section would probably request access to the new building. "Please omit my name and Bob Richardson's name when you tell facilities director Erle Barnes the news. Say you heard it from somebody else" was my request.

Steel started arriving on April 4, not just for the KC-135, but for the 707 body jigs as well. Then chaos broke loose. The whole Manufacturing Department, with eighteen thousand employees, suddenly realized that production could begin ahead of schedule in the unfinished 360,000-square-foot building.

A huge "early-move-in committee" was established. Production plans were updated. Everyone claimed it was their idea, especially the top brass. Richardson's boss was told what to do by his boss, but each of them claimed it was their idea in the first place. I didn't care who got credit.

Overhead Cranes

The early move to the 10-50 building began on April 1, 1957, when Boeing tooling fabricators began setting the bases for KC-135 and 707 body jigs into the concrete floor. Mobile cranes on wheels were used for the first two weeks while the crane subcontractors finished installing the permanent 10-ton bridge cranes over the area Boeing was using. On April 15, 1957, the overhead cranes above the tooling mechanics were released for use. Cranes in the remainder of the building were still being installed.

Two days later, all hell broke loose. "Something's wrong with the cranes," said Haselwood when he returned from a staff meeting, "They drip oil and slow down. No one knows what's wrong. Our inspectors refuse to climb and look at the problem. Austin (the general contractor) says its Star Machinery's fault. Star Machinery says it's the Louden Company's fault. Now people are asking me why we bought Louden bridge cranes. I don't know that answer because the cranes were on order when I got this job. I think the guy who ordered the cranes is off building Bomarc bases somewhere on the East Coast. It doesn't matter where he is. We've got the problem."

My desk was next to Haselwood's. He often shared thoughts with me. I could tell he was worried the problem would reflect poorly on him; however, climbing was not feasible for him because it might trigger a heart attack.

I thought a moment and said, "Bridge cranes are the province of the structural engineering group at Boeing. We both know who those guys are. They're at Plant II, and they're not capable of doing fieldwork."

Haselwood laughed, "Yeah, Vern is disabled and J. V. has the shakes from drinking too much. Our own field inspectors should be investigating, but they refuse to climb."

I continued, "I talk to them every day when I deliver prints. They're out of shape or can't stomach high work. If I was part of the inspection team, I'd be glad to be the crane inspector. I don't know much about the guts of a bridge crane, but I could learn."

Haselwood suddenly remembered that my résumé included six months' experience with the 10-ton cranes at Plant II, high rigging as a lineman, and window washer on tall buildings. "Hey John, why don't you go up and troubleshoot the problem?" he said. He looked me in the eye and continued, "I know you want to get some fresh air. I'll call Ted Fulton (supervisor of Boeing inspectors) and tell him you're willing to inspect the cranes part time. I still need you here most of the time."

The call was made. I grabbed a set of blueprints for the 10-50 building to look official. When I entered the building, a Boeing hook tender first pointed to some oily drips on the concrete below and then shifted his eyes skyward and said, "That's the stranded bridge crane. The damn thing dripped oil and now it can't move. They're changing the fluid drive."

"How do I get up there?" I asked.

"Climb the ladder," he replied. "Take the catwalk to the main truss. Climb over the railing. Walk on the beams. When you're over the bridge, jump down on it."

The ladder rose 60 feet vertically. It was caged above the 10-foot level. I felt secure that I could lean back and rest if I wanted to. It had been almost four years since I earned a living washing windows in Spokane. It was there that I climbed an 80-foot uncaged ladder connected to a fire escape that got me to the top of the eleven-story Paulson building.

I leaned back on the long strips of smooth steel that made the caging. It felt comfortable when I stopped briefly to rest. I stepped off the ladder just above the 50-foot level and onto a catwalk that ran the length of the building, almost disappearing into the distance some 600 feet away. I took my time walking on the catwalk to allow my mind and eyes to become accustomed to the height. I knew from years of working up high that it's best (at least for me) to concentrate on nearby things and not think about the ground, which in this case was a hard concrete floor 50 feet below.

It had been five years since I hung out over the vertical face of Hungry Horse Dam and walked the beams of the Bonneville power line towers. I hesitated momentarily. I'd been seriously sick since then. It had taken a year to recover. Was I fully recovered? When I did the high work, I was in terrific physical condition. Now I was an office worker assigned to a desk six days a week, ten hours per day—with no time for jogging or workouts.

THE BOEING COMPANY CRANE MANUAL

D4-1005-1030

December 1976

In the interest of standardization and safety, many updated versions of the Crane Operators Guide were released by Boeing over the decades.

Delivering a load to the Plant II balcony in December 1937 yielded a unique situation whereby the bridge crane operator and his counterpart, the hook tender, could both appear in the same photograph.

Could I walk the beams to the stranded bridge unit? Could I jump down to it? Could I scramble back when it was time to return? Here I was wearing coat and tie, up in the factory trusswork, inspecting cranes—when I was professionally dressed for business.

I clambered over the catwalk railing, stepped onto the lower chord of the truss, balanced myself with one hand on a diagonal brace, let go, and carefully took several steps to the next diagonal brace. Arriving at the bridge unit, I carefully bent over, grasped the steel I was standing on, and jumped easily onto the deck of the bridge, about 2 feet below.

I heaved an involuntary sign of relief because I could walk beams again. My instincts for high work returned. The bridge unit was 60 feet long, and the top had a deck of wooden planks about 4 feet wide—which was plenty of room to work. Near the end, two men knelt on the planks, unbolting a round object about the size of a basketball.

They looked up when I landed on the bridge but continued working. I knew the mechanics were employees of Star Machinery working on behalf of Louden Cranes. I walked to them and asked, "How are you guys doing?"

They both glanced up again. One answered in a Brooklyn accent, "These goddamn fluid drives are a piece of crap."

I said, "Is that what your boss thinks?"

"I don't care what my goddamn boss thinks or says. This whole goddamn crane system is crap" came the response. I would learn much about bridge crane systems in the next eight months. About half of my work time was spent walking the beams in that lofty but lonely world 60 feet above the factory floor. Furthermore, the varying view below came to influence my thinking regarding future factories.

I summoned the subcontractor, worked with his people, worked with the Boeing crane operators, and operated the cranes myself, rewiring them when the subcontractor couldn't get there. I learned to change the fluid drives. A pair of coveralls were stashed up in the trusses along with wrenches, screwdrivers, and a heavy lead hammer to knock the interlocks and crossovers into line when they wouldn't work. Basically, I maintained the huge and complex crane system because Boeing maintenance people would not touch the cranes until they passed final acceptance.

One day, while peering down from the trusswork above, I witnessed something memorable. A crane pulled an upper-half body section from the jig. Rather than a KC-135 solid curved metal tube—this section had a long, neat row of windows of perfect size and shape. I realized that it was the fuselage of the first 707 airliner, and that the world of transportation would be changed forever.

Other Construction

Other facilities projects were accomplished at Boeing after World War II:

- **1954:** To shelter B-52s undergoing flight test, a large, new hangar was constructed at the north end of Boeing Field. Covering about 5 acres and built at an expense of $5.8 million, its unique cantilevered roof allows simultaneous opening of all the overhead doors along the entire east side. To this day, building 3-390 remains the Puget Sound operational home for flight testing.

- **1955:** The former Navy bombing range at Boardman, Oregon (consisting of 47,000 acres), was acquired as a test site for handling dangerous and explosive rocket and missile technology. Some of this land was leased to farmers for agricultural purposes. Barge access is available via the Columbia River.

- **1956:** A $21 million complex called the Developmental Center (or DC) was created at the south end of Boeing Field. The original purpose was to host Boeing's entry into the Weapon System 110A competition. Later, the DC housed the SST mockup and a series of military projects. Bob Kimbrough was the senior supervisor in charge of facilities design in 1956.

- **1956:** A $15 million "Renton Office and Manufacturing Facility" project began under direction of Bob Haselwood. Sprawling low-rise buildings housed general-purpose office space, executive offices, a theater, and a cafeteria.

Both the Developmental Center and Renton expansions were handled by the Austin Company under a "cost plus fixed fee" (abbreviated CPFF) contract.

Other Postwar Weapon Systems

Bomarc, a 58-foot-long, antiaircraft, trapezoidal-wing ramjet, was an early win for the Pilotless Aircraft Division. It was an Air Force project that competed for Defense Department sponsorship with the Army's Nike Hercules surface-to-air missiles. A total of fifty-two launching sites all across the US were envisioned; however, a waning Soviet bomber threat made it a prime target for reductions.

Weapon System 110A, dated 1955, was a specification for a new strategic bomber that would replace the B-52. Yet, the B-52 program was huge and still flight-testing when the Air Force released the first of many solicitations for its replacement. Boeing dutifully went to work on its proposal with the Developmental Center, earmarked to house the program. However, North American Aviation of Los Angeles won the contract in 1957. The result was the triple-sonic (Mach 3) XB-70A Valkyrie. Only two prototypes were built at Palmdale's Air Force Plant 42 and test-flown from nearby Edwards AFB.

As the decade of the 1950s gave way to the 1960s, the XB-70 program became mired in controversy regarding cost and role—partly because the Boeing Minuteman ICBM had stolen much of its intended mission and enhancements to Soviet air defenses. Airplane number 2 was lost in a freak midair collision during a staged photographic flight on June 8, 1966. The NASA logo was applied to the sole survivor, and it performed research flights on behalf of SST technology.

Systems Management Organization (SMO)

SMO was created in the wake of the loss of Weapon System 110A. During the 1950s, a cadre of thinkers, strategists, and leaders believed the future for Boeing resided in space. Therefore, the company name was shortened from Boeing Airplane Company to the Boeing Company. A "Systems Management Organization" (or SMO) was created to seek out and manage space-related projects. Leaders of the new organization included Clyde Skeen, T. A. Wilson, and George Stoner.

A portfolio of projects soon resulted. They included Dynasoar (a man-in-space project) and, most notably, Minuteman. Previous intercontinental ballistic missiles were liquid fueled, which was dangerous, accident prone, and demanding of constant attention. In contrast, the solid-fueled Minuteman could sit in an underground silo virtually untended for years. T. A. Wilson was placed in charge, and the program became a model for cost-effective development of complicated weapon systems.

Meanwhile, my own position, salary, and job status were incrementally improving. I was transferred to Facilities long-range planning in September 1957 because construction on the 10-50 building was complete. I returned to the Harvard Business School in 1958 and this time completed the curriculum. Important events transpired at Transport Division before, during, and after the nine months of my educational leave of absence.

CHAPTER 5
Transport Division at Renton

The J. B. Connelly Era: 1956 to 1960

They will someday regard airplane travel

to be as commonplace and

incidental as train travel.
—*William E. Boeing, 1929*

John B. Connelly (1907–1990) was vice president and general manager (VP & GM) of Transport Division from 1956 to 1960. Other American companies also entered the new airliner fray, including Lockheed with the turboprop-powered Electra and Convair with models 880 and 990; however, the biggest competitive threat resided with the well-entrenched Douglas Aircraft Company (DAC) of Long Beach, California—which seemed initially complacent with DC-7 production humming along.

Connelly aggressively took on the challenges thrown at him by Lockheed, Douglas, Convair, and the Europeans. The dapper salesman of Irish background was alone at the storm-tossed Boeing helm during the vicious dogfight for sales of first-generation turbine-powered aircraft. Connelly especially catered to the Europeans and secured Lufthansa as an early and influential customer for the 707. The reputation of the B-17 cast a long shadow over the postwar Germans. To Lufthansa president Gerhard Holtje, the 707 (and later 727) represented outstanding engineering matching German high expectations for elegant design, manufacturing excellence, and reliable performance.

The Dash 80,[1] with the oversized numbers "707" emblazoned on its tail, was a persuasive marketing tool. Airline officials of every ilk were irresistibly drawn to the Dash 80 because they instinctively knew it represented the future of air travel. Like visitors to a new car dealership, they came to inspect it and kick the tires, and those who were either lucky (or influential) were invited aboard for a ride.

Douglas was initially slow in reacting to the 707 challenge. Finally grasping the threat, DAC emerged energized for a marketing battle with archrival Boeing. The competition was hardball. The DC-8 was a four-engine jetliner of similar size, configuration, and appearance to the 707. The initial advantage of the 707 was a flying prototype, greater speed, and a head start. It would be in airline service a year sooner than the DC-8; however, as with model 247, this fleeting advantage was insufficient for the long haul.

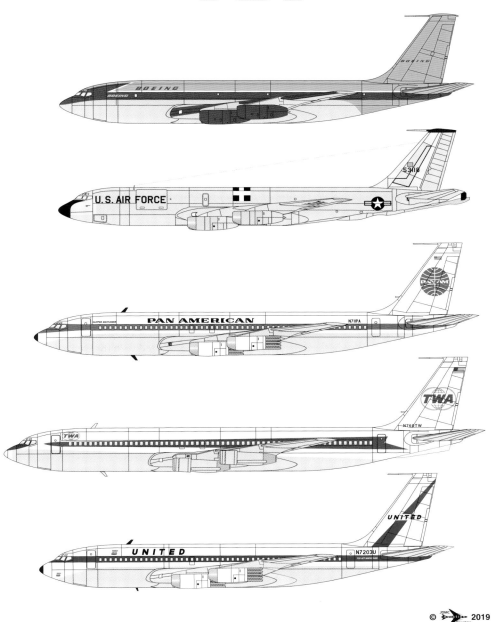

The single Dash 80 prototype (top) of 1954 was the patriarch of the Boeing family of aircraft. For decades, the KC-135 (*second*) was the primary aerial refueling tanker of the USAF. Airliners began with the 707-100 series (*third*) with the 707-320 Intercontinental (*fourth*) at the apex. Model 720 (*bottom*) was faster and intended for routes of medium range. Airlines requested improvements including 6 abreast seating, more powerful engines, and longer-range wings. These changes increased market share—but at the expense of near-term profits. *Graphic by Jack Morris*

Manifesting the attributes of grace, utility, and longevity, the Boeing KC-135 Stratotanker joined the elite club of legendary military aircraft with a service life measured in decades rather than years. The orange markings (conspicuity paint) were a fleeting safety of flight idea.

Bill Allen and the other Boeing executives remained wary of Douglas Aircraft Company and especially its very capable founder—Donald Douglas (1892–1981). They well remembered being outfoxed by Douglas in 1935, when Boeing leadership harbored dreams of sweeping not only the airliner marketplace with model 247 (an all-metal, twin-engine monoplane capable of seating ten passengers) but also capturing the Army Air Corps heavy-bomber contract with the B-17. Instead, Douglas handed Boeing stinging defeats on both counts.

Boeing made a couple of strategic mistakes starting in 1933. The company lacked a suitable wind tunnel, so testing was contracted to a facility in Los Angeles. It was reported that Douglas engineers used purloined access to Boeing data to craft the DC-2 design and perfected it with the follow-on DC-3. Furthermore, when Donald Frye of TWA sought model 247 aircraft from Boeing in 1934, he was told they were all committed to United Air Lines.

Frye received a warmer reception at DAC. The teachable moment was to establish and hold open production line positions for uncommitted potential customers. It is vital to get those first few aircraft placed with an airline because it is a toehold from which follow-on orders flow.

Donald Douglas, founder of Douglas Aircraft Company (DAC). The fierce competition between Boeing and DAC began in the 1930s and continued unabated for a half century.

Recognizing their jetliner bargaining strength, airlines evaluated options in their quest for the optimum airplane and then bargained hard for those considered most important to their own situation. Juan Trippe, president of Pan American, decided to prod both Douglas and Boeing into doing their best by simultaneously ordering twenty model 707 and twenty-five Douglas DC-8 aircraft. Salesmen from both Renton and Long Beach fanned out and camped on the doorstep at each of the world's major international airlines.

Back then, major airlines employed larger engineering staffs than today. The result was a fresh list of demands—which included a wider fuselage for six-abreast seating, complete redesign of the wing, and more-powerful engines. New wings and a wider fuselage required reengineering, wind tunnel validation, and new tooling for the factory. The goal of commonality between KC-135 and model 707 evaporated.

The wish list varied by customer. Boeing proceeded to win airline respect and loyalty by offering customer-specific solutions. Model 707-138 was important to Qantas because the Australian carrier needed less weight to achieve more range on its long Pacific flights. Northwest Airlines also wanted nonstop range between Tokyo and Seattle. Model 707-220 allowed Braniff to substitute Pratt & Whitney JT-4 engines (the civilian designation for the military J75 turbojet found in the Vietnam War–era Republic F-105), while British airlines stipulated Rolls-Royce Conway engines. Hence, the 707-420 was born.

The near-term financial damage inflicted upon the airframe builders was of no immediate concern to the airlines; however, the inevitable winnowing of the weakest would limit future competition on the basis of price. The "sticker price" on a factory-fresh airliner became as fixed as the CAB (Civil Aeronautics Board) prescribed airfare between LAX and Chicago. Even the exact fuel load at delivery was defined by contract. Concessions were sometimes negotiated regarding sundry services such as initial provisioning, other spare parts, or crew training.

The fierce marketplace competition with Convair and Douglas forced evolution of the 707 design beyond adequacy and onto greatness. Furthermore, the final 707 fuselage diameter (cross section) became standard for every subsequent Boeing single-aisle airliner, thus yielding factory efficiencies and customer benefits when refurbishing interiors.

Relatively few people are aware of the pathfinder service provided by the Dash 80. In an era when most other civilian propeller airliners plied lower-altitude routes over the icy-cold North Atlantic, the Dash 80 most often found itself mostly alone in the cold, inky-dark stratosphere above. Its mission? Gathering data for the introduction of the 707. Winds aloft, temperatures, and routing options all were being evaluated, while accurate timetables relied on the flying time between major trans-Atlantic city pairs.

Milestone: On October 26, 1958, the first Boeing 707 revenue load of 111 enthusiastic passengers departed New York on their way to Paris.

This trio of interiors mechanics install sidewall panels, ca. 1968. The common fuselage diameter between 707, 727, and 737 simplified parts inventory both for Boeing and the airlines.

This Pan Am 707 airframe entered service fully broken in, because it had accumulated 1,700 flight hours during flight testing. Domestic service between New York and Miami followed in December. American Airlines was flying the 707 between New York and Los Angeles starting in January 1959. While living in Boston, I was heartened to witness the universal respect that Boeing was garnering. The demise of propeller-driven aircraft on long-haul routes came quickly. With larger wings, the model 707-320 Intercontinental became the final configuration—which seemed to appease most everybody.

A market niche in the medium to short ranges became evident with the sales success of Convair models 880 and 990. The Convairs flew fast. By shortening the 707's cabin and adding more wing sweep, the Boeing 720^2 became an interim attempt to meet this need. Orders from United, Eastern, and Northwest arrived quickly. The responsiveness of Boeing won market share for Boeing at the expense of the others, but the cost of reworking the fuselage, new wing tooling, and adapting the emerging turbofan engines was adding to Transport Division's bucket of red ink.

John O. Yeasting (1905–1970) was appointed VP & GM of Transport Division in January 1960. By the time J. B. Connelly was demoted, the European airliner builders were in full retreat; Convair, after suffering a $350 million financial loss, was a fatality of the joust with models 720 and 720B. A leading-edge "glove" yielded the speed necessary to kill the Convair 880, and the Pratt & Whitney turbofan did in the 990.

The airliner business units within Douglas and Lockheed were also wounded and bleeding. The future held bankruptcy and a government bailout for Lockheed. McDonnell Aircraft Company of St. Louis, holding a balance sheet rich in cash resulting from profits earned building F-4 Phantoms for the Vietnam War, acquired Douglas Aircraft in 1967.

Transport Division earned customer trust as market share grew. Connelly was denied the recognition he deserved. While retained as a salesman, he was pushed aside as VP & GM because of too many customer-specific variations within the model 707 family. Like a swordsman thwarting multiple attackers, Connelly prevailed by reworking the 707. As in warfare, it was essential to gaining market share, fending off the competition, and leaving them financially wounded. Corporate leaders at Boeing headquarters failed to fully appreciate Connelly's marketing victory and simply expected Yeasting, a rigorous accountant with a sharp eye for numbers, to keep a better lid on costs—thus stemming Renton's hemorrhage of red ink.

Upon arrival as VP & GM in 1960, John Yeasting correctly perceived airlines were hungry for a better medium-range solution, and sponsored creation of model 727. Starting in 1964, the Boeing 727 delivered on that vision and began to dominate medium-range routes. This time, Boeing had done its homework in collaboration with the airlines, thus avoiding the major rework, retrofits, and expense that dogged model 707. John E. "Jack" Steiner (1917–2003) and his team worked magic. No other builder could muster such an elegant design. Other airframe builders simply stood by flatfooted. If they glanced upward, skies filled with Boeing jets created a new form of aluminum overcast.

John Andrew Returns
from Leave of Absence

In late April 1959, I phoned my former supervisor at Boeing from Boston to let him know that I was about to graduate. I was on an unfunded leave of absence, and under no obligation to return. "Do you have a job for me?" I asked.

"Yes, I think so," replied Bob Schneebeli, a thirty-one-year-old graduate of Purdue and head of the long-range business planning unit for J. B. Connelly. "I have a senior supervisor opening reporting to me. I won't kid you though. You'll have no one to supervise because it's a staff job, and your title will be Staff Planner."

"What's the pay?" I asked. "I'll try to get you $8,000 or $9,000 per year," was the response. "I was making that much when I left," I complained. "When you talk to personnel, tell them I need $10,000."

The next phone call was from Tom Sheppard, the same personnel manager who processed my leave. "I'm glad you're coming back to Boeing," he said. "The division planning staff has lots of promise. Most guys would give their eye teeth to work at that level."

"What's the offer?" I said. "In dollars and cents—I can't eat prestige."

"Nine thousand three hundred and fifty," he responded, repeating the numbers slowly. "We'll send a formal written offer in the mail."

"Can't you do better than that?" I wheedled. "I won't be eligible for overtime, so I've got to get it in base salary. Remember, I've got an MBA from Harvard."

"I'll remember that and see what I can do," he replied. "You know we'll pay travel expenses from Boston and move your household goods." He went on to assure me my government security clearance for working on military projects was still in place.

The written offer arrived at $9,500. I was disappointed and unwilling to accept the offer until talking to some recruiters who came to campus. Lockheed offered me a job in Sunnyvale. They were mum about the project, but I assumed it was working on undersea Polaris missiles. Electric Boat sent a recruiter from Groton, Connecticut. At least they admitted their business was nuclear submarines. Both jobs required paperwork, including a security questionnaire that would take more than a day to complete. These chores were already behind me at Boeing.

I discussed the offer with several classmates. Harvard kept an anonymous running score on high, low, and average offers, and nearly everyone was open about their salaries. My $9,500 offer was quite reasonable. It was slightly above the median, and when I told them it was from Boeing at a very high reporting level, they seemed much more impressed than I was.

It's funny how distance changes perspective. I still retained my provincial Seattle attitude about Boeing. In Seattle, many people considered the "Lazy-B" to be the last resort. It seemed like everybody in the Pacific Northwest had a horror story or two about working at Boeing. Some dated back to World War II, when thousands of men and women crowded into the giant aircraft factories located in South Seattle and Renton.

Now, in 1959, the factories were back to their wartime levels, with forty thousand souls almost elbow to elbow in the Seattle Plant II complex and another twenty-six thousand packed into the Renton plant 10 miles away. I'd been part of the anthill of humanity, first in Seattle and then in Renton. I'd also seen a good bit of stupidity—at least what looked like stupidity—especially in "management."

At Harvard, 3,000 miles from Seattle, everybody I met had an entirely different view. My classmates gave me deference and respect when I mentioned Boeing. To them, Boeing was the big mysterious company tucked away in a remote corner of the USA that somehow filled the sky with giant planes and rockets—and a Boeing 707 had just made the first commercial flight across the Atlantic. In the end, it was my classmates' attitude, and not wanting to fill out another security clearance application, that tipped the scales in favor of Boeing.

Nancy and I discussed the job search at our duplex in Bedford, Massachusetts. "I like the idea of going back to Seattle," she said. "I've just talked with Doreen Weber. George is quitting Boeing and going into the family business in Spokane. Their home on 57th Street near Green Lake will be available in June. We can pick up the lease and move right in."

"That's a little far from Renton but convenient to the University of Washington, so you can finish your degree," I responded.

We decided to skip the graduation ceremonies. After I took my last final, I was about to put the luggage carrier on the top of our station wagon when I said to Nancy, "We'll leave early tomorrow?"

"Yes, I think we can," she answered, "but maybe we should visit the cemetery this afternoon."

Two infant sons were separately conceived during our stay in Boston. Tragically, both arrived prematurely without the requisite lung development to survive. Their passing weighed heavily on each of us. I hoped to leave in peace but knew I wouldn't. The passing of two infants, a mountain of debt, and five years down the tube was a high price to pay for a Harvard degree.

Nancy and I both seemed to recover from dismal thoughts, because we were in high spirits the next morning. In reality, we had accomplished a tremendous amount. I'd done well in my second year and received "distinction" in several courses. Nancy had accomplished a lot too. She'd recovered from whatever caused her to give birth early, before the babies were ready to survive for more than a day or two. We had Jack to prove that. He was strong and healthy. We put our youngsters, five-year-old Kathi and one-year-old Jack, into the car and set off for Seattle in faraway Washington.

I was glad Boeing was paying for our relocation. With no air-conditioning in the car, we had hot weather all the way across the continent. Hot and windblown, we crested Snoqualmie Pass and dropped into a cool foggy rain. We both cheered. We were home.

When we arrived, the place on North 57th Street was furnished and ready to go, with everything we needed except groceries. Nancy visited the registrar at the University of Washington. It was her turn to go to college. I would be supportive. I drove to the Renton plant and found it to be one hour and ten minutes away. Other than the Alaskan Way viaduct, there were no freeways in Seattle in 1959.

At Boeing, a small corporate headquarters (as measured by both building size and head count) presided over the two much-larger operating units: Commercial Airplane Group (CAG, also called "Transport Division") and Aerospace Group (ASG).

Sentimental Journey

I met Tom Sheppard in the Personnel Building outside the gate. My badge was ready. Tom didn't need to explain payday. I already knew it was every other Thursday. Other aerospace companies paid weekly on Friday. Why was Boeing unique? Nobody seemed to know, but the two best theories were that it allowed second-shift workers to cash their checks before the weekend, or the cost accountants would have computer-generated priced labor reports in hand first thing on Monday morning. Maybe the truth was a mixture of both.

As I clipped the badge onto the left pocket of my suit coat, Sheppard said, "I'll take you to Earl Combs's office. You'll be working for him."

"Who the hell is Earl Combs?" I asked.

"He runs the Operations and Scheduling unit. Schneebeli's budget got cut. Combs has budget."

The 3,000-mile perspective was gone. I was back in Seattle. Boeing management remained all screwed up. But a call to Earl Combs's office determined that he was gone to meetings. I collected my parking pass and other paperwork and set out to kill time with a self-guided tour.

The Personnel Building was a tiny part of the old plant, which stood by itself on the edge of a vast parking lot. It was a simple, flat-roofed, single-story structure built hurriedly in 1942 as a hiring hall and daily processing center for new workers. A long, porch-like extension sheltered dozens of turnstiles where, over a period of three shifts, armed guards checked twenty thousand workers in and out.

The Boeing Renton site was bisected by railroad tracks. On the east side of the tracks was the new plant, the one I'd been involved in constructing two years prior. Combs's office was in the 10-80 building. It would be my last stop later that afternoon. Instead, I drove to the north end of Renton's Logan Avenue. In any case, it would be fun to have a few hours to visit my old haunts and relive my days as a facilities engineer. I wrongly anticipated that designing and building factories was over for me.

The first logical opening will be the development

of a commercial flying boat.
—William E. Boeing

My station wagon was dwarfed by the gray corrugated-steel side of the main assembly buildings numbered 4-20 and 4-21. Boeing is a company where rooftop size can often be expressed as acreage. It was a massive structure of 2.2 million square feet, originally conceived in 1939 to build ocean-spanning flying boats.

The Boeing Airplane Company made a foray into float planes in the late 1930s. Boeing signed a contract with Pan American Airways for six model 314 Clippers for $538,846 each on July 21, 1936. Pan Am also operated flying boats built by Glenn Martin and Sikorsky. Pan Am called them all "clippers"; however, Boeing model 314 was the gold standard for range, performance, and opulence. Pan Am ordered six more of the Boeing Clippers, bringing the production run to twelve. All were built outdoors at Plant I. At a time when air travel was special and airliners were considered more than buses with wings, a spiral stairway tied the multiple decks of the luxurious interior together. The design, generally attributed to Wellwood Beall, combined the four engines and wing derived from the experimental XB-15[3] long-range bomber with a floating hull.

The California Clipper commenced trans-Pacific service from San Francisco to Singapore on March 20, 1939. The arrival of World War II halted production when a mere dozen had been fabricated. Most were commandeered for military service. They accomplished four thousand wartime ocean crossings. When either Winston Churchill or Franklin Roosevelt needed safe airlift across the Atlantic, the model 314 was the aircraft of choice.

I paused my unescorted sojourn to look squarely at this imposing structure, only eighteen years old but already steeped in history. Just over 1,100 B-29s emerged from the large doors facing Lake Washington. The workers were sent home when Japan capitulated, and the plant briefly sat idle. A traveling circus sometimes rented space to give the elephants a place to work out.

Production of model 314 ceased with the arrival of World War II; however, its features, including spiral staircase, multiple decks, and unprecedented levels of opulence, triggered nostalgic expectation within Juan Trippe (and others) at Pan Am that model 747 would resurrect that golden, bygone era for travelers.

As my self-guided solo tour continued, I glanced upward at the sawtooth roofline of the quarter-mile-long building. I loved those sawteeth and had ventured there occasionally two years before—on my own, alone, and without permission—partly because it was a challenge to climb a 60-foot caged ladder and partly because of curiosity about how the old Depression-era factory was built. Up there, among the giant sawteeth, there was absolute isolation from the teeming mass of humanity in the factory below. The place reminded me of an uninhabited desert of rolling black sand dunes, each with a sharp cliff on the lee side. Getting around from tooth to tooth meant walking up the slanted roof and down a 20-foot vertical ladder to the next tooth, again and again, eighteen times in all. Near the center of the roof, catwalks spanned the peaks from tooth to tooth, making negotiation of the entire 30 acres of roof a little easier.

As I looked up, I remembered exploring the maze and finding an abandoned barracks hidden from view between two of the sawteeth. It was basically a large tar-paper shack. My skin still crawled when recalling the spookiness that came over me when I first opened the door and entered the dark, stifling wartime relic. I witnessed rows of bunks stair-stepping one above the other on the slanted roof that was the barrack's only floor.

When old-timers were asked about the ghostly place high on the roof above, they told me that a platoon of black soldiers, probably about forty in number, had been assigned sentry duty at machine gun platforms on the building's four corners while the remainder of the unit stood by as firemen on the ready to handle any of the two-dozen fire hoses, in case of sabotage or incendiary attack. The assignment of black-only soldiers to the isolated roof duty and the construction of their flimsy wartime barracks with its slanted floor was a decision made solely by the segregated United States Army, and not Boeing. Never in my wanderings or inquiries did I find any evidence of segregation within Boeing at its Seattle-area plants.

Another reason I loved to go up into the giant sawteeth was because they marked the end of an era. For over a century, since before the Civil War, the most practical way to bring light and fresh air into large, flat buildings had been the sawtooth design. The slanted part channeled rainwater away, while the vertical part had windows for sunlight and ventilation. In 1939, that tradition still guided the industrial architects designing the huge flying-boat factory on the south shore of Lake Washington; however, just as the building was completed in 1941, tradition was thrown to the wind as more than fifty thousand glass windows in the sawteeth were painted black and then sealed shut. Not one beam of light could escape to reveal the location of the factory during wartime blackout conditions. The plant must remain hidden from the bombsights of marauding Japanese bombers launched from their aircraft carriers (which never arrived) off the Washington coast.

For workers inside, newly perfected fluorescent lights provided around-the-clock day-light, and forced-air blowers pumped fresh air in and stale air out far more efficiently than opening overhead windows in the sawteeth. The Depression-era Grand Coulee Dam was still new in 1942. It would provide plenty of hydroelectric power not only to run machinery and illuminate the workspace but also to refine bauxite into aluminum after the metal shortage of 1942. From my occasional perch up on the obsolete roof, I could look eastward across the tracks and see the new factory rising. It had a flat roof. Sawteeth were history.

I continued along the east side of the Renton factory and abruptly came to the shore of Lake Washington and, by looking west, could gaze upon the three lake-facing (or north) doors. There were only three of them—but what huge doors they were. Each was as wide as the length of a football field. They filled the entire 900-foot width of the building. I marveled at their size the first time I witnessed them in 1956, and I was awestruck when they folded up into the roof, revealing three open assembly halls with bridge cranes sweeping back and forth overhead all the way to the far end of the building—1,000 feet distant.

As a freshly minted civil engineer in the year 1957, I wondered why the span was 300 feet wide when the airplanes under construction were 131 and 145 feet, respectively. A 200-foot-wide assembly bay would have exceeded even the B-52's 185-foot span. A "takeaway" from engineering school and construction experience told me that the amount of steel in a structure increased roughly in proportion to the square of the span. So, the volume of steel required to span 300 feet was double the amount of steel needed to span 200 feet.

For a year, when sitting at my desk, I would occasionally look up and wonder, "Why would an engineer waste so much steel?" The hint of answer arrived in the form of Harold Mansfield's book titled *Vision*. The business history professor at Harvard dismissed Mansfield's book as not rising to the true standards of a business history tome, because it did not include profit and loss statements and the like. Nor did the book offer factory-building design guidance.

The answer to my question was derived by inference. By the 1930s, military-oriented aeronautical engineers had gathered data and crunched numbers. By 1933, the Army Air Corps began reaching for the "Holy Grail," a 10,000-mile bomber. Such a bomber would be truly intercontinental because, at a wing loading of 30 pounds per square foot, it had the fuel needed to fly 5,000 miles, drop bombs, and return to home base; however, it would require a wing 300 feet in length. To test the theory, a half-sized experimental aircraft was designed, built, and tested. The Boeing XB-15 of 1937 had a wingspan of 149 feet. While demonstrating the sought-after range, it was slow, fragile, and vulnerable to attack. The B-17 Flying Fortress was already flying, laden with armaments and much better suited for combat.

In any case, the theory was validated, but the means of propulsion for the full-sized aircraft was yet to be invented. The wings and engine configuration from the XB-15 found their way onto the model 314 Clipper. It could haul seventy passengers, or forty people in a luxury sleeping/dining configuration. The 314 had the range to make the 2,400-mile nonstop crossing from San Francisco Bay to Honolulu, the litmus test for trans-Pacific flight operations.

Eventually, twelve Clippers were built at Boeing's old Plant I (Ed Heath's former boatyard) on the Duwamish waterway, a few miles downstream from the recently established, and still growing, Plant II. Production was centered in an ancient wooden building with an assembly hall only 100 feet wide. The hall was far too narrow to contain a plane with a wingspan of 152 feet. The attachment of the wings to the fuselage had to be accomplished one aircraft at a time in a drydock-like appendage outside the factory, which extended over tidewater. It was a miserable way to build airplanes in Seattle's frequently rainy weather, and especially during wintertime cold snaps when snow and ice prevailed. The untoward conditions may have been yielding world-class airplanes, but engineers, workers, and management were all fed up with the situation.

It can be surmised that Boeing's Depression-era business plan envisioned three assembly halls, each with a production line of flying boats launching down the three concrete ramps that still make their way into the fresh water of Lake Washington. In their dreams, flying boats were expected to tie the world together, because far more global destinations then hosted harbors rather than adequate airports.

The Army Air Corps hired Boeing to build an experimental long-range bomber—the XB-15. It was deemed too fragile for combat and performed the wartime role of transport. The wings and engines were adapted onto model 314—one of the legendary Pan American Clippers—a flying boat.

The existing commercial seaplane base at Renton had gained notoriety in 1935, when Will Rogers, the humorist and popular Hollywood actor, along with Wiley Post, a famous aviator, took off on their ill-fated trip to Russia and died in a crash near Point Barrow, Alaska. Across the river was 200 acres of vacant swampy ground that seemed to be an ideal location for a flying-boat factory. The tract fronted on the lake and seemed a place where a flying boat with wings spanning nearly 300 feet (and a 10,000-mile range) could be built.

Boeing needed such a factory but lacked internal funding. That's when the US Navy stepped in. There existed a perpetual interservice rivalry between the Navy and the Army. A 10,000-mile seaplane would allow the Navy to rule the seas and project power that would otherwise be ceded to the Army if their Air Corps first reached the "Holy Grail" of long-range flight.

In July 1940, the Navy awarded Boeing a contract to build fifty-seven smaller PBB-1 Sea Ranger[4] patrol bombers for maritime surveillance missions. They were to be assembled in the new Boeing-operated factory on Lake Washington. Money for the factory came from federal funds via the Reconstruction Finance Corporation, with assignment to the Navy.

Size and attributes of the building were specified by Boeing. Oliver West, a Boeing factory production expert who favored multiple assembly lines for the same aircraft, dictated the

Despite a short (but wide) runway at Renton Airport, every Boeing-built aircraft has departed, but virtually none of them ever return. The general aviation airport continues to host a seaplane base with strange-looking pullout vehicles. *John Fredrickson photo*

The Navy's huge investment in the Renton sea plane factory yielded a single floatplane, the XPBB-1 Sea Ranger. The only Boeing model 344 constructed became known as the "Lone Ranger" when, after a rethink of wartime strategy, the Renton factory was turned over to Army Air Forces in preparation for B-29 production.

factory layout. Wellwood Beall was probably responsible for the 300-foot door span. Construction was by the Seattle branch of the Austin Company.

Although the Sea Ranger had only a 139-foot wingspan and 5,000-mile range, the Navy agreed to make the assembly bays wide enough to build a 10,000-mile patrol bomber in the future. To ensure the Navy would retain ownership and keep the Army's Air Corps at bay, absolutely no provision was made for a runway, other than the lake itself.

However, in the aftermath of the stunning Pearl Harbor debacle on December 7, 1941, the Navy abandoned the Sea Ranger concept. An intraservice deal was brokered early in 1942 to swap factories. The Navy would receive land-based, medium-sized aircraft for maritime surveillance from the newly constructed Kansas City B-25 factory. Army Air Forces then assumed ownership of the Renton plant—which was operated by Boeing. The B-29 was the nation's highest wartime priority, and the budget exceeded even the Manhattan Project, which yielded the world's first atomic weapon.

I noticed a 707 and a KC-135 beside me, as my lakeside meanderings continued. They had probably rolled out of the big doors in the wee hours of the morning on third shift. That is when moving the production line disrupted the fewest workers. Log-sized wheel chocks painted yellow ensured that the big birds would not accidentally roll into the lake. A tow team would soon arrive to pull them over a bridge across the Cedar River and onto the Renton Airport.

The bridge and airport were there courtesy of the Army Corps of Engineers. In 1940, the Navy planners did not believe a runway could be built in the narrow confines of the Cedar River delta. With no runway, the Renton plant would be a captive Navy factory for manufacture of Navy and Marine aircraft. For more than a century, the Army Corps of Engineers built levies, dams, locks, and canals by moving thousands of yards of hydraulic fill. Within a year after the war began, the narrow, swampy west side of the Cedar River became flat land filled with sand dredged from the bottom of Lake Washington, and ready for the first B-29 to take off.

As I walked under the wing of the KC-135 sitting at the lakeshore, a worker glanced at my badge, said nothing, and went on his way. I had an orange supervisor's badge, and on the bar were engraved the numbers 6-1000. The black numbers told him I was cleared for Secret and could be near a military airplane. The number 6 told him I worked in Transport Division, and 1000 designated the office of vice president and general manager. That badge combined with the spiral-bound steno pad I carried was my passport to wandering anywhere in the plant while looking official.

It was nice to be under the wing of an airplane again. I recalled my first job at Boeing as a junior engineer, grade B. Supervisors and above were exempt from punching a time clock. I was now a member of this elite category.

When the KC-135 I was standing beneath was towed to the Renton flight line it might get parked over the old sawdust pit if no other stall was available. Army engineers, in their wartime haste, demolished a large sawmill and simply paved over the sawdust pit. Therein was a dichotomy. When business was slow, there was no money to dig up the pit up properly fix the problem. When business was busy, every aircraft parking stall was needed. Some other junior engineer, grade B, was probably out there—counting cracks to ensure a brand-new (and never-flown) KC-135 would not sink into the pavement.

Now that I'd seen the factory building from the outside, I couldn't resist entering the huge final-assembly building. The biggest doors are for aircraft. Medium doors are for industrial vehicles—aircraft tugs, forklifts, and jitneys. Food service trucks bring coffee, donuts, and sandwiches to workers at break times. The smallest entryways are pedestrian doors.

All my senses were assaulted as I entered. My eyes brought back the familiar feeling of sheer volume. The temperature was comfortable. My nose conveyed the somewhat pleasant scent I call "new airplane smell," no doubt a complicated (but diluted) mixture of manufacturing solvents, sealants, fresh paint, and adhesives. But it was my ears that were filled with the nearby whine of air-driven drills at work, overlying the more distant din of rivets being bucked and the clatter of dollies laden with parts being towed. Yellow lines painted on the floor delineate separate space for pedestrians and items on wheels. The largest spaces were angled parking positions for aircraft under construction.

I walked along the KC-135 final-assembly line and then the 707 line. Production rates were higher than when I departed the year before. I noted that the KC-135 line had doubled in the west assembly hall from one to two. Preparations were under way to do the same on the 707 side. A single 300-foot bay, with its overhead cranes, comfortably held parallel assembly lines for these large airframes. This grand old building, designed for flying boats and completed before jet airplanes were invented, had gracefully entered the jet age. Maybe Harold Mansfield was correct: those old-timers—who seemed to do everything right for the wrong reasons—must have had a larger-than-life vision when they built the old Renton sawtooth plant.

H. Oliver West

H. Oliver West returned to Boeing with P. G. Johnson in 1939 and was soon executive vice president and a voting board member. His specialty was aircraft production. Mr. West was an advocate of multiple "short" production lines.

Jerry Sanford enlightened me regarding the wartime savant who spearheaded Boeing manufacturing. Sanford had recently been involved in CX and was also experienced with 707 and KC-135 production. While his peers donned uniforms and marched off to World War II, Jerry Sanford instead came to Boeing in April 1942, just five months after the attack on Pearl Harbor.

For the next three years, Sanford, an industrial engineer, worked under the direction of the legendary H. Oliver West. West hired into Boeing in 1921 as a receiving parts inspector. A brilliant mind rapidly earned him respect, more responsibilities, and the attention of P. G. Johnson—who recruited West to join him at United Air Lines. Later, in the aftermath of the Air Mail Act of 1934, West accompanied Johnson to Trans-Canadian Airlines. Oliver West was a master of organizing either aircraft construction or maintenance. West once again followed the jovial Johnson back to Boeing in 1939.

Under P. G. Johnson's sponsorship, H. Oliver West was soon executive vice president of operations (a Boeing term for manufacturing) and a voting member on the board of directors. Archival documents credit West with wartime plant construction and layout at Seattle, Renton, and Wichita.

The wartime practitioners of aircraft construction were of two divergent camps. One faction favored long production lines—which were successful at many sites; however, West wrote scholarly magazine articles advocating the multiple short lines in evidence at the Renton sawtooth factory, as manifested by those three adjacent sets of 300-foot-wide doors. He further argued for building aircraft in sections, putting everything possible into those sections, and joining them only as late as possible before rollout. This revelation convinced me that future aircraft factories with doors on both ends would provide maximum flexibility for manufacturing executives to establish either short or long production lines. That would become one of my contributions to the factory of the future.

Tour of Renton Continues

I then took the stairs to the balcony where it overlooked the wing line. Overhead cranes were carefully lowering wing skins into heavy steel wing panel jigs, where workers riveted on the spars and stiffeners, creating upper and lower wing panels. At the time, nobody anticipated that the service life of the KC-135 would match or exceed human life expectancy. Until then, airplanes either wore out or became obsolete within a few years.

Then, the cranes transferred the panels to nearby wing jigs to be completed. This activity took place with the panels and wings standing on their sides, upright, in a multiple series of steel jigs with platforms and catwalks for workers. The heavy riveting from so many guns, in such a compact place, was deafening.

On my trips around the factory in past years, I'd often gone to the edge of the balcony and listened to the din. It always reminded me of the roar of ocean surf in a storm. The noise was constant but seemed to rise and fall in regular waves. The teams worked in pairs, a riveter on one side of the wing panel and the assistant, the rivet bucker, on the other side. Separated by the thick wing skin and deafened by the noise, they could hardly communicate, yet their rivets had to be perfect and fuel-tight because fuel is carried in the wing. Not many women worked on the wing line. It was so hellish that it attracted men who were proud to go deaf just to say they worked there. They were respected as the "tough guys" of the factory. They could take it and survive—but eventually go deaf. Yes, they all wore ear plugs and earmuffs of the best quality, but twenty years on the wing line seemed to defeat even the finest-available hearing protection.

I left the balcony overlook reluctantly. It was time for lunch. I knew I'd find some of my old buddies heading for the cafeteria at 11:42 a.m., noon break time for the facilities department. The old-style cafeteria was 60 feet east of the big assembly building. I waited a few minutes and then joined Bruce Macklin and Claude Sourbeer, who were walking together. Bruce ran the layout unit, where dozens of large boards, each the size of a table tennis board, recorded the location of every desk, table, machine fixture, or airplane in the entire 4-million-square-foot complex. He

A Wichita bridge crane makes lifting an entire fuselage look easy. The hand signals previously stipulated in the Crane Operators Handbook have been superseded by handheld two-way radios.

knew everyone. He was the master of the yellow lines painted on the factory floor, because it was in his unit where bargains were struck on who got what regarding space, equipment, and layout. They also allocated everything else, from corner office space to parking lots.

I was happy to see them because they'd bring me up to date before I became immersed in my new job as staff planner at the division level. We filled our trays, found a table, and spent the remainder of the forty minutes discussing their work. Before lunch was over, it seemed like I hadn't been gone at all. The problems hadn't changed, the people hadn't changed, and the work hadn't changed.

I made my way to the 10-50 building after lunch. I wanted to walk through the factory I'd helped build. The new 10-50 building was "my" factory, especially the 10-ton bridge crane system in the high bay. I was still a junior construction engineer when the crane newly installed in the unfinished building malfunctioned.

It was with a sense of pride that I walked into the high bay of the 10-50 building again. When asked, a worker stated, "The cranes are running great." I looked up and waved at a crane operator. I think I recognized him. He waved back. Maybe he recognized me. I left the building all pumped up and headed for Earl Combs's office. He was a tough bastard? So was I.

Needed: An Outsized USAF Airlifter

With war in Vietnam approaching, constant tension in Korea, and the ongoing Soviet threat in Europe, the Pentagon needed modern airlifters. The Douglas products (C-54, C-124, and C-133) were obsolete. On April 7, 1955, the Georgia Division of Lockheed first flew a four-engine-turboprop, high-wing transport designated C-130 Hercules. With a takeoff roll of a mere 800 feet, it was a great tactical airlifter but lacked the range, speed, and capacity for long-haul missions.

The Air Force let a "request for proposal" (or RFP) for what became a swept-wing, turbojet-powered, elongated C-130. Lockheed won the contract to build the C-141A Starlifter. Transporting a Minuteman ICBM, dropping troops or cargo, landing on Antarctic ice, or medical evacuations were all within the C-141's daily repertoire. Pending delivery of Starlifters starting in 1965, Renton provided interim airlift in the form of C-135 cargo planes, which had the speed and range to quickly deliver heavy loads of cargo where needed; however, the Army and Air Force preferred the Lockheed Starlifter's high-wing design. It was better suited for airdrop of supplies or troops, and the cargo floor was low to the ground, which facilitated loading of wheeled or tracked vehicles.

A new Air Force requirement emerged and then began to evolve. It started as "CX" (Cargo Experimental), then CX-4, next becoming CX-HLS (Heavy Lift System), and finally

Now retired, the versatile Lockheed C-141B Starlifter was the first airplane to bring military airlift into the jet age. After retrofitting for aerial refueling in the 1970s, it could deliver heavy loads anywhere needed. *Museum of the Air Force photo*

Freshly landed amid storm clouds at U-Tapao Airfield during the waning days of the Vietnam War, this Lockheed C-5A is delivering a large load of priority cargo. The largest airlifter in the USAF inventory remains hobbled by poor reliability, as measured by "mission capable" metrics published in the *Air Force Times*. *John Fredrickson photo, ca. 1972*

was designated C-5A—a tiny moniker for such a massive airplane. The requirement stipulated an airlifter large enough to transport outsized cargo, including large helicopters or main battle tanks, plus passengers in the form of technicians and operators. Boeing opted to go all out to win the competition for the world's largest military transport.

Three thousand people were assigned to the proposal effort, which was led by T. A. Wilson (1921–1999), who had recently earned the internal celebrity status as leader of the very successful Minuteman project. By 1965, Wilson's team intended to use existing facilities at Plant II in Seattle.

Like bees swarming about their hive, Plant II had evolved into the ancestral home for everything Boeing. The plant was adequate for B-17 manufacturing during World War II, so it remained at the crux of the Boeing cultural universe. However, the proposed C-5A aircraft, with a footprint in excess of a B-52, would overwhelm the 1930s-vintage sawtooth factories. Wilson persisted in his quest to stuff a giant airplane into an obsolete factory. Partial teardown of Plant II was required. Rebuilding would then be needed to increase the final-assembly bay head height from 40 to 70 feet, along with installing heavier overhead cranes.

Expanding to Kent and Auburn

Under the proposed C-5 scenario, the fabrication of aircraft parts would be displaced from Plant II and require a new home. The logical site was Kent, where several hundred recently purchased acres of rich farmland, bordering the Green River, were in excess of the proposed construction footprint for the new Boeing Space Center; however, in a demonstration of the schism between military and commercial segments of Boeing, Bob Regan, director of manufacturing for Commercial Airplanes, wanted sole jurisdiction over parts fabrication. He did not want to be subservient to the growing space operations in Kent, or to their NASA customer.

Our facilities group proposed buying 260 acres in Auburn from Vic Markov, an ex-Husky All-American football player, who had gone into the tire business and other ventures. He purchased the property as surplus from the US government and tried unsuccessfully to make it into an industrial park. There were 600,000 square feet of empty warehouse space and another 100 acres, plus a million square feet of warehouse space adjoining land Commercial Airplanes leased from the Air Force. I made a layout of the Auburn fabrication buildings on the Markov property.

Meanwhile, the Aerospace Division had ideas, which included placing the fabrication buildings at Kent—where there was adequate road access, proximity to Seattle's airport, and plenty of suitable land for offices, plant, and employee parking. With construction of a campus of small manufacturing buildings in mind, their facilities director wanted to be forced to take the fabrication center as an unwelcome interloper; therefore, he made no effort to actively promote this opportunity. He was unaware that Commercial Airplanes had an alternative plan of their own.

Both competing plans were taken to Boeing president Bill Allen for adjudication. Allen valued input from expertly qualified outside consultants and opted to engage a longtime trusted source, the Austin Company. Al Waidelich, Austin's senior vice president in Cleveland, was invited to Seattle for on-site evaluation, alternatives analysis, and providing an opinion. Waidelich was also a visiting professor at MIT. I had worked with the Austin Company, established a relationship of trust, and knew that Allen deferred to them for his most-important decisions, in preference to the advice of his own facilities managers.

Waidelich was intercepted. We showed him our scale models of Auburn and the associated site logic. We also demonstrated a scale model of the Boeing Kent Space Center, with big fabrication buildings that would detract from the campus setting of a new space center, conforming to still-fuzzy NASA expectations.

The Austin Company had done the original plan for the Kent site and constructed the space chamber building, but the Aerospace Division facilities department eschewed "fast track" design construction; they preferred design-bid construction and therefore excluded Austin from any further work at Kent. Waidelich knew this. He also was aware that Transport Division was forced to expedite construction because we too often got late approval from headquarters, which left no time for design and bid. He grasped and fully understood the message embedded in our meeting—the Austin Company would probably get to build a new parts plant in Auburn—but only if that site was selected. The next day, Waidelich advised Boeing president Bill Allen that Auburn was the best site for the Fabrication Division.

Our group was responsible for facilities planning for the new site in Auburn as well as the assembly plant in Renton. On September 9, 1965, under a Transport Division contract, the Austin Construction Company broke ground at Auburn for a process assembly building, followed immediately by a huge spar- and skin-milling building, a large numerically controlled machining building, and, later, a sprawling tooling building. When expansion was complete in 1967, the new Auburn plant totaled 2.9 million square feet.

Sections of wing skin and spar are typically assembled as a unit in an automated manufacturing process. The units can be both long and wide. Protective coatings are applied by dipping the assemblies into tanks. The dip tanks at Auburn measured up to 115 feet long and 12 feet deep; however, the soil conditions at Auburn were perfect for manufacturing. As a floodplain, the site was flat and level. Furthermore, the moraine deposits were rich in heavy gravel, perfect for providing a solid building surface. Meanwhile, the soil at the downstream Kent location was great for farming, with a mix of volcanic ash and silt. Buildings there, like Renton and the Duwamish corridor, required the driving of pilings beneath them.

Henceforth, plant sites would typically belong either to Aerospace or Commercial Divisions—and not be shared. This reduced haggling with the government regarding allocation of overhead expenses. Auburn, Everett, Renton, and Plant II came under the commercial umbrella. Kent and Developmental Center were Aerospace.

The Boeing Auburn plant derived from a mixture of "greenfield" (or agricultural land) and US government surplus warehouses repurposed into a modern industrial complex.

Hidden away in the back shops of Fabrication Division, a typical automated milling machine grinds away on an aluminum forging while leaving behind a mountain of shavings, all of which will be recycled.

The aerial view of Auburn belies the fact it is sitting on gravel, the only remaining evidence that the site once hosted retreating glaciers extending all the way from Mount Rainier, a nearby 14,411-foot dormant volcano.

CHAPTER 6
Welcome to the 1960s

For Americans, the 1960s was a memorable decade of euphoric accomplishment, humbling defeats, chronic frustrations, and societal change. Young men grew long hair as British music and pot smoking invaded North America. An unpopular military draft dispatched many of them to a vicious war of insurgency in the tropical heat of Vietnam. Separately, a trio of vexing assassinations (John F. Kennedy, Martin Luther King Jr., and Robert Kennedy) rocked the nation's psyche even as President Lyndon Johnson attempted to redress a legacy of racial and economic injustice by declaring war on poverty.

The apex year was 1969. The 747, which would change air travel worldwide, made its maiden flight on February 9. US technology prevailed and JFK's goal was met when Neil Armstrong stepped onto the lunar surface and planted the US flag in July 1969.

U-Tapao Airfield was SAC's most forward-operating base during the Vietnam War. A globe-spanning B-52D is cleared to land at sunrise for refueling, rearming, and a fresh aircrew. The standard load was 112 conventional bombs weighing 60,000 pounds. *John Fredrickson photos*

Mounting machine guns on airplanes started in World War I. The B-52D tail gunner sat alone with an aft scanning radar, four .50-caliber machine guns, and 2,400 rounds of ammunition. *Museum of the Air Force photo*

As a wartime defensive measure B-52s were rearmed, refueled, and otherwise serviced in revetments. The SAC crews manifest shined shoes, regulation haircuts, and proper uniforms despite performing daily combat sorties.

The Boeing-built CH-47 Chinook entered military service during the 1960s and remains vital to US Army air operations. Boeing acquired the Philadelphia company named VERTOL (acronym for vertical takeoff and landing) in 1960. *Boeing photo*

A skilled and experienced munitions load team could load 60,000 pounds of high-explosive munitions onto a B-52D in less than an hour, despite rainfall and temperatures of 90°F.

A crew arrives by bus to begin preflight tasks. In Air Force lore, the crew chief (shirtless in the tropical heat) "owns" the airplane. He lets the aircrew borrow it, expects it to be flown hard in combat, but wants it returned in good order.

Boeing products played a significant role in the Vietnam War. Older B-52s were culled from SAC's (Strategic Air Command's) nuclear fleet and retrofitted at Wichita for the dropping of conventional bombs. KC-135 tankers were rotated from their home base for aerial-refueling duty in the Southeast Asia war zone. Despite a politically divisive, mismanaged, and unpopular war, SAC-trained ground crews and air crews remained resolute in the performance of their combat roles. Tens of thousands of sorties were flown. Both the B-52 and KC-135 excelled in their wartime assignments.

Called On by Surprise

Meanwhile, back at the factory in Renton, I had worked on Transport Division's president John Yeasting's staff as long-range divisional planner for the three years since graduating from Harvard Business School. Yeasting was an accountant and almost bloodthirsty in his desire to beat all competitors. He told me in 1961, at a private meeting in his office regarding divisional goals and objectives, that his personal goal was to shut down the Douglas Aircraft Company production line. He said, "I can't write that down, but that's my goal. We've doomed the Convair production line. We've shut down the Lockheed Electra [model L-188] production line. Next, I want to shut down Douglas Commercial."

However malicious Yeasting was as a competitor, he issued ultraconservative sales forecasts and was a very frugal operator. His way to control the internal business plan was to slash the sales forecasts. I observed this propensity first in 1961 and then again in 1962. This was the primary reason I departed Division Offices and transferred to Facilities' long-range planning under Erle Barnes, where I had the freedom to look way ahead.

Tell 'em what long-range planning is, Johnny.

I was stunned and not prepared to speak. The month was January 1963, and as a thirty-one-year-old planner, I had just transferred into the Facilities Department. With barely time to unpack my belongings, I was told to attend this semiannual luncheon for some thirty top managers of the two-thousand-employee facilities department.

The luncheon, held in a room adjacent to the Renton factory executive dining room, was intended to be informative and motivational. I had been seated between the manager of plant transportation and the manager of plumbers and pipe fitters. The server had asked us to write either salmon or steak on a blank slip of paper. Out of the corner of my eye, I saw one of them writing "samon." The other wrote "STAKE!" with so much gusto the pencil broke when he hit the dot on the bottom of the exclamation mark.

Wanting to fit into this largely blue-collar department, I waited a moment until their attention was directed to Erle Barnes, the department director, who began to speak. Only then did I unobtrusively print "steak." I was so pleased at hiding my education that Barnes's first words were barely heard—distracted as I was by thoughts about being in a department that was 85 percent unionized hourly workers. I relaxed, sat back, and prepared to savor a free executive luncheon in my new department.

Suddenly, Barnes dropped it on me. "Tell 'em what long-range planning is, Johnny." Startled, I stood up, looked around the room, and attempted to gather my thoughts.

How could I explain long-range planning to the two men sitting beside me and about thirty others when I didn't know what it was myself? Attempting to speak, I hesitated. My vocal cords, damaged by polio, responded with a long "uhh," followed by silence.

People shifted in their chairs, waiting uncomfortably. Another "uhh." Finally, words came slowly. "Buildings last forty years. Uhh. They depreciate slowly. They'll be on the books for, uhh, forty years. We use sum of the years' digits, uhh, to depreciate buildings. Uhh, and double-straight-line declining balance on vehicles, uhh. Vehicles depreciate in three years."

I continued stumbling, describing tax effects and how military investment is short range due to appropriation uncertainty, while commercial business allows long-term investment.

After about five minutes of gibberish, Barnes rescued me by interjecting, "By god, we're going to quit building doghouses, aren't we, Johnny? We're going to get ahead of the curve. I'm tired of building lean-tos and doghouses."

I knew I had done a terrible job, and returned to my office discouraged. I was embarrassed that a Harvard Business School graduate would do so poorly. I had been trained to always be prepared—but failed on this instance.

J. W. Maulbetch, Barnes's staff assistant, entered my office, closed the door, and said, "Your speaking needs improvement. You said 'uhh' twenty-three times."

My boss, Don Davis, sensed how disappointed I was. He was next to enter my office and said with a smile, "Cheer up, John. Barnes has just helped write your position statement. Your job is to quit building doghouses."

"Yeah," I said, "that's the result he wants. How do I write that into a position description?"

Davis continued apologetically. "I had no idea Barnes would ask you to speak. I'd have advised you to prepare some talking points, had I known."

"I need more than talking points," I replied.

"Take your time thinking about long-range planning," continued Davis. "We have a lot of work to do. Your help is needed guiding the planners in their daily work. Spend about half your time working long-range and half helping others."

When Davis left my office, I continued to ruminate about my terrible performance, as a concept resonated within my mind—"Buildings last forty years." I knew that was arbitrary, but it provided an approximate planning horizon to work with. I decided to resurrect every study I'd done that had a forty-year horizon.

The standard civil engineering problem of college days at Gonzaga University asked a student to size a new water supply for a town of ten thousand people. What will be the future size of that town? Is it growing? How fast? What will be the population in forty years? The same, less, or more? The available information is plotted on an S curve. The gamble is where to place the town on the standard S curve.

Translating that to Boeing Transport Division, where is Transportation Division on a standard S curve with a forty-year horizon? I had attempted to plot that two years before, when I became chief of long-range planning for Boeing Commercial.

I solicited the help of two economists from Marketing Research. They readily found records of US population from 1790 to 1960. They projected the trend line to the year 2000 and forward another forty years to the year 2040. They estimated the population was growing about 1.5 times every forty years. At that rate, the population would grow from 180 million in 1960 to 270 million in 2000 to 405 million in 2040.

They cautioned that gross domestic product (GDP) was growing much faster—at least four or five times larger every forty years. They said economists had been working on this for thirty years, ever since the Great Depression, and had adjusted for inflation. With the US economy at a half-trillion dollars in 1960, that would be about $2.2 trillion in 2000 and $10 trillion by 2040 (all in 1960s dollars).

When asked about the aircraft market, they responded that passenger and cargo aircraft were considered prime transportation, and that prime transportation normally led the GDP, citing the growth of railroads and ships during the age of steam, the rise of automobile transport, and the huge growth of telephone, telegraph, and radio in the transporting of messages.

As a result of this study, I could confidently state that the Boeing Transport Division, if it maintained its 70 percent market share, would be five to ten times as big in the year 2000 as it was in the year 1960. And this was only the United States. The world was growing too, and Boeing had the lion's share of that lucrative marketplace.

At the division level, where a ten-year horizon prevailed, the forty-year study was discounted as dreaming, so I just put it on the shelf and almost forgot it. Now, three years later in 1963, Boeing was nearing 75 percent commercial market share, and my horizon had shifted to forty years. Renton was almost full, with all 4 million square feet fully utilized. This simple study showed that in forty years, the need would be somewhere between 20 and 40 million square feet. A doghouse or two would never suffice. Four or five new plants would be needed.

Erle Barnes

My relationship with Erle Barnes had gotten off to an embarrassing start at the luncheon. At a company with an intense focus on the most-advanced aerospace products, it's easy to see the opportunity for congenial people who could reliably oversee the more mundane overhead functions such as paying bills, staffing libraries, mowing grass, and washing windows. Boeing was a place where an occasional smart, savvy, and persistent person—with no education beyond high school—could make it into the executive ranks.

Affable Erle Barnes, director of facilities, was such a person. Lacking the gravitas of an advanced degree, I harbored qualms about his leadership. But, at over 6 feet in height, lean, and with a dignified bearing, he had a calm demeanor, quick wit, great instincts, and a knack for managing people. His pedigree included a stint with Greyhound as a bus driver. He told stories about applying tire chains to buses stalled atop Snoqualmie Pass in the rugged Cascade Range during wintertime blizzard conditions. His reputation for staying on schedule while remaining level headed and polite under stress yielded him a promotion to Greyhound bus system dispatcher for their Seattle district.

The war intervened. Boeing needed experienced transportation supervisors to organize and manage fleets of trucks, pickups, buses, forklifts, overhead cranes, and even the tractors that towed the heavy bombers. Other than hand-carried items, nothing moved at Boeing without the massive operation that came under Erle Barnes.

When the Renton plant was reactivated to build propeller-driven aircraft for the newly formed United States Air Force in 1950, Barnes's assignment was expanded beyond transportation and into the new role of maintenance custodian for the entire Renton campus. During that era, engineering and other office functions remained in Seattle. Things began to change starting in 1955, as orders for jet-powered transport aircraft began to roll in. New office space was needed at Renton to host engineers and every other white-collar skill needed to gear up production to match rising customer demand.

Barnes's job suddenly changed from transportation expert to responsibility for all Boeing Commercial's facilities. After ten years of hastily constructing buildings at the last instant, Barnes wanted rational planning that anticipated emerging requirements.

Boeing Transformation

Meanwhile, what changed at Boeing during the year 1965? "Old Boeing" was dependent on government contracts for most of its revenue. A series of rejected contract proposals, concurrent with ascendancy of the commercial airliner business, shifted the business base like an earthquake. The jolt hit Aerospace unit senior management the hardest because they tended to be rooted in the business of defense. First-line supervisors, their workers, and the engineers were more flexible. They could readily transition between the two worlds whenever the need arose.

To this day, few observers (including insiders) have understood that like a lowly leaf-eating caterpillar that metamorphoses into a beautiful butterfly, "old" Boeing adroitly transformed itself into "new" Boeing. An internal overhaul was performed, analogous to a magician

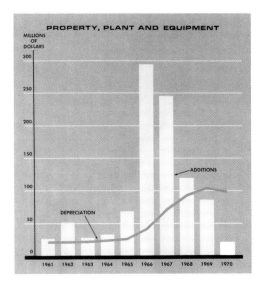

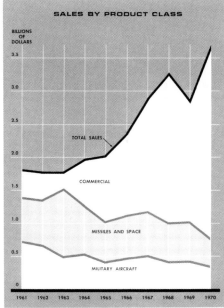

Spending on property, plant, and equipment spiked in 1966–67. This new capacity, combined with increased worldwide demand for jetliners, shifted the Boeing sales mix away from military, missiles, and space and into commercial airliners. *Boeing Annual Report, 1970*

cloaked in a cape—with everybody watching but nobody seeing. On the basis of rapidly unfolding events, the climax of the transformation played out over the second half of 1965 and the first half of 1966, which is the nexus of our story.

The Pentagon's demand for military hardware may have been big, but global demand for personal and business travel remains overwhelming. For example, Lockheed built 131 C-5 Galaxy wide-body transports, while B-52 jet bomber production ended at 744. Model 747 deliveries bested 1,500, and model 737 lifetime production exceeded ten thousand units in January 2019. Meanwhile, airlines are worldwide and plentiful. Even the loss of a failed longtime partner (such as Pan Am) is mitigated by emerging new air carriers.

Critical Mass

The infrastructure at Boeing was especially interchangeable. The original Renton sawtooth factory is a classic example. Built to accommodate globe-spanning floatplanes, it gave birth to B-29 bombers during World War II. Now, eighty years after construction, it houses the heavily automated model 737 wing line. A transonic wind tunnel dating to 1943, aircraft parking stalls, paint hangars, and concrete runways make no distinction between airliners and military aircraft.

Business continued to grow, and both the Seattle and Renton sites were overflowing with humanity, traffic congestion, and lack of parking.

The solution was to decentralize the workforce. The Seattle suburbs soon hosted various office buildings, aerospace laboratories, warehouses, and manufacturing plants that sprouted like springtime weeds on hundreds of acres of greenfield. The investment spiked in 1966. Henceforth, the airliner business was deeply rooted into the eastern shore of Puget Sound. "Critical mass" had been achieved. Frequent change created a nimble infrastructure. Everything

A Boeing 707 in TWA livery departs LAX in the early days of jet transportation. Pan Am exclusively handled overseas routes, while TWA had a mix of domestic and international destinations. Neither company survived airline deregulation.

needed to spawn a new model was instantly available. If the 707 variants are counted, by 1959, new airplanes were arriving at a pace of one new model every two years.

Human skills, including product development, design engineering, and manufacturing talent, were plentiful. Then, there were physical components: final-assembly bays were located on three separate airfields, parts plants and back shops filled with the most-advanced automated machinery abounded, while labs and wind tunnels facilitated experimentation and rapid refinements to existing technology. Flight testing leading the FAA certification became a core competency. All forms of customer support—ranging from crew training to spare parts, documentation, and on-site repair of a damaged airframe—were instantly available.

An educational system evolved in the geographically isolated northwest corner of America, which delivered young people well suited for either white-collar work (college graduates) or blue-collar industrial work (high school graduates). Capable employees were recruited and then inculcated with the specialized skills needed to master their own tiny part of the far-ranging enterprise.

A mild climate, wonderful nearby outdoor recreation, and lack of other nearby aerospace employers delivered to Boeing a stable, competent, and reliable workforce willing to make a lifetime commitment—despite the perpetual threat of layoff on the next market downswing.

CHAPTER 7
Buildings 4-81 and 4-82

In February 1965, I directed the creation and distribution of a "limited" fifty-page brochure titled *Long Range Facilities Site Plan: Boeing Renton* ("limited" is a Boeing term for sensitive or restricted information). Internal documents rarely received glossy covers or were printed on premium paper. But this important document traced the twenty-five-year history of the site and was intended to guide its future for at least the next twenty-five years. Designed like a family photo album, the document was long on images but short on words.

During the first twenty-five years, the Renton site had produced four thousand large aircraft and doubled in size. It had grown from 2.3 million square feet on 95 acres to 4.3 million square feet on 190 acres. The last two-thirds of the document showed, step by step, how the plant might again be doubled, growing to 8.6 million square feet on 400 acres, all the while remaining modern and producing future aircraft of much-larger size.

The summary had a Renton land acquisition plan, which listed thirty-three parcels totaling 222.2 acres. Two parcels had the highest priority. One was a 22-acre parcel owned by the railroad that had recently been listed as for sale. Its role for us was to provide employee parking, thus alleviating a current constraint. The other was a 60-acre tract with an obsolete power generation station owned by Puget Sound Power and Light Company, the local electric utility. This tract was essential for expansion of Renton's aircraft final assembly.

My department leader, Erle Barnes, was extremely pleased with the document. He finally had a long-range plan to use when the need for more space arose, thus avoiding the hodge-podge of temporary lean-to and doghouse structures scattered about the site. Barnes hated "doghouses," a derisive term for temporary structures.

Senior factory manager Bob Regan liked the plan because it expanded the original flying-boat factory with its three big doors extending on both the south and east. Regan's plea had always been for "one-roof" manufacturing. He maintained that the most efficient way to build airplanes was to do it under one roof with an integrated overhead crane system.

The brochure contained no surprises for Boeing president Bill Allen or CAG president John Yeasting. Both were members of the board of directors. Most of the senior management at Boeing sat through one or more of my presentations about the future and growth. In the manner akin to houses or hotels on a *Monopoly* board game, scale models applied to oversized aerial photographs were a powerful tool to show how the Renton site must grow, and how even that growth could not contain the Transport Division for very long. Jet transports had been eagerly embraced by the traveling public starting in 1959. Now, six years later, passenger seat miles were growing at 10 percent per year, with no end in sight.

My message had been loud and clear. Boeing would need to expand at Renton. Furthermore, a much-bigger factory would soon be needed on another airport. All the top managers who saw my presentation said they enjoyed the look into the future, and that a new plant was logical, but not probable, within the current five-year planning cycle.

The planning base for 1965 dated back to 1964 and established the budgets, staffing, technology, and need for facilities. The planning base, as approved by the division president, John Yeasting, went beyond conservatism into pessimism.

Slashing of the sales forecast for 1965 in mid-1964 triggered corporate top managers to think that Commercial was going out of business. If Yeasting's intent was to look good by exceeding the airliner sales forecast, it was a dangerous form of bravado that instead yielded an inadequate number of workers, insufficient working space, and operating constraints everywhere. Furthermore, this contradicted my own forecasts regarding the need for more land and new facilities.

Thus, on the day the glossy brochure was published, only two tiny new buildings were in work. One was a small, shedlike, 24,000-square-foot, open-air trucking terminal with roof. The other was a 10,000-square-foot, sheet-metal, prefabricated building for the 737 program master models (master models, as full-sized replicas of airplane sections, were reference tools). The 737 was a new program just getting underway that would backfill the KC-135 tanker that was phasing out. These buildings were the little "sheds and doghouses" that Erle Barnes detested.

The remaining 4 million square feet of expansion shown on the long-range site plan for Renton had no timetable. A new plant on another site, a factory for the future, with millions more square feet, was in fantasyland. What a shocking difference twelve short months can make! Had I gone to sleep in February 1965 and awoke a year later, I would not have been surprised to learn that

- Boeing had a huge new building under construction at Renton for increased production of 707 and 727 airliners.
- The 737 program would require an entirely new factory on the Thompson tract, plus a big stake within Plant II.
- The 747 program would move into the world's largest building at the "factory of the future" on Everett's Paine Field.
- A new cadre of shops in Auburn would fabricate clips, angles, brackets, ducts, skins, spars, and the myriad of larger assemblies (not otherwise vended but) necessary to produce airliners at the other sites.

These were the actions I had been predicting and advocating since 1963. My nightmare was to awake and find that I was charged with accomplishing this. It was not a bad dream. I could not go back to sleep. There was too much work to be accomplished! Luckily, I had the full support of my bosses—Don Davis and Erle Barnes. After delivering copies of the glossy brochure to corporate headquarters, I met with them.

"We agree," Barnes stated, "with your assessment that land acquisition is paramount. The brochure drives a stake and puts them on notice. What's the next priority?"

Purchasing land from the railroad for employee parking on the east edge of the Renton site was first. It was bogged down because Bill Allen and his real estate consultant, Elmer Sill, opted to haggle regarding price and delayed acquisition from May until December.

Davis answered next: "The most important thing is expansion of final assembly. We need to know in detail what a new building will look like and how much it will cost. We advocate hiring the Austin Company to perform an engineering trade study and preliminary estimate. John is best suited to manage this task."

The first 737 is seen in flight. It was acquired for research by NASA and then, after decades of service, delivered to the Museum of Flight, where it is on public display bearing NASA livery.

Business Is Booming

As the calendar flipped to April 1965, we were ready to go in Renton. The existing factory was bulging with work. Customers were clamoring to get delivery of the model 727. Every US trunk carrier would eventually operate it. The trijet was delivering 15 percent better fuel efficiency than promised. It was faster than any other commercial plane in the skies, flew like a swept-wing fighter, and dominated the world market for midrange jets. With three engines, it was certified for overwater routes off limits to twin jets.

Government assistance in the form of the Export-Import Bank fostered a growing offshore market for airliners. Savvy marketeers befriended potential customers and wooed them with the latest offerings, ranging from hundred-passenger short-haul passenger jets to aerial freighters and the globe-spanning 707-320. People worldwide gradually lifted themselves from a subsistence-based existence into the middle class. Citizens of Asia, Europe, and the Middle East were achieving levels of affluence never previously imagined.

United Airlines announced the largest commercial order ever placed by an airline on April 5, 1965. The order for aircraft to be built in Renton was for sixty-six jetliners, options on thirty-nine others, and leasing of twenty-five more. Financial data made public indicate the Commercial Airplane Division backlog at the end of 1966 was worth $4.4 billion. It swelled to $5.9 billion by the end of 1967 as airlines raced against each other to secure aircraft for their fleets.[1]

Yet, the pessimistic planning baseline for 1965 had not been changed. Wes Mauldin was a forty-five-year-old production expert from corporate headquarters with a curious reputation for working in a darkened office during daylight hours and a becoming a party animal after sunset. Wes paid Transport Division a visit and took one look at the growing manufacturing backlog, and his eyes grew wide. He hastily returned to headquarters to report that Yeasting had a tiger by the tail!

Who Was the Austin Company?

Samuel Austin, a recently immigrated British carpenter, founded the Austin Company in 1878. The business prospered. With at least twenty regional branches, the demonstrated core competency was engineering and rapid construction of factory buildings. Their clientele included automobile plants, food processing, chemical production, and more. Owning a major steel fabrication plant was a key success factor to achieving speedy construction.[2]

During the 1960s, the Austin Company, in aggregate, had about five thousand engineers and sometimes fifty thousand construction workers on the payroll. Each branch was a mirror image of the home office in Cleveland, with Austin Associates as the professional arm and the Austin Company as the construction operation. The Austin Company was privately owned by its senior partners. Most of these partners were professional engineers or architects with licenses that allowed them to sell engineering and architectural services. Professional licenses are issued by each state and are governed by that state's board of professional engineering examiners. This is much like state bar associations, which hold bar exams and govern the practice of law in that state.

The Austin Company was also composed of a huge construction company. Construction companies do not need professional licenses. Instead, they must abide by various state and local covenants, including electrical, mechanical, plumbing, structural, and other codes. The top people in a construction company are often master craftsman, such as carpenters, plumbers, electricians, ironworkers, steamfitters, and laborers. Sometimes a tradesman would work up to the presidency of the branch construction arm and become a senior partner in the overall Austin Company.

Austin guaranteed schedules because of their unique strike avoidance strategy. Their "no strike" clause was predicated on a national agreement with labor unions, whereby Austin abided by the locally prevailing rates of pay and work rules.

To deal with all this complexity, the Austin Company was organized into two separate legal entities: Austin Associates, which did the professional planning and design, and Austin Company, to do construction. The Cleveland headquarters presided over both entities. Seattle was the home of Austin's Pacific Northwest region.

On the basis of past performance, the reputation of the Austin Company was impeccable. Their résumé with Boeing started during the Depression and included Plant II, Renton, Developmental Center, Kent, and Wichita—plus various expansions at these same sites. Starting with my first construction assignment at Renton, I came to respect the Austin Company because they were capable and honest.

Wally Engstrom, about seventy years of age, was a semiretired partner who maintained an office at Austin's Seattle office and stayed informed on major projects. Cy Prideaux was not well known by Bill Allen because Prideaux only recently had taken over the reins of Austin in Seattle (in 1960). Their sustained performance at Boeing over the years by Wally Engstrom (and staff) over thirty years had gained for them the complete confidence of Bill Allen and the other top executives.

Cy Prideaux, about fifty-eight years old, was senior partner and vice president actively in charge of the Austin's entire Pacific Northwest regional operation. Prideaux's background was engineering, augmented by three decades of hands-on construction projects with large factories for other industries.

Al Waidelich, also about fifty-eight years of age, was the senior partner responsible for site planning, architectural design, and structural design at Austin's Cleveland headquarters. Waidelich managed construction at the Developmental Center in 1956, while Engstrom was simultaneously in charge of the Renton expansion. Mr. Waidelich was also a visiting professor of architectural design at MIT (Massachusetts Institute of Technology). The remuneration of these three construction industry moguls probably matched or exceeded any Boeing senior executive.

Client relationships built on trust at the executive level were a part of Bill Allen's internalized system of Industrial Age chivalry. That's why law firms keep their semiretired senior partners on the payroll until they die. Allen remained an invisible partner at Perkins Coie law firm. So also are engineering firms organized as partnerships. For that reason, Engstrom, Waidelich, and, separately, real estate consultant Elmer Sill were so influential with Bill Allen. Prideaux, the active senior partner in charge of daily operations, was my primary contact at Austin and critical both to me and the Boeing Company.

I had studied the history of Boeing facilities far more than any other senior facilities manager. I quickly realized the way to bypass the morass of headquarters bureaucracy was to use the pipeline of Prideaux via Engstrom directly to Allen.

Aware that Engstrom came to the Austin office almost every day, and his office was adjacent to Prideaux's, obviously Engstrom was observing everything going on and was familiar with all the major problems. I assumed that Bill Allen telephoned Wally Engstrom on a weekly or monthly basis to get Engstrom's opinion about construction progress.

I never mentioned this to others and used the relationship very sparingly, but I always asked Prideaux to make sure Engstrom was prepared to address any current construction problems that would likely make their way into Boeing headquarters. The Austin executives were as vital to the transformation of Boeing during the 1960s as anybody—either inside or outside Boeing.

Planning a New Renton Factory Building

Major building projects start with the conceptual phase, advance to preliminary design, then to budgeting and final design. Only then can construction and occupancy take place. For years, I had operated much like a management consultant. Now I was charged with molding my concepts into something realistic.

In June 1965, I rounded up assistance from the Austin Company in the form of Cy Prideaux and his lead structural engineer, named Dennis Koskinen. They took immediate interest in our project, especially after informing them of the likely need for the new 747 assembly plant (with a location yet to be determined).

"The study we need is pretty simple," I said. "Two new assembly bays, each 300 feet wide and 900 feet long, on Puget Power's property, just east of the existing final assembly. We have not yet purchased the property. This is just a study." I placed an approximate scale model on a simulated aerial photo. "The bay width is firm at 300 feet. The overhead height, the tonnage of the cranes (either 30 or 60 ton), and hook height (either 75 or 100 feet) remain to be determined."

As they pondered the scale model, I further explained, "Note the doors. We are specifying something unique—hangar doors on both ends. Having back doors on 900-foot-long bays will allow us to produce on a single production line 1,800 feet long, if the need arises." The Austin people paid close attention and took notes, as I concluded, "The building we are now studying may be the first step into the future. We need to get this building right. Our future factories will probably be more of the same." Prideaux thanked me and requested a tour of the existing factory.

"That's a good idea," I said. My engineering assistant, Jim Laws, set out on the walking tour with Prideaux and Koskinen.

Two days later we met again. "Our preliminary analysis indicates problems with the columns," said Prideaux. "We use star columns for buildings with 10-ton cranes and 40-foot hooks. They are inadequate for 30- or 60-ton cranes at 75- or 100-foot hook height. The choices are concrete bridge piers or heavy steel lattice columns."

"The place will look like a cathedral," I said. "You can rule out concrete bridge piers. I won't have concrete in any factory that I am charged with designing—except the floor. I had too much trouble trying to modify a concrete building and guessing where the reinforcement was—when I was a structural engineer."

"You were a structural engineer?" asked Koskinen.

"Yes, I only practiced for three years here at Boeing. That was before they made me into a planner. I've designed in steel, timber, and concrete. I also know the overhead crane system's maintenance from a time when no other engineers in our group were willing to go up high and walk the beams to rescue a stranded crane."

"Good, then you'll understand what we're talking about," said Koskinen. "We're talking slenderness and shear loads. If we didn't have to put doors on both ends, we could use the end of the building as a shear wall for earthquake and wind loads. With no end wall, the columns take the shear (sideways resistance). That's one reason they must be big. The other is slenderness or buckling under load."

"We want hangar doors on both ends," I replied. "Big doors are like escape hatches. We might want to deliver planes out of the back door as well as the front—or have one long serpentine assembly line that uses both bays. I don't want to sacrifice backdoor flexibility."

Prideaux, sensing an impending argument between structural engineers, interrupted in a convincing tone: "John, I don't think the big lattice columns will interfere with your factory operations. While on the factory tour two days ago, we noticed the column lines are used for parts storage and support operations. In places, two or three decks have been built along the column line. A large lattice column will hardly be noticed when surrounded by storage decks and other support activities."

"Yes, I know," I replied. "Over the years, we've added more and more decks along the column lines. We call them 'tower stores.' Some of them stick out 20 feet from the columns on each side of the bay. It's a hell of a poor way to use the 300-foot clear span—to take up 40 feet with a damn warehouse—but factory managers insist they're efficient."

A cluster of pilings driven into the mucky lakefront turf underlie this structural steel column. With strength far in excess of a mighty oak tree, this (and other) columns will support the weight of roof, walls, and overhead cranes for many decades.

No fewer than five construction cranes are on hand to hoist trusses into position. Puget Sound Energy Company sold to Boeing the land that previously hosted an obsolete steam power plant. If undertaken today, current wetland restrictions would seriously hamper this project.

"Then we'll proceed on the study using big lattice columns," said Prideaux.

I hesitated to answer quickly because Prideaux had reminded me that tower stores of some kind would probably be added to any final-assembly area. I decided to beg for time to think about how a line of large lattice columns at 100-foot spacing would work surrounded by tower stores. "Don't go with lattice columns yet," I said. "I want to think about it overnight. I'll give you an answer tomorrow morning. I don't want to hold up the study."

That night I stayed up late, sitting at our family kitchen table with an engineering pad and pencil in hand. My goal was concepts rather than detailed engineering. I wanted to look at human factors. Humans would use this big assembly building. How could I best help them? Big lattice columns would be a barrier to work around. I sketched a 10-foot lattice column to see what it might look like. There would be an "X" brace every 10 feet. The center of the "X" would be at eye level for the average human. He or she would have to walk around it. The 100 square feet within the column would be useless and probably become a trash repository that would be hard to clean. Fencing with a tight mesh would be required to keep people and objects from falling from the storage decks that would likely be built. These things would be easy to fix.

Nevertheless, the human was still on my mind. I remembered a picture I'd seen in McGraw-Hill's *Engineering News Record* of a newly completed skyscraper in Chicago with giant "X" braces on the outer walls, just inside the windows. From a distance the boxy hi-rise looked like a huge lattice column that was 800 feet tall, with four giant "X" braces each on top of the other. The two thousand humans working inside would hardly notice the "X," except where an occasional window had a large steel girder running on a diagonal.

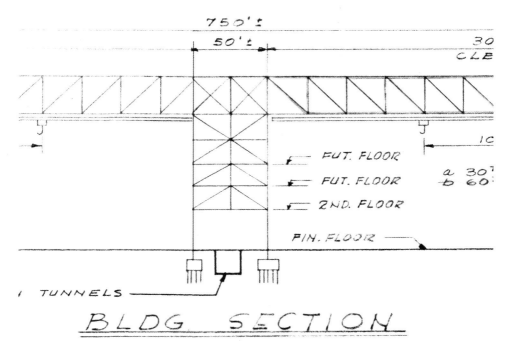

This sketch documents the lattice necessary to stabilize a factory with doors on both ends against wind and earthquake, while also yielding valuable working space.

I realized that on a giant scale, humans could walk around, under, and through a giant lattice column and work with little impediment. I sketched a lattice column with a footprint of 50 by 50 feet instead of 10 by 10 feet. Its diagonals, at 45 degrees (the most structurally efficient angle), crossed 25 feet above the floor. Then I remembered that Dennis Koskinen had said that the 300-feet-wide load-bearing trusses would probably repeat every 100 feet. If the lattice column was 50 feet wide and 100 feet long, each corner would support the end of a 300-foot truss.

Now the lattice column had a footprint of 5,000 square feet, the size of a medium-sized city lot, with the potential for multiple floors. With lattice columns this large, there would be no need to build storage decks protruding into the clear-span assembly bay. The storage decks, to which Cy had called my attention, could be contained inside the lattice and multiplied several times.

Quick hand calculations revealed a clear-span factory floor of 540,000 square feet. By adding four internal floors, the workspace doubled to 1 million square feet. Creating more space would please Bob Regan of manufacturing. Better organizing the hodge-podge of decks, foreman's offices, tool rooms, and blueprint rooms cluttering the final-assembly bays would please Erle Barnes—the man who despises flimsy lean-tos and doghouses. For me, using space more efficiently would be a godsend—if it would work.

The next morning, my boss Don Davis and I made a conference call to Cy Prideaux at Austin. After explaining the concept and getting agreement, my instructions were as follows: "We want the oversized lattices capable of supporting multiple permanent decks, each

The new final assembly buildings are nearing completion as a pair of 707s and pair of 727 airframes sit on the apron overlooking the south shore of Lake Washington. Floating log booms provide evidence of a waning local lumbering economy.

poured-concrete deck capable of supporting 100 pounds per square foot. Make sure the pile foundations are designed strong enough to carry the added load."

Prideaux replied, "I can tell you right now that this should solve the stability problems." Planning continued. I wanted to ensure the cost and schedule estimate contained everything needed. The list included large freight elevators to the decks, one elevator all the way to the roof, another elevator to the crane maintenance bay high in the trusswork, an assembly floor 1 foot thick, fireproof stairwells paralleling every elevator, catwalks above all crane bridges, large utility and fire escape tunnels running the length of the building and connected to the fireproof stairwells, and ample toilet rooms both for men and women (at office capacity, which exceeds building-code requirements for factory space). The estimate also needed to have allowance for utilities, compressed air, steam, power substations, power distribution, high-intensity lighting, and more.

Within four weeks the preliminary estimate for the various combinations of crane tonnage and hook height arrived. My decision was to pick 30-ton cranes lifting to 75 feet. This was deemed adequate for any aircraft likely to be built at Renton into the 1990s. Furthermore, if the need arose, it would have easily housed the C-5A aircraft being planned for new assembly space at Plant II.

I never mentioned much about the extra decks. I said only that there was potential for extra decks. I wanted the building to seem smaller than it really was. Nobody counted the square footage in the lattice until the building was in use. Then, it would seem "free," which it was.

CHAPTER 8
Probing for New Models

The recent face-off between the Boeing 707 and Douglas DC-8 had vanquished Convair, with their models 880 and 990, from the marketplace. The turboprop Lockheed model L-188 also failed to gain traction. But airlines like choices because it gives them bargaining leverage.

Bill Allen Ponders the Short-Haul Market

Serving the world's largest cities, model 707 was the initial Boeing jet airliner. The interim medium-range 720 was displaced by model 727, which could operate out of medium-sized airports and carried its own onboard power supply (auxiliary power unit or APU), which provided electricity, air-conditioning, and starting power for the main engines. The rear ventral airstair eliminated the need for step trucks, and the baggage bins were close to ground level. Without peer, the 727 deftly handled routes of intermediate length.

Meanwhile, regional airlines were hungry for bigger equipment for their short-haul routes into smaller cities. The ubiquitous DC-3 (seating 24–26) were either worn out, obsolete, or undersized. Adequate (but uninspiring) regional airliners could be obtained from multiple sources.

In any case, the arrival of the Douglas Aircraft DC-9 (which entered airline service on December 8, 1965) made the Renton executives, Bill Allen, and the Boeing board of directors sit up and take note because it was fresh, bold, and selling like hotcakes. DAC laid claim to the niche immediately below model 727 and was exploiting its full potential. The T-tailed DC-9 seated a hundred passengers five abreast. Self-contained forward and ventral staircases and an onboard APU made the aircraft self-sufficient at the smaller airports it frequented. Squat landing gears allowed easy access to the baggage bins, without requiring conveyor belt devices.

In 1964, two competitive teams had been chartered within Boeing to independently seek the "best" new design. The red team was managed by master aircraft designer Jack Steiner, and the blue team was under the direction of his subordinate, Joe Sutter. The design was to be completely new and not merely a DC-9 clone.

The parameter for each team was a product with six-abreast seating for 100 to 120 passengers, and a 500-mile range. The consensus recommendation was to place the engines under the wings, apply a conventional empennage, and increase manufacturing efficiency by recycling the nose section and fuselage diameter from the 707 and 727 designs—thereby yielding common seat tracks, sidewall panels, overhead bins, lavatories, and a small galley for beverage service. Cockpit commonality with model 707 was measured at 64 percent. Cabin commonality was even better, at 76 percent.

JT8D PRINCIPAL CHANGES

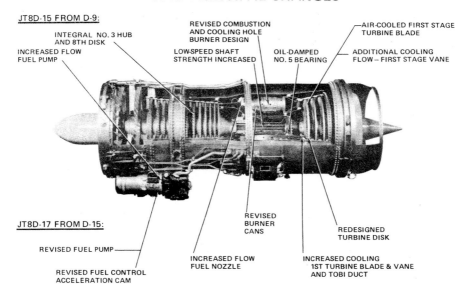

JT8D-15 FROM D-9:

INTEGRAL NO. 3 HUB
AND 8TH DISK

INCREASED FLOW
FUEL PUMP

REVISED COMBUSTION
AND COOLING HOLE
BURNER DESIGN

LOW-SPEED SHAFT
STRENGTH INCREASED

OIL-DAMPED
NO. 5 BEARING

AIR-COOLED FIRST STAGE
TURBINE BLADE

ADDITIONAL COOLING
FLOW – FIRST STAGE VANE

JT8D-17 FROM D-15:

REVISED FUEL PUMP

REVISED FUEL CONTROL
ACCELERATION CAM

INCREASED FLOW
FUEL NOZZLE

REVISED
BURNER
CANS

REDESIGNED
TURBINE DISK

INCREASED COOLING
1ST TURBINE BLADE & VANE
AND TOBI DUCT

ADDITIONAL IMPROVEMENTS IN MATERIALS
AND HEAT TREAT THROUGHOUT THE ENGINE.

The Pratt & Whitney (P&W) JT8D jet engine powered every 727, the DC-9, and early versions of the 737. It was ultimately obsoleted by other quieter and more-fuel-efficient engines. The first 747s utilized the much-larger P&W JT9D turbofans.

Despite the shared attributes, fuselage fabrication for model 737 was assigned to Wichita. All other single-aisle fuselages were built on-site at Renton. The firm of Dorwin Teague & Associates traditionally handles interior design for many Boeing customers, thus ensuring that colors, patterns, textures, and fabrics are durable while conforming with the latest fashion trends.

The selection of the Pratt & Whitney JT8D engine was a safe bet. Three of them were factory installed on every model 727. The Douglas DC-9s, already entering service, were powered by a pair of aft-mounted JT8Ds. This engine was embraced within Boeing, while also popular with the airlines. Simplicity was the 737 watchword. For instance, main landing-gear doors were eliminated by applying a hub cap to the wheel and leaving the horizontal surface of the retracted tires exposed on the bottom of the airplane.

Despite the recent loss of market share, the Douglas Aircraft Company remained a very accomplished and highly respected foe. In any case, the Seattle gang (and especially Jack Steiner) was eager to renew the joust. With competitive juices flowing, Boeing was about to march into the short-haul fray. But first, a resolution by the Boeing board of directors was required before any new model could be sold or committed to production. The board members took their work seriously. The Great Depression had left them fiscally conservative and skittish regarding risk.

This model of the famed World War II B-17 Flying Fortress is being tested in the Eddie Allen Wind Tunnel. Built in 1943, the transonic wind tunnel remains a vital developmental tool for aircraft designers and is part of the "critical mass" necessary for a successful company.

Launching the 737:
Board Meeting, February 1, 1965

Starting at 8:30 a.m., the board met in a conference room at the National Bank of Commerce located at 210 Barrone Street in New Orleans' Ninth Ward, where Boeing was constructing the first stage of the massive Saturn V moon rocket. Aging board member Claire Egtvedt did not make the trip from his home in Seattle.

The agenda for the meeting was scripted by Boeing president Bill Allen, a board member since personally appointed by company founder Bill Boeing in 1930. George Schairer, a gifted aerodynamicist (but not a board member), was invited to join John O. Yeasting in making the 737 presentation.

The discussion was raucous. A heated debate ensued. Boeing was a strong contender to win contracts to develop the government-funded Super Sonic Transport (SST). Everybody at Boeing, at the airlines, and in government considered the SST as the future of air travel. Why waste time with a little airplane like the proposed 737 when multiple competitors were already filling the fragmented niche and delivering airplanes?

As stated in board minutes, Boeing market analysts forecasted the 737 to garner half the anticipated future demand for one thousand short-haul twin jets. Estimated sales were 500 airplanes—plus another hundred for the military. The design was expected to be viable for a production run of ten to twelve years. On the basis of dialogue between Boeing salesmen and various airlines, some combination of Lufthansa, Eastern Airlines, and Western Airlines, or possibly United Airlines, was anticipated to be lead customers. Mr. Schairer was then excused from the meeting. Consensus on 737 was lacking. Extensive and sometimes passionate discussion between board members continued. The future was clouded with "SST and a large subsonic aircraft employing the technology of the [Boeing] C-5A."

The board broke for lunch at 12:20 p.m. and resumed at 2:30 p.m. The primary purpose of the gathering in New Orleans was a tour of the Michoud facility, where Boeing was then manufacturing the massive first stage of the Saturn V moon rocket. It was 33 feet in diameter, fabricated on its side, and on the list of NASA components so large that they could be moved only aboard barges attached to oceangoing tugboats. With the Michoud factory tour completed, the board returned to conference.

The competition, and especially Douglas Aircraft Company of Long Beach, California, was always of intense interest to Boeing management and the board of directors. The directors were briefed on an elongated DC-8, designated DC-8-62. With a maximum capacity of 260 passengers (or eighteen cargo pallets), it was informally dubbed "Stretch 8" by airport workers. John O. Yeasting and Ed Wells informed the board of the potential for competing airplanes from Boeing—designated 707-620 and 707-820. With a developmental price tag estimated at $20 million, the project was soon outprioritized by 747.

The board then returned to the vexing 737 proposal. Under questioning, it was disclosed that breakeven was estimated to be at 375 airplanes. Furthermore, a premature production line shutdown, after only fifty units, would yield a $150 million loss. A tepid agreement finally emerged only because it was getting late. "Resolved: Management is authorized to go ahead with the model 737 program upon obtaining a satisfactory arrangement with Lufthansa, if in management's judgment it is deemed advisable." An exhausted board of directors finally adjourned at 6:15 p.m.

Breakeven points meant little to the people who would design, build, and certify the 737. Their unshakable priorities were excellence of engineering, fabrication, and assembly. Schedule commitments were next in line. The cost would be what was needed. The finance people would sort that out later.

There were holes in the Boeing product lineup, and the Commercial Airplane Group was about to plug one of them—even if the 737 turned out to be a loss leader. The 737 was intended to handle lighter loads on shorter routes, while the still-hypothetical 747 would span oceans heavily laden with passengers, high-priority cargo, or both. That decision would come before the board in thirteen months.

In the end, Bill Allen prevailed by force of will and stellar reputation—but barely. He returned to his brownstone home in the Highlands in an angry mood.

737 Milestones	
February 1, 1965	Approved by board of directors
April 9, 1967	First flight
December 15, 1967	FAA certificate awarded

Given the excellent experience with their 707 and 727 aircraft and rosy promises from the Boeing marketing department, Lufthansa's Gerhard Holtje signed up for twenty-one of the Model 737s on March 15, 1965. The price was $63 million, or $3 million per airplane. It was the first time a foreign airline was the lead customer for a new Boeing design. An order from United Airlines for the "baby Boeing" arrived shortly thereafter.

A Collective Panic Attack

Both the 707 and 747 utilized well-understood technology. It was obvious to industry observers that a 747 type would make the intercontinental and transcontinental 707s and DC-8s obsolete in little more than four years, which was possible only if a go-ahead decision was made either by Boeing, Douglas, Lockheed, or Convair within the next six months. Boeing's decision had to be made quickly—or the long-range market would be lost.

In August 1965, we in facilities planning learned that Steiner's preliminary design group had configured a big new transport to be powered by the proposed P&W high-bypass turbofan engines. All internal factory and facility groups monitored preliminary design activity for quick response to changes or new products.

Industry observers and company leadership assumed Boeing was most likely to win the C-5A contract; however, the Pentagon under Robert McNamara delivered to Boeing another unsettling defeat. Boeing executives were thrown into a tizzy as word of the devastating loss of the C-5A contract sank in.

A temporary catatonic state engulfed the company. It was like both feet were mired in quicksand. Bill Allen and others departed on vacation (or otherwise disappeared) to lick their wounds. Allen was reported to be in Bermuda. I refer to the resulting turmoil as the "collective panic attack." It began two weeks later, on October 2, 1965, when it seemed no one knew what to do. Rhetorical feathers flew as executives of every ilk flailed about for a "go forward" strategy. The major leaders in the company were Bill Allen, John Yeasting, T. A. Wilson, Ed Wells, and two extremely competent preliminary designers of commercial airplanes—Maynard Pennell and Jack Steiner.

My own leadership, specifically Erle Barnes, must be commended for maintaining their own aplomb—no matter how adverse the circumstances. Driving the Greyhound bus over Snoqualmie Pass during winter blizzards must have earned him immunity from workplace anxiety. In any case, the term "panic attack" is a bit unfair, because the dilemma was genuine and huge. All the people involved were very intelligent and dedicated to Boeing.

Super Sonic Transport (SST): Model 2707

Boeing won the government-sponsored project to build the Supersonic Transport (SST), a Mach 3 airliner. It soon became mired in environmental and political controversy. The funding was killed in the US Senate before the evolving design became firm.

Maynard Pennell was the father of the 707, having shepherded the program for a decade, starting with the Dash 80 prototype and continuing through all the subsequent versions. It was under Pennell's guidance that Jack Steiner designed the 727. There was no personal animosity or competition between the pair. Both men knew that the secret to commercial airplane success was seat miles per hour.

For example, the 707 carried 150 passengers at just under Mach 1, which generates about 105,000 seat miles per hour. The upcoming Concorde carried eighty passengers at Mach 2, which generates about 112,000 seat miles per hour—which is not much better than a 707 or DC-8. (Note: Actual speed is slightly less than Mach number, and seats installed varies; however, for purposes of illustrating the dilemma, the concepts are valid.)

Two years before, in 1963, Yeasting had asked Pennell to form a design team devoted exclusively to SST. The Renton plant was crowded. In early 1964, Pennell moved his SST team to the nearby Developmental Center, where he planned to design and build a prototype.

Pennell fully understood the seat-miles-per-hour concept. He decided against a Mach 2 airplane to match the Concorde. Instead, he took a huge leap and went to Mach 3 with 300 seats. Model 2707 was an SST that could produce an astounding 630,000 seat miles per hour.

It was obvious that model numbers were no longer assigned sequentially but instead had become marketing tools. Pennell called it a 2707 because it had twice the seats of a 707. He could have called it a 6707, because it was about six times as productive as a 707 or a Concorde.

Meanwhile, Steiner's team in Renton saw the promise of a 747. It was only a glimmer in January 1965, but by October 1965 the potential availability of the P&W engine made the 747 a real possibility. The 747 would have 450 seats, about 315,000 seat mph, three times more productive than the 707 but half as productive as a Boeing SST. Each aircraft has four engines, and assuming cruise is twenty-five of takeoff thrust, a comparison of the three shows the following:

707	105,000 seat mph, thrust 80,000 lbs.	thrust per seat mile 0.76 lbs.
747	315,000 seat mph, thrust 160,000 lbs.	thrust per seat mile 0.50 lbs.
SST	630,000 seat mph, thrust 240,000 lbs.	thrust per seat mile 0.38 lbs.

The SST wins on all counts, including the least thrust per seat mile.

All the numbers can be refined by experts, but relationships will remain the same. Passengers also prefer speed. An airline's costs are incurred per flight hour, making a faster airplane best for them too.

Despite data then being gathered by the experimental triple-sonic North American XB-70A at Edwards AFB, building an SST remained unknown technology. Therefore, it required a prototype and flight test before production could begin. At least eight years would elapse before a highly productive SST could carry revenue passengers, but when it did, it would make all Mach 1 long-range transports obsolete, including the 747. Thus, the 747 would have only a four-year useful life as a passenger transport. Nevertheless, it had to be built to retain the market in which Boeing was so heavily invested.

By October 1, 1965, we had in hand the 747's approximate size and estimated sales price. Project go-ahead was required to beat the competition. February 1966 was less than six months away. Obviously, every estimated parameter was subject to growth. Nothing seemed to shrink.

Chaotic Requirements

On the basis of revenue of $100 per square foot times annual revenue, I quickly estimated the need for at least 10 million square feet; however, 3 million square feet was already planned for a new fabrication plant to support a C-5A. That would have to continue. I dropped a bombshell-sized requirement into the dilemma. At least 7 million more square feet was needed, which meant building a new assembly plant the size of our expanded Renton plant. My demand was no surprise. I had been predicting the need for a new plant for two years. Every top executive in the Boeing Company knew me and had seen my plans for an ideal aircraft plant. I was well known to all as "the new site guy." They also knew that I favored buying 300 acres of private rural land just east of McChord Field, south of Tacoma.

On the same day the C-5A was lost, Yeasting pronounced his own shocking revelation when he finally reversed his pessimistic prognosis and released a commercial planning base that doubled the 707, 727, and 737 deliveries. Existing production lines required immediate expansion to meet committed deliveries already sold to airlines. The 707 had come back to life at nine per month; each 707 delivery was extremely profitable. The long years of red ink shifted to black. The 727, with a rate of twenty-one per month, was now also finally profitable. The planned 737 assembly rate was now fourteen per month instead of seven. It could no longer fit into Renton. The 737 needed 4 million square feet somewhere. Plant II in Seattle could supply about half of that.

Then T. Wilson dropped two stunning wishes of his own: the 747 new plant must be built outside the Seattle area, preferably somewhere in California, and the 737 must move to Wichita. Almost everyone knew that Allen was about to name Wilson as executive vice president and a member of the board of directors. Wilson was already beginning to manage by decree, instead of by consensus.

Wilson's reasoning was logical but oriented to the military market. Presence in more states yields a broader political footprint, which is vital to congressional appropriations. He had never been part of Boeing's commercial activity. His customer experiences were with the US government—mostly military, and more recently with NASA. All government contracts ultimately rely on Congress and are often awarded to the location with the most political clout. Wilson had just lost the C-5A to Lockheed of Marietta, Georgia. Wells, who was recognized as Boeing's most senior airplane designer, had lost the TFX (F-111) to General Dynamics in Texas. The B-58 supersonic bomber went to Convair, also in Texas, and the XB-70 contract was awarded to North American Aviation of California.

In the background lurked two more bombshells. Yeasting's new planning base featured a "family of airplanes" concept. The 747 would be followed by a go-ahead on a large, twin-aisle trijet at the end of 1968, and a go-ahead on a wide body with twin engines in 1970. World seat mile forecast demanded a new high-capacity family of twin-aisle airliners well before the SST production could begin to absorb any significant portion of the seat mile market. Those two revelations were real to Facilities management. We would have to triple the space at Everett or maybe establish another new plant.

As the stampede began in early October, Wilson ordered me to send all my plans for a new plant to his headquarters planning staff. I was the only planner with a coherent answer to the needed facilities expansion. The requirement had been predicted by me for two years, and I had the plans and engineering ready to go. They now intended to determine its location.

Preliminary Specification as of October 1, 1965		
Boeing Model 747		
Body style		Double Decker
Fuselage		19' wide, 26' vertical, 210' long
Wingspan		164' Tail height: 62'
Weights	Gross takeoff	554,000
	Empty	265,000
	AMPR	225,000
Rate		8.5 per month, 100 per year
Sales price		$16.5 to $17 million
Annual sales revenue		
Annual sales revenue	1969	$221 million
	1970	$1.360 billion
	1971	$1.734 billion
Subcontract		Aft body, tail, wing tips, flaps, engine pylons & nacelles, and landing gear

AMPR was then a measure of aircraft structural weight less the weight of procured parts including tires, wheels, brakes, engines, electronics, and interiors. *Data from John Andrew collection*

This model of a 747 preliminary concept demonstrates the double-deck, passenger only, approach—which was quickly discarded in favor of a more cargo-friendly configuration.

The Transport Division VP & GM finally awoke about October 15, 1965. The 747 was not identified in the Commercial Division's business-planning summary, which ironically was released on the same day the C-5A was lost. Apparently, John Yeasting did not realize how quickly Steiner was developing a commercial version of an outsized airplane using the proposed Pratt & Whitney large fan—which suddenly looked not only promising, but also available.

The executives stampeded, and I was about to get trampled in the debacle. It was now realized that the 747 was a real and likely prospect. Pan American expected to introduce it to the flying public in the spring of 1970.

Another rising executive at Boeing was an outsider, Malcolm T. "Mal" Stamper (1923–2005). Mal was hired away from General Motors in 1962 and then placed in charge of Boeing's Turbine Division (intended for powering trucks or helicopters, but never achieving success). I was next ordered by corporate planners to drop what I was doing at bustling Commercial and make a long-range plan for Mal's floundering Turbine Division, Boeing's anemic engine operation. Stamper invited me to be his facilities director, but I politely declined the offer.

It was now December 1965, with the holiday season approaching, but there was tension in the chart-lined Industrial Engineering control room at the Renton site. Unlike the still-hypothetical 747, model 737 was real, sanctioned by the board of directors, and the configuration was firm. It was time to review planning assumptions necessary to keep the project moving forward. I wandered in and took a seat in the front row. Trouble was brewing and a feud was about to erupt.

"Your forecast isn't worth a damn." Gordon Link aimed his words at Ron Fraser, who was the head of Industrial Engineering (IE) at Boeing Commercial. Link's comment rudely interrupted Fraser's subordinate, who was explaining several charts propped on easels in front of the meeting hosted in the IE Control Room.

The charts showed the number of factory workers (almost ten thousand) needed to build the first two hundred Boeing 737s.

Ron Fraser rose from his seat, took the pointer from his subordinate, tapped it loudly on a chart, and slowly and emphatically said, "Our man-loading is correct at every jig, every tool, every fixture, and every position." He waved the pointer toward another easel that held a stack of flip charts. "And the learning curves are also correct."

Turning from the displays, Fraser squarely faced the man who had just implied that a year's work by four hundred people in the Industrial Engineering Section wasn't worth a damn. Fraser's face flushed. He took a deep breath. His nostrils flared. A vein bulged above his necktie as he glared at Gordon Link.

Link was lounging on a chair in the middle of the front row, head back, arms at his sides, legs outstretched, as if he was bored with the presentation. Fraser stepped toward Link, close enough to kick his outstretched legs.

I was sitting at the end of the front row, two persons to the right of Link. I moved my chair forward and turned it slightly, allowing me to see both men.

Link was a manufacturing expert from Boeing's corporate headquarters in Seattle, who had come to Renton to review the Commercial Division's need for factory workers. He was considered a genius in industrial engineering with such things as time and motion studies, human factors, and how to translate those into logarithmic learning curves that predicted the number of man-hours for each aircraft or missile on the assembly line. He'd come to Boeing twenty-five years before, during mass production of prop-driven wartime bombers, and had stayed to help with mass production of postwar B-47 and B-52 swept-wing jet bombers. After that, he helped apply aircraft production methods to the manufacture and installation of Minuteman ballistic missiles. Most recently, he'd spent a year on a Boeing proposal team that bid on the huge C-5A military transport plane—a bid lost to Lockheed just three months prior—in September 1965. The ego wounds to those involved were still fresh and painful.

Link's genius was negated by an obtuse personality that no subordinate could tolerate. This prevented him from becoming a manager of people. Nevertheless, he held great power in the company as an advisor to senior corporate executives, including Wes Mauldin and T. A. Wilson.

The meeting had been delayed ten minutes awaiting Link's arrival. He finally walked in with a threatening, ponderous gait and plopped himself into an empty chair reserved for him in the front row. He gave no nod of recognition to anyone. He was a large man, about fifty years of age, bald on top with graying sides that blended with a gray complexion and a lugubrious manner that quickly changed from mournful to sneering. He was at his sneering best as he looked up at the angry, red-faced Fraser. He said, "You guys in Commercial don't know how to man-load the assembly positions. You haven't the foggiest notion about learning curves or how to use them."

Ron Fraser was about forty, lean, athletic, and slightly over 6 feet tall, with a stiff crew cut and a disciplined bearing. He'd been with the company fifteen years, the last ten at Renton on the commercial side of the business. His career had been stellar. As section manager of industrial engineering, he now reported to a manufacturing director. Fraser's team of four hundred industrial engineers planned and scheduled the 707 and 727 assembly lines and the new line being established for the 737. He also had been estimating how many assembly positions and factory workers would be needed for a much-larger airplane, the 747—not yet approved for final design or sale.

Ron Fraser leaned toward the lounging Link, almost yelling in his face. "I don't know why you're here anyway, telling my people they're all screwed up. You military guys are the ones that screwed up. You just lost the C-5A."

Link moved his feet about 6 inches. I saw a squint of his eye and a flinch in his gray poker face. Everyone in the room knew the massive C-5A military transport was lost because of factory cost, which was Link's specialty. The Air Force wanted the Boeing airplane, but Lockheed bid the lowest price.

Fraser turned to the stack of learning curves propped against one of the easels. He took the pointer in both hands, like a baseball bat, slammed it broadside onto the stack, and said, "If you military guys had used learning curves like these, you might have won the C-5A."

"Yeah, and if we did, would have bankrupted the company," replied Link, quickly regaining his sneering composure. "Your learning curves are too optimistic."

"By god, this is what we forecast a year ago, and this is what we are going to do," said Ron Fraser.

"Last year was different," replied Link. "Last year you assumed production rates would go down on 707 and 727 lines. Instead, the production rates are doubling. You don't have experienced people for the 737. If you rob people from the 707 and 727 lines, their learning curves will go to hell—and you guys are talking about the model 747 following right behind the 737. The Seattle area doesn't have enough factory workers to do what you're trying to do."

"We'll hire and train them," said Fraser.

"Not without learning curves going to hell and bankrupting the company," said Link. "The only place we have experienced people is in Wichita, Kansas. The last of the B-52s are now on the production line. The factory will be empty. Fifteen thousand skilled factory workers face layoff. The only way to prevent disaster in Seattle is to move the 737 to Wichita."

"Moving it to Wichita will bankrupt the company, for damn sure," retorted Fraser. "We're halfway into the program. We're cutting parts and building subassemblies. The first unit must roll out of final assembly a year from now. Production rate buildup is right behind. The Wichita workers will lose a year on the schedule. Their learning curves will begin all over again. They lack the commonality with the 707 and 727. We are already hundreds of units down the curve."

Link retracted his feet, sat upright, slowly rose, and joined Fraser at the stack of learning curves. The top chart was a summation, a cumulative curve showing total man-hours per pound of aircraft structure for each unit to number 200 and beyond.

"This curve ought to be closer to 90 percent than 80 percent," said Link (a high percentage indicates inexperience and slow improvement).

"I'll show you how we can get below 80 percent," said Fraser as he turned over the top chart and exposed supporting detail. The two men faced each other, nose to nose. Link's gray complexion took on a reddish tinge as he tried to convince Fraser to adjust the learning curves and admit the 737 would take more factory workers than forecast. Fraser remained adamant that the forecast was accurate, and that a move to Wichita was not only bad but disastrous. Hot tempers on the part of both men erased any chance of communication or compromise.

I wondered, Why was I asked to attend this meeting between two of Boeing's top industrial engineers? My job had nothing to do with scheduling production lines, applying learning curves to head counts, or making factory-staffing decisions. Yet, the bosses of both Link and Fraser had separately invited me to the meeting to "lend support"—but was it to Link or Fraser?

As a thirty-four-year-old manager of Facilities Planning for Boeing Commercial, assisted by a staff of forty planners, it was my job to allocate factory space for thirty thousand workers and office space for twenty thousand aircraft design engineers and administrative personnel. If needed space was unavailable, my group controlled the capital budget, and it was our job to request funding for new construction from the board of directors.

It was unlikely that Fraser would retreat from his optimistic forecasts, because those estimates were already baked into the initial 737 sales contracts—twenty-one airplanes for Lufthansa at $3.2 million each and forty slightly longer versions for United at $3.5 million per copy. Anybody who read Seattle's newspapers could deduce that the first two hundred aircraft would need to be built for $700 million to break even. That's what Fraser had committed the manufacturing department to do. A move to Wichita in the middle of the program would wreck the financials; however, lack of enough experienced workers in Seattle would snarl production.

As a very busy manager with a full plate at home and at work, I was about to excuse myself and walk out of the stalled meeting when Gordon Link suddenly looked at me and said, "There's not enough space for the 737 anywhere in Seattle or Renton, is there, Andrew?" Link's remark was posed more like a statement than a question.

Before I had a chance to collect my thoughts, Fraser interrupted, "There's plenty of space at Seattle's Plant II, now that you lost the C-5A, Link! The 737 can be assembled at Plant II. Isn't that correct, Andrew?

Now it was stunningly apparent why both sides had invited me into this rhetorical face-off. If the esteemed industrial engineers ended at loggerheads, the deciding factor might hinge on factory space. Link swung his verbal sword yet again: "No, there's not enough space at Plant II. Our requirement was to tear down half of Plant II and build two new assembly bays for the C-5A. That was to consume two years. There is no time for that! The only available factory space is in Wichita. That's true, Andrew . . . Isn't it?"

The previous summer, I was temporarily assigned to the C-5A proposal team to help document facilities requirements, and I was familiar with their plan. I had found Gordon Link to be abrasive, but intelligent, in our previous interactions. I remained deferential to his age and experience, and he reciprocated by respecting my judgments. This was after I reduced many facilities requirements to basic parameters such as revenue per square foot of factory space. It was a technique that allowed me to size facilities for a new program as quickly as Link quantified manpower.

Fraser continued his tirade: "You C-5A guys had to build new bays because the jumbo airlifter was so big. The tail was 65 feet tall. Plant II has only 38 feet of headroom. The 737 is much smaller, with a 37-foot tail. It will fit in Plant II—correct, Andrew?"

Thus far, I had not been able to get a word in edgewise. Fraser was correct. The 737 was small enough to fit inside the assembly bays, which two decades prior hosted wartime B-17s, but we were having trouble finding space for sixteen of them. Sixteen was the magic number of manufacturing spaces needed to achieve a production rate of fourteen airliners per month within two years. The issue was further complicated because of an improved way to build wings, using two huge automatic riveters on railroad tracks. These riveting machines and the tracks they ran on would consume much of the space previously utilized for final assembly within the aging 1930s-vintage factory.

I realized that I was being asked to cast my vote whether to move 737 assembly to Wichita. There was a high-level feud afoot between the powerful T. Wilson and the equally powerful John Yeasting, head of Boeing Commercial. I hadn't realized how bitter and acrimonious it had become until I witnessed the vicious argument between Link and Fraser, which played out before an audience.

I needed time to think. My answer would soon echo about—both at corporate offices in Seattle and commercial headquarters in Renton. I decided to delay my response. "My people have not finished laying out the production lines in Plant II. An option is to split the work between Renton and Plant II, because barging large sections between the locations is feasible. I'll get back to you in a week, when there is a better understanding of where things fit; however, I know it will fit in Wichita." Now it was my turn to ask the questions. "So far today, the discussion has been only about factory workers. What about the three thousand engineers working on the project? Right now, we're moving them into the South Seattle engineering building because that's where the vacant office space is located. Under the Wichita 737 scenario, do we relocate either the engineers or their work?"

Link played an ace card by invoking the name of Thornton A. Wilson: "'T' says he wants the engineering to move to Wichita along with the production. He ran the Minuteman program, and it was spread all over the country."

The friction underlying this unfortunate exchange needs to be explained. Boeing Aerospace Group had been making money year in and year out on various products (warplanes, missiles, rockets, satellites, and a helicopter plant in Philadelphia). Meanwhile, their counterparts in Commercial Airplane Group in Renton had been losing it as they hammered away at the hard-to-penetrate airliner business.

Boeing lost out on a string of bids during the 1960s. The two respected senators from Washington, Henry "Scoop" Jackson of Everett and Warren Magnuson of Seattle, were often dubbed by the press as the "senators from Boeing." Despite their best efforts, government business was clearly flowing to the big states of California and Texas. President Lyndon Johnson was a friend to Texas.

Robert McNamara's Revenge?

On the basis of recurring office chatter, the people at Boeing were convinced that Robert S. McNamara (1916–2009) bore a long-standing grudge against Boeing. McNamara left Harvard University as an assistant professor to join the Army Air Force's Office of Statistical Control as a captain in 1943. The "whiz kid" enjoyed an inborn mastery of numbers and the demonstrated ability to weaponize them by beating into submission anybody who dared challenge him.

McNamara was a member of a postwar group of gifted consultants recruited by Ernest Breech, president of Ford Motor Company, to unravel the damage done by the mercurial founder, Henry Ford, and bring the modern management disciplines needed by a family-held company. McNamara quickly ascended the corporate ladder and assumed the top job at Ford. The election of President John F. Kennedy in 1960 soon followed. Positive chemistry between the young president and Robert McNamara, bolstered by their separate wartime military experiences, yielded a top cabinet post for Mr. McNamara. His term as secretary of defense spanned the inauguration of JFK in 1961 until the Vietnam fiasco wrecked the political reputation of Lyndon Johnson by mid-1968.

Checking further into the allegation on unfair treatment at the hands of Robert McNamara, the late Alwyn Lloyd, in his 2005 book *Boeing's B-47 Stratojet*, relates the following story on pages 48–49:

In July 1951, the Air Force issued three contracts . . . directing Boeing to subcontract with the Ford Motor Company for the manufacture of B-47B wing box sets. . . . But Ford did not prove up to the task. A survey conducted at the Ford Plant in Kansas City, Missouri[,] on October 21, 1953, revealed that Ford was behind schedule. . . . Ford's major problem was a lack of personnel experienced in aircraft production. . . . When the first shipsets of Ford wings arrived at [Boeing Wichita], they underwent routine receiving inspection. Boeing determined that the parts were not built to design specifications[,] and rejected them. McNamara offered to send a team to fix the discrepant parts, but Boeing stated that they were beyond salvage. The wings had to be scrapped and a

Robert McNamara joined the administration of President John F. Kennedy in 1961 as secretary of defense. In this role, he was an architect of the war in Vietnam and no friend to Boeing. The dearth of military contracts in the 1960s redirected Boeing from bomber builder into the much-larger role of airliner provider.

protracted battle of words ensued. In the end, Ford had to refund $5 million to Boeing for failure to produce acceptable parts.

Other observers contend that Robert McNamara held no specific animus toward Boeing but simply acceded, without recourse, to the political whims of those appointed over him.

As the decade of the 1960s arrived, three important projects were winding up as they migrated from production to operational status. They were the B-52 bomber, the KC-135 tanker, and the Minuteman ICBM. These three enduring weapon systems formed the nucleus of the Strategic Air Command (SAC) and proved themselves to be an excellent long-term investment both for the Air Force and taxpayers. Contract losses included the following:

- Despite the Air Force's preference for the Boeing design, McNamara selected General Dynamics to build the F-111 over the Boeing's version of TFX in November 1962.
- DynaSoar, a space orbiter (also known as X-20), was canceled by McNamara on December 23, 1963.
- Bomarc, an antiaircraft missile program, was shut down on December 20, 1963.
- Manned Orbiting Laboratory (MOL) was lost on August 28, 1965.
- Lockheed won the bid to build the C-5A Galaxy in September 1965.
- The HiBex antimissile project. The contract, awarded in 1963, was canceled on January 13, 1966.

Orders booked but not yet delivered are called "backlog." Henceforth, the commercial airliner backlog greatly exceeded the combined value of all military and space contracts. Despite the losses, government business remained a vital tool for technological advancement and diversification of the Boeing product portfolio. Even if Boeing lost a prime contract, the Aerospace unit frequently landed a lucrative subcontract for some combination of weapons, structures, or sophisticated electronic systems. In any case, the unprecedented shift in the business base from military to commercial unhinged more than a few Boeing executives.

Profitable Air Force contracts for sustainment of the nation's fleet of B-52 bombers, KC-135 tankers, and Minuteman ICBMs would continue for decades. Old-technology analog systems were replaced by digital avionics. New weapons such as SRAM (acronym for short-range attack missile) replaced older AGM-28 Hound Dog missiles. Airplane modifications were frequently performed at Wichita and included repair of cracked or failing wing panels. Tankers received new turbofan engines that were quieter, more powerful, and fuel efficient.

Boeing built the first stage of the Saturn V moon rocket and the lunar rover, a moon buggy. Fewer people are aware that Boeing shouldered a vital Apollo recovery role after the fatal Apollo 1 fire of January 1967. NASA administrator James Webb covertly called on Bill Allen to provide Boeing oversight to assist with the Apollo project reviews resulting from the fire in which three popular astronauts died. The schedule for the moon landing, a national priority, was torn asunder, and public trust was shaken.

Key people with recent relevant experience gained on the Minuteman program were tapped on the shoulder and dispatched to where most needed, without fanfare. Commercial programs suffered because the expected influx of seasoned engineers from completed military assignments was delayed for many months. The patriotic fact was that both Bill Allen and T. Wilson placed the needs of country above Boeing priorities.

1967
737 ASSEMBLY

K-14648

This is the 1967 floor plan for the Thompson site. Prior to the advent of the nose-to-tail moving assembly lines, airliners were positioned in an arrangement analogous to angle parking on a street.

CHAPTER 9
Charlie Thompson and His Tract

My boss was Don Davis, director of facilities planning and construction for BCA. The thirty-nine-year-old Navy veteran joined Boeing is 1953. After working for Davis for three years—first as long-range planner and then as head of facilities planning, I found him to be thoughtful, honest, and easy to talk with. His door was open. "How did the meeting go?" he asked as I entered.

"It appeared Link and Fraser were going to kill each other," I said. "Each of them tried to drag us into it. The issue is should 737 stay in the Seattle area or go to Wichita."

"What do you think?" asked Don.

"I think the 737 is headed for financial disaster either way, but it is wiser to keep it in Seattle. That helps Boeing achieve the critical mass necessary to fend off the formidable competition in Southern California," I said before continuing. "There's one piece of vacant land near Plant II where we might site a new final assembly."

Don Davis laughed, "I know. It's the Thompson site. Everyone says old Charlie won't sell to Boeing. They say he likes looking at his land and bragging about it. They say he owns it free and clear."

The first 737 fuselage section departed Wichita on February 15, 1967. Over ten thousand followed. Later, the sections would be joined into a single, complete fuselage, sometimes called a "cigar."

The owner of the only tract of remaining nearby vacant land was Charlie Thompson, a foreman in the sheet metal shop located deep within the blue-smoky bowels of Plant II. Charlie started at Boeing in 1919, when the company was barely two years old. He'd built the wooden and cloth aircraft of the 1920s and seen the change to metal, which was now his specialty. People who knew him said he loved banging out clips, angles, and brackets, using shears and brakes, but his real passion was operating the giant presses that bent aluminum ribs to the radius of an aircraft's fuselage. He was on a first-name basis with every other Boeing old-timer—including company president Bill Allen.

Somewhere in his forty-five-year career, Charlie acquired 16 acres of vacant land that spanned the gap between the Duwamish waterway and Old Highway 99 and Boeing Field to the east. Isaacson Steel was on the north and the Kenworth truck plant adjoined on the southern property line. The primary runway at Boeing Field had been expanded during the B-52 program, and it now measured 10,007 feet long by 200 feet wide. By 1965, halting vehicular traffic briefly for aircraft-towing operations across Highway 99 was a routine event.

I told Don Davis, "A deal is needed to acquire the Thompson site. We know Bill Allen is notoriously frugal and delegates real estate matters only to his consultant, Elmer Sill." Meanwhile, I committed myself to get with Cy Prideaux, to see what kind of rapid schedule the Austin Company could support.

The proposed building had structural steel and internal dimensions exactly like the 10-50 factory building in Renton, which was built by Austin ten years earlier and was since expanded three times. They had the plans. It was designed for a pile foundation, which would

To this day, the Thompson site sits on East Marginal Way (Old Highway 99) with access to barge, Boeing Field, Union Pacific Railway, and highway. Currently, it is where Navy P-8 Poseidon aircraft receive their mission equipment.

be required on the mucky land adjacent to the Duwamish waterway. The 120-foot span exceeded the 96-foot wingspan of the 737. The 10-ton overhead crane system has a hook height of 40 feet, which was greater than the tail height of 37 feet. I thought Austin could break ground within two weeks, if needed.

I arrived in Cy Prideaux's office at 8:00 a.m. the following day. We both knew that Austin had other commitments to Boeing, including planning for a 747 factory building (location still undetermined), new assembly bays at Renton, and major construction at Auburn. The layout I'd prepared the day before was reviewed. It showed a building 780 feet long with two parallel bays 120 feet wide, and a four-deck support structure 40 feet wide—making the total width 280 feet.

Cy Prideaux wasted no time. Events were moving quickly, and a seasoned construction company willing and capable of maintaining stride with the world's leading builder of jet aircraft was truly a blessing. It was a partnership forged over the decades and reinforced during wartime. Cy promised a letter proposal the following day, preliminary design and estimates in a week, and a reservation for structural steel fabrication at their plant for February 1966. As anticipated, the rough cost estimate was $30 per square foot times 300,000 square feet—or $9 million.

I instructed Earl Bowden, my lead supervisor for factory planning, "Lay out the 737 assembly line in a new building on the Thompson tract, just like we discussed yesterday evening. The Austin Company said they might be able to build it by June 30. Act like we've got a go ahead. Move forward with everything you need to do. We can't sit around and wait. We've got to push."

Ron Fraser of Commercial Airplanes industrial engineering was happy with the plan, but I knew the corporate types could easily kill it by delaying the funding approval. But there were no delays. Events were moving at breakneck speed. I was told to prepare for a wide-ranging meeting with Bill Allen, who had much-bigger fish to fry and was tired of the incessant bickering regarding the location for 737 assembly.

Meet Juan Trippe

Juan Trippe (1899–1981) was a high-energy early airline tycoon some considered ruthless. The first name of "Juan" suggested Hispanic heritage; however, Trippe was the son of a well-to-do Wall Street banker of northern European lineage. Growing up, few knew what was going on behind his laconic facade. Nicknamed "the mummy" by friends, the outbreak of World War I found him as a student at Yale. His burning desire for military service was thwarted by a weak left eye, but Trippe persisted and was commissioned as an ensign in the Navy. The war ended before he saw overseas duty. Trippe wisely returned to Yale and completed his education. Then he followed the family tradition by taking a Wall Street job that he came to loathe—bond salesman.

As founder of Pan American Airways (abbreviated "Pan Am"), Mr. Trippe set about to establish international routes headed in most every direction. After Charles Lindbergh earned celebrity status in 1927 by being the first to cross the Atlantic nonstop and solo, Lindbergh became a trusted consultant to Pan Am on everything from scouting early routes to covertly checking on technical issues at Boeing. Lindbergh made secret visits to Boeing in the late 1960s under an assumed name. Trippe always savored the leading edge of aviation technology. Pan Am had their own engineers and used them to taunt both Douglas and Boeing by ordering both the competing DC-8 and 707 and then made future orders contingent on technical improvements.

By 1965, both Trippe and Allen were the elder statesmen of commercial aviation as they departed together on their annual fishing trip to Alaska, where they bunked aboard John Wayne's classic yacht named *Wild Goose*. Like William E. Boeing and Conrad Westervelt (fifty years earlier), the two old anglers conceived an idea for a better airplane on their own and in a vacuum. Based on the tradition of the Pan American model 314 Clippers, it would be a big airplane with multiple decks tied together by a spiral staircase, thus providing additional seating, cargo capacity, luxury accommodations, and longer range pending arrival of the SST into daily service. The jumbo-sized interim airplanes would then be relegated to tramp freighters of the sky, hauling cargo between continents, until their airframes were finally worn out.

The glory and excitement of bringing model 707 to fruition in 1959 had faded. With nostalgia on their minds, both men were at retirement age, and each understood it would be the last opportunity to cement their own reputations into aviation history while concurrently pushing their respective companies onto further greatness. Building the airplane envisioned by Juan Trippe would require a contract between a willing buyer and an equally capable seller. Trippe was known to drive a hard bargain, but he understood the need to remain within the bounds of "Industrial Age chivalry," a dogma shared with Bill Allen.

After over two decades as president, Bill Allen intimately understood the capacity of his company. Boeing had neither the financial capital, factory space, nor human resources necessary to simultaneously maintain 707 and 727 production while undertaking every new project on the horizon (e.g., 737, SST, Trippe's 747, and the Air Force C-5A).

SST and C-5A would ultimately fall by the wayside, leaving only 737 and 747 as new projects; however, even this pair of youngsters would demand cash expenditures that would bring Boeing close to bankruptcy by 1970.

Others at Boeing were convinced of the apparent synergy between military and commercial models, as was demonstrated by the Dash 80, when it was simultaneously adapted into both a military tanker and a civilian airliner. Lockheed won the C-5A contract in September 1965 and assigned model number L-500 to the civilian version. T. Wilson advised Bill Allen that Lockheed intended to evolve the C-5A basic design into separate jetliners suitable for cargo or passenger service; therefore, Wilson (a man devoid of an iota of commercial airliner experience) may have had civilian variants in mind for the Boeing version of the C-5A.

Bill Allen had endured many surprise business setbacks during his long Boeing career. They included the audacious Air Mail Act of 1934, the humbling loss of the B-17 fly-off in 1935, and the gut-wrenching failure of model 247 at the hands of Donald Douglas. Upon hearing of a potential coup by Lockheed, Bill Allen was nudged closer to launching the new wide-body jet, but only as it was envisioned between him and Juan Trippe. If a 737-sized aircraft was necessary to plug the gap created by the runaway success of the Douglas DC-9, then it was equally essential to establish a beachhead in the emerging marketplace for wide-body jets.

Lockheed Airlifters

Was the perceived civilian wide-body threat from Lockheed credible? With a long history of building the L-1049 Constellation, L-188 Electra, and other airliners, Lockheed was in the early 1960s dual-certifying the C-141 Starlifter both for military and commercial service. Having completed rigorous flight testing and earning dual certification, the first Lockheed C-141A assigned to McChord Field touched down in nearby Pierce County on August 9, 1966, and immediately entered long-haul trans-Pacific military service.

Furthermore, starting in 1964, over a hundred C-130s (civilian designation L-100) were sold by Lockheed into corporate hands. They served well in rugged cargo service on remote construction projects—including the Alaskan Alyeska pipeline project. These were impressive airlifters. Market analysts at Boeing and Douglas took note of Lockheed's accomplishment; however, no civilian C-141 or C-5 was ever sold.

While both the Lockheed C-130 Hercules and C-141 were superb transports, the C-5A Galaxy came up short. Airliners are measured by "dispatch reliability." Operating history shows every type of Boeing airliner approaches 100 percent. Very rarely is a departure delayed or canceled because of a mechanical failure. Meanwhile, military aircraft are tracked by a similar metric called "mission capable" rate. The Lockheed C-5M Galaxy struggles to achieve 60 percent (as reported by the *Air Force Times*). Some of the blame resides with the Air Force acquisition process. Lockheed underbid Boeing but was then stuck with the consequences. Lockheed exited the airliner business after building 250 model L-1011 Tri-Star wide-body jets between 1968 and 1984.

Doing business as a Pentagon prime contractor is a challenge. Multiyear projects rely on annual appropriations. Furthermore, the contracts bring with them thick and daunting manuals called "Federal Acquisition Regulations" (or FAR). These Byzantine tomes are akin to reading Internal Revenue Service (IRS) code both in complexity and massiveness. Nothing is sillier than watching tax dollars being squandered as a government auditor searches for a "gotcha" by pawing through a thick stack of travel expense reports in search of a glass of wine (to accompany an evening meal in a faraway city) improperly accounted for.

Congressional appropriations intended for military projects can disappear in a heartbeat. A fickle Congress may abruptly cease funding a weapons system when the other political party sweeps into Washington, DC. Or, a new president or secretary of defense might take the military in a fresh direction.

The military expected an outsized C-141—high wing, four engines, and low main deck for ease of loading. With the C-5A contract lost in September 1965, the way was cleared for Boeing to move forward aggressively with the 747. The Boeing design team was now unshackled to conceive a much-better configuration. Consistent with other Boeing airliners, the 747 wing-to-body join is below the main deck.

When Boeing lost the C-5A contract, three thousand people on the proposal were ordered disbanded in one week. Existing organizations were directed to take on the people, absorb them, and lay off the lowest-producing people of the resulting mix. Fifteen facilities planners showed up outside my office the following Monday. I knew all of them and further knew they were wondering who would be laid off.

This model represents one rendering of the Air Force C-5A as envisioned by Boeing; however, Lockheed underbid, won a contract, but suffered the resulting red ink. Better still for Boeing, they were then free to join forces with engine builder Pratt & Whiney and move forward with the much more lucrative 747. *John Fredrickson photo of an artifact in Boeing Archives*

I took them into my planning room and said, "I need every one of you. You guys were on the little program. The C-5A has a rate of two per month. We have a program in the works that almost no one knows exists—not even our top management. They've had their eyes on C-5A and SST. Our lead factory planner, Earl Bowden, has just attended an advance meeting between industrial engineering and preliminary design. We will build a big transport plane, as big as the C-5A, but the rate will be seven airplanes a month—or eighty-four airplanes a year."

Other than massive size, did any attributes of the rejected Boeing C-5A make it forward to the 747? First, a cockpit placed above and atop the forward section of main deck with useful space behind. Second, the option to swing the entire nose assembly skyward for straight-in main-deck cargo loading on the freighter version. Third, four big engines; however, the greater wing sweep of the model 747 contributes to the fastest cruise speed (normally Mach .86) of any other transport aircraft currently in service.

Let's Make a Deal . . .

Pan American's Juan Trippe was known to drive a very hard bargain. Status as launch customer had been leveraged on the 707 purchase to justify a lower unit price. In addition to an eager launch customer, Bill Allen also knew the board of directors would also need a full suite of facts and data before a 747-sized project would be approved.

With activities at a fever pitch, most everybody at Boeing was awash in meetings as 1965 became 1966. I recall two large meetings attended by Bill Allen. The first, in late December, was to update him for discussions with potential customers—primarily Juan Trippe. The second, in January, was to prepare for the upcoming February 1966 board meeting.

The agenda for a crucial December meeting was set. This would be a gathering too large for the boardroom. The theater-sized New Employee Orientation Hall across the street was reserved. Meeting topics for my group included if the 747 could be built at Renton, an update on the two big new final-assembly buildings in Renton (numbered 4-81 and 4-82), a presentation showing 737 production at the Thompson tract, and a review of site studies for an entirely new factory for 747.

William "Bill" Allen selected his own replacement. It was the legendary engineer who ramrodded the Minuteman project, Thornton A. Wilson (*seated*, who liked to be known as "T"), who was elevated to president of Boeing in 1968.

CHAPTER 10
Decision to Delay a Decision

Preparations began for what would turn out to be one of the strangest meetings of my Boeing career. This would be an important meeting, and memorable for its size. It seemed all the important people then on the Boeing payroll were invited. The various groups selected their speakers. Presentations were prepared, rehearsed, timed, and critiqued. Revisions were made and the process repeated.

Rich Archer, a Coast Guard veteran with five years of service in the Boeing facilities organization, was nominated to present the 737 factory plan. He had personally laid out 737 production in Plant II with spillover into the proposed Thompson site. Archer's presentation was not previewed by the headquarters staff.

A youthful appearance belied his thirty-two years of age. Designating a younger presenter was an effective technique for handling controversial topics. The exposure and experience were good for the speaker, and the executives were unlikely to shoot a messenger who was merely a low-level spokesman. Best of all, it allowed individual managers to embrace a new direction and quickly move on without losing face.

I said, "If Archer's going to carry the ball, he must be disciplined, follow instructions, appear to be neutral, and stick to a factual message. I'll help with preparing his presentation." I was assured that Rich Archer would do fine, and was especially thankful to my boss for shielding me from this donnybrook, thus preserving my image as the "new site" guy.

I had previously phoned Cy Prideaux at Austin Construction immediately after the meeting with Fraser and Link: "Now that you've had a week to study the project at the Thompson site, are you willing to commit to a six-month schedule? I am depending on you not to let me or Boeing down . . ."

Cy responded, "We can make our schedule if you guys make your schedule. The design is a remake of the 10-50 building; our steel plant in Cleveland is already preparing shop drawings and has reserved fabrication capacity—but we need written go-ahead before cutting structural steel. We're getting bids from the pile-driving and foundation subcontractors. The location is under nondisclosure, and they probably think the work is at Renton." We also discussed budget and concluded that transformers would be a close-watch item because the incoming line voltage was different at Renton than at Seattle plants.

I further took the time to review the plan with Wally Engstrom, the recently retired Austin executive who had earned the complete confidence of Bill Allen (and the other Boeing executives) dating back to World War II. This assured me that any phone call from Bill Allen to Wally would not yield a surprise. Sometimes it seemed Bill Allen put more trust in Austin than in his own facilities experts. After twenty years as CEO, Bill Allen, no doubt, had been told misleading stories more than once.

Within a week, the Austin Company committed to construct a new 737 final-assembly building[1] on the Thompson tract in six months for $9 million. Furthermore, I knew the next few years would approximate wartime for the Austin Construction Company, me, and thousands of others at Boeing.

Preparing for a Memorable Meeting

That night I stayed up late, sitting at our family kitchen table, and crafted a presentation. Section 1 would be the planning base, which showed 737 shop completion, supported flight testing and certification, and delivery schedules, beginning with Lufthansa German airlines and continuing with United Airlines and others. Section 2 was Rich Archer's 737 factory layout. Section 3 was the construction schedule. Section 4 was the capital budget and ending.

I knew my job was to utilize existing facilities rather than build new ones; however, it was the demographics that prevailed in my mind. I didn't yet fully realize how downtrodden the model 737 was within certain factions at Boeing. "Why should Boeing be distracted by a small, short-haul airliner when bigger and sexier projects like SST and 747 were afoot?" they asked. To me, it would be necessary to keep the twenty thousand people (a third professional engineering and two-thirds hourly workers) all together if this fragile infant airliner still in gestation was to be kept viable. My boss, Don Davis, agreed with me on the importance of "critical mass"—but the concept was unprovable and argumentative.

While pondering the upcoming meeting, it became clear in my mind that the main subject of review was 747. Bill Allen wanted to know the latest thinking about cost and feasibility before talking with the board of directors and our lead customer—Juan Trippe of Pan American World Airlines. I knew Jack Steiner would present the latest 747 configuration.

There had been a big change. Initial factory layouts in November 1965 showed a very large but stubby-looking double-deck airplane. Now, the latest rendering was a single-deck airplane, with a wider and longer body. Earl Bowden would cover that presentation.

The first set of 737 layouts showed the airplane in Renton; however, production rates were rising rapidly. Model 707 was at 10.5 aircraft per month, and twenty-one of the slightly smaller 727s were rolling out every month. A dearth of factory space left 737 assembly out in the cold. Further complicating planning was the assumption that SST would eliminate model 707 on long-haul routes. The big bays in Renton were intended to host SST final assembly. It seemed the Thompson site was necessary to keep the 737 in Seattle. The pair of bigger and faster models (707 and 727) was pushing the little 737 out of Renton.

Furthermore, the Thompson site was unique in that it offered access to four modes of transportation: an international airport, an interstate highway, a railroad line, and barge loading. The Duwamish waterway connected to the Ballard Locks, which made possible the economic shipment of outsized major assemblies between Seattle and Renton by barge. The goal was to demonstrate the Thompson site as viable for many purposes—which has been borne out over the decades.

The 737 situation was forcing Bill Allen to side against either his trusted financial guru at Renton (John Yeasting) or his heir apparent (T. A. Wilson). I decided to offer Bill Allen an escape route. Rich Archer's presentation would be called "Decision Delay Plan." The conclusion would say, "The decision to send 737 to Wichita[2] can be delayed six months."

Our company had grown to 103,762 employees in 1965 and would hit 150,000 in four more years, as recruiters scoured the nation in search of qualified job applicants. The facilities department would be called on to find each of them workspace.

The time for the big meeting arrived. Discussions with Pan American were ongoing. The next board meeting would be in Renton on February 28, 1966. Launching the 747 program was expected to be on their agenda. Boeing held 71 percent of world airliner market share and was after more. Time was of the essence.

My chain of command, up to John Yeasting, were already in their chairs. Each of the top airplane engineers began to file in. They were accomplished airplane people worthy of high esteem. Ed Wells, a designer of the B-17 and B-29, was on the board of directors and was Bill Allen's primary source of engineering guidance. Next in line was Maynard Pennell, designer of the KC-135 and 707. He was now assigned to SST. Of course, there was Jack Steiner, designer of the 727 and 737, who—as a designated speaker—would present the latest version of the 747.

T. A. Wilson, legendary program manager of doomsday weapon systems—B-52 and Minuteman—arrived with his own entourage of corporate men. Each of them took seats. The lower-level subject matter experts also made their way into the meeting room. Dick Welch of Commercial finance arrived to present the 747 cost estimates. George Sanborn represented Sales and Marketing.

The big room was now filled with the key people of Boeing. The excitement was palpable. Never had I witnessed so many at the same time and in the same place. Each was uniformly attired in a business suit with a white shirt, skinny necktie, and closely cropped hair. They were strong willed, accustomed to tight deadlines, and commanding organizations sometimes numbering into the tens of thousands. They engendered respect at work and in the community.

Caffeine sped them up in the morning. Cigarettes, stress, and bad diet shortened some of their lives. Their pay was modest by the standards of today—but it was enough to provide their families comfortable lives and tuition for college-bound offspring. They knew how to tell a joke, laugh, or orchestrate an occasional office prank. For them, life was good, and to them, work was fun. Each was narrowly focused on some aspect of bigger and faster airplanes. For many of us, a lifetime within Boeing easily became all consuming. Workaholics abounded.

The place remained strangely silent as everyone waited for the absolute boss—William M. "Bill" Allen—to walk in. The last of the great leaders personally hired and mentored by the founder was about to launch Mr. Boeing's company onto a trajectory that would take it far into the next century. But first, he needed the benefit of the group's wisdom before fine-tuning the details.

Graciously, Bill Allen timed his entry to be five minutes late, so as not to embarrass latecomers who might have been tied up in traffic. Allen, despite his autocratic ways, was always smooth, polished, and very polite. Everybody in the meeting strove to be on their best behavior. Even T. Wilson stifled his propensity to emote four-letter expletives whenever Allen was within earshot.

Bill Allen was all business; in a gentlemanly way, he simply said, "I'd like to see the latest on 747 configuration." With that, Jack Steiner arose and proceeded to explain a slick sales presentation on card stock, rather than flip charts. He went very slowly so Allen could absorb the important details and be primed to respond to questions from Juan Trippe, whether it be face to face or over the phone. Everybody knew these two industrial titans were close to the deal of the century. Steiner said the cargo 747 should be priced at $19.9 million, the passenger version at $20 million, and the combination cargo/passenger at $20.1 million each. An average selling price of $20 million seemed important. This presentation, including questions, took less than an hour.

"Could I see the cost estimate?" Allen next asked. Dick Welch of the finance department launched into a very detailed presentation. Welch asserted that a larger airplane would take fewer man-hours per pound than smaller aircraft, which backed up estimates from Manufacturing, thus avoiding the embarrassment of a rehash of the recent heated argument between Fraser and Gordon Link regarding learning curve. Welch (who later become BCA president) priced the manufacturing hours as derived by Ron Fraser's group, and estimated the engineering effort and overhead expense—which totaled about $4 billion (in 1966 dollars). This meant the program would break even at two hundred units—if each airplane was offered at Steiner's price of $20 million. Dick Welch's explanation took forty-five minutes.

"Now, I'd like to see if the 747 can be built in Renton with a minimum of new construction," asked Allen. That was Earl Bowden's cue to speak. Bowden went in the front of the room, where Mr. Allen was seated, and placed his board of flip charts on the easel. The contrast with Steiner's slick individual charts on heavy card stock was obvious. We limited ourselves to only red felt-tip titles with occasional red bullets. Our staff had to look austere because we were presenting internally. Steiner could use fancy charts because he sold externally.

Bowden carefully went through a series of layouts showing the 747 program building up in Renton. Even if we added two huge assembly bays to the two already under construction, the wide-body airplane would squeeze out production of the smaller 707 and 727 jets. "And what's the price tag on that?" asked Allen. A precise answer was rendered—but it didn't make any difference. Allen lamented, "I don't think we can afford to limit 707 or 727 production. They are in positive cash flow now, and we need them to pay for the 747 until it makes a profit six years from now."

Allen looked at me and at John Bixby, corporate director of facilities. He said, "I think we need to keep looking for a new site." The meeting was now more than two hours old.

Allen had obviously been prebriefed when he now broached the topic from hell: "I'd like to discuss whether to move the 737 to Wichita. I understand it's an employment issue and a facilities issue. I think we'd better settle it and get on with the program." O. C. Scott, head of Commercial Division's industrial-relations department, which was responsible for recruitment and hiring, explained charts showing employees needed division wide. He explained, "No problem. We did it twenty-five years ago during the war, and again ten years ago on the B-52 program. Please be assured we can adequately staff both 737 and 747 programs."

This brought Mr. Thornton Wilson to life. "What about the learning curves? All these new people will be green." I noted again how gentlemanly Wilson was in Allen's presence by the absence of profanity. Allen asked John Yeasting to have someone address T. Wilson's question. Ron Fraser got up with his stack of flip charts, but before he turned any over, he simply said, "We don't think there will be any deterioration of experience. The fuselage section is common with existing programs, and the wings will be done with automatic riveters, which will cut down manpower."

Wilson then asked Gordon Link to respond. Link[3] stood up and said, "There's no way to escape learning-curve problems with the new workers we're planning to hire. Wichita has factory workers available. According to my calculations, the 737 will overrun its budget on the first two hundred aircraft by $75 million."

Fraser's immediate retort: "The disruption of moving it to Wichita in the middle of buildup will cost $75 million." In this meeting there would be neither beating of pointers onto flip charts nor screaming at one another. The adversaries agreed on one thing—a $75 million loss whether it stayed or went. No senior people on either side of the issue had the guts to come to either man's rescue in front of Bill Allen. Allen, now into his sixty-fifth year, sat in silence and seemed somewhat bewildered.

Over three hours had elapsed since the start of the meeting. Everybody was getting tired. "I'd like to see the facilities plan" were the next words Bill Allen uttered. Rich Archer got up with his stack of flip charts. He would be the last man standing. Archer placed them on the easel and uncovered the title, "Decision Delay Plan." I wondered if Allen would bite the bait.

Rich Archer proceeded in a very businesslike manner. He quickly went through the charts showing the 737[4] buildup in Plant II and overflowing into the new building on the Thompson tract in six months. "The cost will be $10 million," said Archer, "which includes one million dollars for Charlie Thompson's land." The section on alternative uses demonstrated how the new 14-01 building could benefit other programs, including 747, if the 737 was not built there.

Allen snapped back into his best form when he succinctly wrapped up the meeting, "Thank you, gentlemen. We'll delay the 737 decision by six months. Meanwhile, we'll continue looking for a new site for the 747. I guess I'll have to talk about real estate with Charlie Thompson." With that, Bill Allen abruptly stood up and departed.

Wilson and his entourage stayed behind only briefly—but long enough to lament, "If we wait six months, it'll never move," and then shuffled off in disgust. T. Wilson and his corporate people lost this skirmish. The center of gravity within the company had just shifted further toward Commercial. The team from Renton, savoring victory, exited in a state of euphoria.

Creators of the 747 could not imagine their creation would be so enduring. The Special Performance version (1975) traded seats for longer range. Sales were expected to be 100 units but achieved only a third of that goal.

Mr. and Mrs. Juan Trippe arrive at Boeing Field on the evening of July 14, 1966, ostensibly to attend the Boeing fiftieth-anniversary celebration the next day; however, Trippe was also seeking details of the still-evolving 747.

CHAPTER 11
Inheriting a Firestorm

The Commercial team from Renton had won the battle to keep 737 in Seattle. I thought I could relax. Boeing shifts people rapidly. That's the advantage of having critical mass.

Within two weeks T. Wilson had a new assignment: he was charged to win the SST. He had the pick of subordinates. He picked my boss, Don Davis, to be his facility director. Davis could not refuse. He was drafted. As Davis packed his belongings, preparing to move from Renton to the Developmental Center, I was called to Erle Barnes's office.

"You are replacing Davis, as of this moment," Barnes said. "You are now director of all facilities planning and construction for the Commercial Airplane Division."

I was stunned. Davis and I were a team. Now I was alone. Barnes, noting my silence, continued, "Johnny, you've done the planning; now you've got to do the construction."

I was thirty-four years old and had two brand-new aircraft plants to build—one at Auburn and a giant one at a site yet to be determined. I also had major expansions underway at both Renton and Plant II. The 737 building on the Thompson site would be a drop in the bucket.

I left Erle Barnes's office with mixed feelings. Pleased to be promoted, I remained apprehensive about the job. I felt alone with the task of building two new aircraft plants while expanding two others. It was my job to bridge the gap between Boeing and the construction company.

I thought about the organization, since it was now configured and reporting to me. The planning section, with its team of fifty people, would pose no problems. I'd come to know each of them well over the past six months. The administrative section, with capital-budgeting, legal, and audiovisual units, also were of little concern. It had forty people and I was on solid ground with all of them.

My greatest concern was the two-hundred-person engineering section, with its estimating, design coordination, and construction management units. A year ago, this section did not exist. Its functions were scattered about. Don Davis invested much of his time during the last six months building the capability of this section. The goal was delivering high-quality new construction on time and within budget.

By 1966, Mr. Barnes's office was in the 10-60 building, headquarters for Transportation Division executives. Five thousand people were in his organization—85 percent hourly and 15 percent white collar. Later, Barnes asked me to move into a top-floor office adjacent to his own and nearby the other top executives. My other workspace was in a nearby leased warehouse called the Overmeyer Building. There were 250 professional people reporting to me. They, in turn, managed seven hundred professional engineers on contract. Add to that the seven thousand construction workers employed by contractors, who were on hourly cost-plus-fixed fee contracts that required daily attention, oversight, and monitoring by Boeing.

Bayne Lamb

Davis had selected a seasoned facilities manager from Aerospace Group named Bayne Lamb to run the engineering section. Davis had consulted with me before bringing Lamb aboard because he knew Lamb would be charged with building what I was planning.

My only previous encounter with Bayne Lamb was a disappointing experience ten years earlier. I was then a young civil engineer charged with designing the foundation of Boeing's first reverse-thrust engine test rig at North Boeing Field. At the time, Lamb was managing facilities support for B-52 flight test and field operations. Supporting flight test is always a stressful job, and apparently Lamb handled it well; however, in a clear violation of "Industrial Age chivalry," Lamb insulted me when I approached him seeking help clearing the area where the test rig foundation was to be placed.

I was left standing in his open doorway while he and three others laughingly engaged in a prolonged conversation about non-work-related matters. As the stalemate dragged on and on, I sensed Lamb was letting a young engineer attired in a gray-flannel business suit

Despite a bumpy first encounter, Bayne Lamb became one of my most trusted colleagues in our mutual quest to get the Everett complex built. Hired during World War II, Bayne enjoyed a long and distinguished career at Boeing.

know he was outranked. I decided to speak up: "If you're the guy that's running this place, I need you to send a crew to clear out the area I've just tagged. We need a solid concrete foundation under the engine test stand to test reverse thrust."

"Never heard of reverse thrust," grumbled Lamb.

"You will," I replied. "The 707s just ordered will need thrust reversers to assist with braking. That's 20,000 pounds of thrust for takeoff and 10,000 pounds of braking assistance on touchdown."

"I'll see if I can break loose a couple of guys. We're pretty busy," he grunted.

My first and only previous brush with Bayne Lamb had been frosty. He would not remember me, but I remembered him as status conscious; therefore, I had been treating Bayne respectfully over the past six months in deference to his greater age and longer tenure.

Barnes and Lamb shared a common background. Both came to Boeing in 1941. Lamb was twenty years younger than Barnes and drove a forklift for the older man. Furthermore, Lamb was athletic. He had been an all-city quarterback for Seattle's Cleveland High School and was recruited with a football scholarship at the University of Washington. An injury ended his football career and disqualified him from the armed forces. He applied with Boeing, got hired, and never returned to school.

It's funny how entry jobs seem to follow people throughout their careers. Erle Barnes was known as the "bus driver" while Lamb was tagged as a jitney operator. Jitney is a derisive term for forklifts and small factory tractors. Lamb's responsibilities grew as temporary wartime bomb shelters were built in the parking lots. He was soon responsible for keeping them stocked, tidy, and instantly available in the unlikely event of an air raid. Meanwhile, Don Davis garnered greater respect and professional status because of his formal education as an architect.

Crew Meeting

Barnes named me as successor to Davis. It was a job I did not want. My peers were all older than me by ten to twenty years. In any case, the assignment was mine, and it was my duty to break the news. I felt lonely as I sat in my pickup truck, waiting to make my entry into the area where the 250 people of the department were gathered. Each of them now reported to me. As I pondered my own formal education, innate talent, and a hard-won blue-collar toughness, I concluded that Barnes had picked the right person for the difficult times ahead. There was no job I could not do. My concern was the reaction of Bayne Lamb. Would he sulk and resist quietly? He seemed to be doing a good job, and I needed an experienced manager in his position.

I knew that neither Erle Barnes nor Bayne Lamb held the academic credentials to assist me on the bumpy road ahead, because neither was formally trained as an engineer; however, despite my initial qualms, the trio of Erle Barnes, me, and Bayne Lamb collaborated to accomplish an industrial form of transformation at the north end of Paine Field that will endure for many more decades.

The workplace stress levels on Boeing executives were significant and building. Like a sergeant receiving a battlefield commission, by demonstrating competence I was rewarded with increased responsibilities, including long-range facilities planning, site selection, and industrial construction; therefore, I was entrusted with greater autonomy than was typical at Boeing.

There were newspaper reports about the vertical-assembly building for the Saturn V moon rocket at Cape Canaveral in Florida. It was the biggest building in the world, with 129 million cubic feet of volume. I multiplied the dimensions of the new 707 and 727 buildings in Renton. A quick envelope-style calculation found it to be about 90 million cubic feet. It would be the second-biggest building in the world when ready for occupancy in late 1966.

Performing the same calculations on the dimensions of the proposed 747 factory, the result was 250 million cubic feet. Only then did I realize that Mr. Allen and the board of directors were being asked for a building twice as large as anything already on planet Earth. I decided to keep my mouth shut. I wouldn't tell my boss, or my subordinates, or anybody else. Bill Allen was a notorious skinflint when it came to capital budget. He had already seen the same small-scale model overlaid nearby the runway on an aerial photograph of each of the potential manufacturing sites under evaluation. Furthermore, the headquarters facilities staff had the drawings—but they (along with everybody else) were fixated on the sideshow called "site selection" rather than the attributes of the factory building.

During this critical time, the ongoing "sideshow" left me free to finalize the design of an ideal aircraft plant without flak from headquarters staffers. My worry was that somebody would find an excuse to declare it "too big" and insist it be divided into three or four buildings to be approved piecemeal. This would scuttle factory manager Bob Regan's desire for "one-roof manufacturing" with overhead cranes moving seamlessly wherever needed. One-roof manufacturing with no doghouses remained my primary goal. Future generations of factory managers yet born would thank me in absentia.

I did not want to risk sacrificing efficiency, capability, and ease of future expansion for the fleeting ego boost of premature bragging. Besides, enclosed volume was meaningless, anyway. Instead, I would wait in silence until thousands of tons of custom-rolled structural steel were loaded aboard trains bound for that yet-to-be-determined location somewhere in the West.

Keeping that secret was only a part of my loneliness. Don Davis, a boss that I revered, was gone to SST, working under T. Wilson. There was nobody to confide in, other than subordinates who looked to me for leadership. Any display of worry or uncertainty on my part would be very disturbing to them. I was working alone and carrying a secret that I dared not share with anyone: Boeing was about to undertake the biggest building project in the world. It would be one-roof manufacturing with no lean-tos or doghouses.

CHAPTER 12
Mr. Allen's Frustrations

A Yale-educated entrepreneur, William E. Boeing, established the company in 1916. Starting on September 1, 1945, an attorney from Harvard University became its most accomplished leader. William M. Allen's long list of product choices was impeccable. Decisions made on Allen's watch launched the company upon a trajectory which sustained it for fifty years beyond his own retirement in 1968. This chapter recounts some of the challenges Bill Allen endured. Whether by passenger train, Greyhound bus, or automobile, Seattle was the end of the line for thousands of young people escaping the backwater small towns of Montana (or the Dakotas) by heading west. Yet, an upbringing in the wide-open spaces of "Big Sky" or "Roughrider" country forever imparts a demeanor of understated self-confidence, independence, humility, and trust in others that endures for a lifetime. Some of these people found their way onto the Boeing payroll. Their ranks included William "Bill" Allen (via Harvard Law School), pilot Jack Waddell, myself, and many others.

An Unexpected Vacancy in the President's Office

Philip G. Johnson was reared in the area of Seattle called Ballard and was educated as an engineer at the nearby University of Washington. Johnson returned to Seattle from exile in Canada (after the Air Mail Act of 1934) to assume the presidency of Boeing in 1939. Claire Egtvedt, another UW alumnus (also class of 1917), was happy to be rejoined with a lifelong friend and embraced his own new position as chairman of the board. Both Johnson and Egtvedt had been handpicked for mentoring by the founder.

H. Oliver West rode Johnson's coattails back to Boeing in 1939. West hired at Boeing in 1921 as a receiving parts inspector. A savant on the topics of parts, maintenance, and aircraft assembly, it was said West could recite from memory the number of every part of the early Boeing airplanes such as model 40. West accompanied Johnson to United Air Lines before their world was devastated by the Air Mail Act of 1934.

Under Johnson's sponsorship, West rose to the position of executive vice president and member of the board of directors, despite being so badly riddled with arthritis that even climbing a few stairs was impossible. Another inside member of the board was engineer Wellwood Beall (1906–1978), who had earned fame as the primary designer of the iconic model 314 flying boat (Clipper, when operated by Pan Am).

Boeing production soared during the war years, and West was given credit for the layout and expansions of Plant II, Renton, and Wichita factories; however, the stresses of wartime had created a festering rift between engineering and manufacturing (called "operations" within Boeing).

Legendary Boeing experimental test pilot Alvin "Tex" Johnston in the flight crew locker room. Johnston was a dichotomy—a swaggering, self-promoting showman at work while simultaneously a soft-spoken family man when at home.

The gregarious Mr. Johnson was returning to Seattle from meetings in Washington, DC, and arranged for a stopover at Wichita. Johnson intended to investigate B-29 production woes. He was prone to walking the factory floor and interacting directly with the hourly workers, which was needed to get firsthand status regarding B-29 assembly. Instead, he felt unwell and opted to remain in his hotel room. It was there that P. G. Johnson was found dead. Cerebral hemorrhage, no doubt stress induced, was deemed the culprit. Word of his passing sent shock waves all around Boeing and beyond.

Commencing with the Civil War, embalmed bodies of the deceased were normally put into a casket, and the casket was secured within a transfer case for shipment aboard a baggage car attached to a passenger train. In this case, a policy deviation authorized the dispatch of an assigned B-17 from Boeing Field to retrieve the remains. A young Wichita accountant named Clyde Skeen later recalled helping load and secure the transfer case into the bomb bay.

With funeral services completed, Claire Egtvedt settled in as acting president and began an executive search to replace P. G. Johnson. Both the rather rotund Wellwood Beall and arthritic Oliver West clamored for the job. However, healing the rift between Engineering and Operations wisely remained a bigger objective for Egtvedt, who, despite the Boeing tradition of promotion from within, was also open for an infusion of outside talent.

Egtvedt had his sights set on Bill Allen, another of the trio personally mentored by the founder, a longtime member of the board of directors, and, best of all, unencumbered by the schism between Operations and Engineering. But Allen, comfortable in his role as partner at the law firm, professed that an engineer was needed. Furthermore, Allen was still grieving the loss of his beloved spouse (and high school sweetheart), Dorothy, to cancer in 1943.

Allen was the son of a prosperous mining engineer and was born in Lolo, Montana (near Missoula). His mother was a suffragist and prohibitionist who closed three saloons and built a church. Historian Eugene Rodgers described Allen as "a brown-eye, brown-haired, slender man . . . slightly jug-eared, ruddy, and balding. . . . Seemingly born in black shoes and a dark-blue three-piece suit, he was a stereotypical archconservative Republican." Outwardly Bill Allen was a shy man. Like William E. Boeing, a reserved demeanor reinforced his image as an unfeeling corporate technician, the antithesis of his affable predecessor, P. G. Johnson, who often strolled about the factory floor exchanging pleasantries with the hourly workers.

Bill Allen finally agreed to accept the job, but his obligations kept him at the law firm until the return of the other partners from wartime military duty. Allen became the fourth person to serve as president of the Boeing Airplane Company, on September 1, 1945. By 1948, Allen's personal life was back on an even keel with his marriage to Margaret Ellen Field (nickname "Mef"). Together, they raised his two daughters.

Having been passed over for promotion, and with his sponsor, P. G. Johnson, gone, Oliver West resigned both the board of directors and his Boeing vice presidency in 1946 to become president of Canadair. Chronic bad health forced him to retire at age fifty-one, and he passed away in 1964 at age sixty-four.

Consistent with western management theory, the Boeing Company is structured like a pyramid. The top layer is corporate headquarters, which sets policy, obtains funding, and allocates budget. The core head count typically numbers fewer than five hundred people. The two largest operating divisions are segregated into "commercial" (tied to airlines) and "aerospace" (government customer). The lowest level is plant site specific. For example, in the Facilities Department, there is a separate management presence at corporate, division, and plant levels.

The economic-investment models embraced by industrial experts of the day included the payback (or breakeven) model, and the standard financial tools of balance sheet and income statement. New commercial airplane programs were risky. When properly bid, a lucrative contract for a new Pentagon weapon system was normally a safer bet.

Unlike T. Wilson, with roots in major Pentagon projects, Allen was a steadfast proponent of ever-better commercial airliners. Allen personally represented William E. Boeing on matters of airmail and airline operations (which ultimately were consolidated to become United Air Lines). Both Mr. Boeing and his attorney (Allen) shared high hopes for the various models launched prior to World War II.

Bill Allen's opportunity to become another victim of Washington, DC, partisan politics came in February 1956, when the US House of Representatives Armed Services Committee held open hearings regarding allegations of price gouging by military aircraft manufacturers. Boeing, represented by controller Clyde Skeen, was called on to testify on the fourth day. Bill Allen attended but sat in silence. At the end, a congressman asked Allen if he had any

While on a trip to Alaska in 1947, General of the Army Dwight D. Eisenhower made a covert stop in Seattle for a firsthand look at the top-secret XB-47. Bill Allen (*far right*) stands back to let his top engineers, Ed Wells (*left*) and Wellwood Beall (*wearing a bow tie*), do the talking.

comment. Bill Allen, no doubt mulled in his mind how William E. Boeing, in February 1934, had been ambushed, berated, pilloried, and ultimately driven from the industry by a separate but similar gang of capital-city thugs.

Bill Allen—slender and dignified, and elegant in dress, speech, and movement—was more given to intent listening rather than speaking. When he rose to his feet, the mental power of the Harvard-educated barrister emerged for the gathered congressmen and their staffers to witness. A monologue heavy with facts and data but laced with pinches of patriotism mixed with dollops of emotion was delivered unabated over the next twenty minutes. He pointed out the small profits, huge risks, and massive R&D investments Boeing was making. In the end, he received a standing ovation from every congressman and staffer in attendance.

As Robert J. Serling put it in his book *Legend & Legacy*, "Allen (of Boeing) seemed to command instinctive respect, a kind of immediate admission that any scandal-seeking congressman was going to get his fingers burned if he tried tangling with the symbol of industrial integrity." The matter of price gouging was dropped like a hot potato. Thus, Bill Allen had skillfully side-stepped the same political quicksand that ensnared his mentor, Mr. William E. Boeing.

Despite its heritage, United Airlines of Chicago came to prefer Douglas prop airliners, as did maverick Northwest Airlines of Minneapolis. TWA embraced the sleek Lockheed Constellation for its service to Europe. Model 377 suffered chronic engine problems. Sales ended at a disappointing fifty-six units. Boeing was then known as a bomber company. Some in the industry wished Boeing would remain so. The postwar Douglas-built prop airliners were fine products, market leaders, and the first choice for many airlines.

Pilot "Tex" Johnston Arrives

A different thin and lanky fellow, Alvin M. "Tex" Johnston (1914–1998), was already an experienced test pilot when he joined Boeing at Wichita in July 1948 to test-fly Air Force B-47 bombers. The soft-spoken Mr. Johnston relocated his young family to Seattle and set about to further embellish his reputation as a colorful character. Wearing cowboy boots and a Stetson hat on the flight line were but a part of the repertoire.

Starting out as a civilian flight instructor during World War II, Tex Johnston was said to be the inspiration for the mythical Air Force B-52 bomber pilot Maj. Kong in the 1964 black-comedy movie *Doctor Strangelove*. A dashing mustache also made him a Howard Hughes look-alike. A fresh pair of cowboy boots were handcrafted each time he took a brand-new version of the legendary B-52 aloft. These boots are now enshrined at Seattle's Museum of Flight.

The annual Seafair celebration was scheduled for August 7, 1955. The ever-popular annual Seattle celebration of summer features unlimited-class hydroplane boat races interspersed with air show events. The roar of war-surplus Rolls-Royce aircraft engines on the water attracted race fans by the thousands. Boeing regularly staged a flyby of whatever aircraft happened to be undergoing flight testing. Bill Allen, a man whose daily actions were deliberate, scheduled, and most often scripted in advance, was about to be eyewitness to an event over Lake Washington that would sear itself into the annals of Seattle folklore as an anecdote to be told and retold.

Always icy cool, Tex Johnston was the pilot in command, with copilot James "Jim" Gannett (1923–2006) seated to his right. The mix of "nice guy" combined with superb piloting skills made Jim Gannett one of the finest aviators to ever wear a Boeing badge. Jim was chosen as project pilot for the SST. A project pilot helps engineer and market and is the pilot in command on the first flight of a new model—thus putting his name into the record books. The fleeting opportunity for enduring notoriety evaporated when the SST got canceled. Two decades after 1955, Gannett soldiered on in anonymity as chief test pilot on separate military versions of the venerable 707-320C. They were the Air Force's E-3A Sentry radar plane and a separate Navy submarine communications aerial platform designated the E-6 Mercury.

Flight testing is also deliberate and carefully scripted. Therefore, as part of a routine workday aloft, the flight plan included a low-level flyby over the racecourse. The barnstormer gene lurking within Tex Johnston emerged when he realized an audience of Boeing management, airline presidents, and a throng of local citizens were awaiting his appearance. A Boeing test engineer named Bel Whitehead occupied the heavily instrumented cabin to the rear. At the appointed time, Johnston aimed the nose toward Lake Washington and, in his usual slow drawl, said to copilot Gannett, "Jim, I'm gonna do a slow roll over the Gold Cup course."[1]

After a moment to process the incongruent words flowing into his headset, Gannett keyed his own microphone and said, "They're liable to fire you."

"Maybe, but I don't think so," countered Tex.

The maneuver, better suited to the Navy's Blue Angel demonstration team, had been rehearsed. It looked dangerous but was perfectly safe—but only when performed by an extraordinarily skilled pilot. The engine oil, fuel sumps, and everything else aboard the big jet would remain at a constant force of gravity (one "g," in technical terms).

Those in attendance at Lake Washington numbered somewhere between 250,000 and 300,000 spectators. Mr. William Allen and several airline guests were aboard a chartered boat and expecting the flyby. A distant spot became visible in the clear blue sky. The visage of a 248,000-pound experimental jet grew rapidly as it closed ground in a shallow dive at 490 miles per hour. The slow barrel roll began at only 200 feet above the watery racecourse as the Dash 80 went into a gentle climb. At the middle of the continuous roll, the bottoms of the wings faced upward and the vertical tail faced downward. Tex turned the aircraft around and repeated the process, this time going the opposite direction—to ensure that the demonstration was not construed as a mechanical malfunction.

Bill Allen had no inkling of the plan and was flummoxed. He had bet the company by investing a scarce $16 million into the Dash 80. Allen, an ultraconservative fellow from Montana, expected "his" airplane to be flown with dignity and respect. This meant the vertical stabilizer pointing upward, engines hanging downward, and people aboard sitting generally erect. Tex Johnston had violated that trust. Under Allen's version of "Industrial Age chivalry," there was nothing that could be done to retrieve loss of trust. The next morning Johnston and a cadre of executives were summoned to Allen's office. Boeing people fretted—would Johnston be fired?

"What did you think you were doing yesterday?" growled Allen.

"Selling airplanes" was Johnston's often-quoted response.

The following evening, Tex Johnston, along with World War I ace and leader of Eastern Airlines, Eddie Rickenbacker, attended a social event at the Allen residence. Rickenbacker mussed Tex's cowboy hat and said, "You slow-rolling son of a bitch, why didn't you let me know you were gonna pull that? I would have been riding the jump seat."

CBS television news anchor Douglas Edwards interviews Johnston at Baltimore Airport regarding the record-setting dash from Seattle in three hours, forty-eight minutes on March 11, 1957. Youthful copilot Lew Wallick (*light-colored coat*) listens in.

Firefighting foam saved the Dash 80 from going up in flames during refused takeoff (RTO) testing. RTOs are an example of the abusive treatment inflicted on test airplanes to ensure the safety of the traveling public.

Bill Allen was much less amused. After investing the company's future into the prototype, he felt betrayed that anybody would sully it by performing cheap stunts. Bill Allen had already mulled the pros and cons of immediately firing Johnston but suppressed his strong urge for swift revenge. Firing, like the death penalty for felons, was a drastic measure to be invoked very rarely. The intuitive caution within the seasoned lawyer had won out; however, any chance for a reconciliation was forever dashed.

Instead, Johnston was slowly pushed from the nest. Soon enough, Tex Johnston was exiled to perform remote assignments and eventually left Boeing for other opportunities. Bill Allen told an audience in 1977, "It has taken nearly twenty-two years for me to reach the point where I can discuss the event with a modicum of humor" (Serling 1992, p. 131). Both Bill Allen and his antagonist, Tex Johnston, lived long lives; however, each was ultimately taken by the same ailment—dementia with symptoms of Alzheimer's disease.

No other Boeing test pilot has ever publicly admitted to slow-rolling a Boeing airliner, but it is commonly assumed by insiders that Johnston's public demonstration was not unique in the lonely remote regions of the vast, uncrowded western skies.

The Air Force purchased 732 of the KC-135 tankers (plus variants, which bring the total to over 800). Public qualms regarding jet travel subsided after a sophisticated Madison Avenue advertising campaign touted the 707. Both the airlines and travelers were, by 1959, eager to step into the jet age. Passengers arrived at the airport in their Sunday-best attire. Airlines reciprocated by serving cuisine on fine china, emulating an elite restaurant. Despite steep airfares, the contrived image of glamour, luxury, and prestige combined to help stoke demand.

Steiner Is Taken to the Woodshed

Bill Allen returned to Seattle in an angry mood after enduring another violation of "Industrial Age chivalry" while at the board-of-directors meeting (as previously described) in New Orleans on February 1, 1965. He suspected Jack Steiner of bypassing him by lobbying directly with members of the board of directors. Steiner was summoned to Allen's office. When confronted, Steiner admitted lobbying three board members on behalf of the 737. One board member was a neighbor in the elite waterfront bedroom community of Medina. Steiner was forcefully told never to repeat these actions.

Test pilots were expendable. The Army (for helicopter pilots), Navy, and Air Force each ran schools that annually transformed

Genius at work: master aircraft configurator John E. "Jack" Steiner (*right*) is seen in this 1961 image at work on a masterpiece, the 727. Note that none of the models hung from the walls bears any resemblance to the finished product.

Steiner's model 727 wing design was subjected to destructive testing. A test rig was fabricated of structural steel and securely attached to railroad track embedded into three feet of poured concrete. This is where a sample wing was bent to breaking.

gifted military pilots into newly minted experimental test pilots; however, aircraft designers of Steiner's ilk were precious. Wellwood Beall had become a problem. Too many instances of bad behavior were attributed to excessive alcohol consumption. Allen banished Mr. Beall from Boeing in 1964. Beall immediately surfaced as a vice president at Douglas Aircraft Company, and in a burst of creativity the stretched DC-8, followed by the DC-9, soon emerged. No, Steiner's job was not at risk. He would be instantly snapped up by the competition and then work his magic for them.

Instead, Steiner, a savant tightly focused on new designs, was made vice president of product development in 1966. The organization chart at BCA was dynamic during this time. The core cadre of Renton executives played musical chairs as they were frequently switched between job assignments. Change was the norm as members of the leadership team were moved up, down, and sideways in the ongoing quest to optimize performance. Stability was achieved only after Ernest H. "Tex" Boullioun (1918–2006) settled in at Renton. Boullioun was popular both within the company and with the airline customers.

Herding Cats

Presiding over a stable of gifted but independent thinkers was hard work. The years 1964–65 found Bill Allen earning every bit of his salary—a mere pittance by the standards of today. Each of them, like Allen himself, was smart, opinionated, and strong willed. Consistent with past completed projects (B-29, B-47, and B-52), Ed Wells and John Yeasting expected C-5A engineering to be performed in Seattle, with fabrication in Wichita.

That expectation lasted until T. A. Wilson took over the project in December 1964. His approach was both design and build in Seattle—and at "ground zero" of the Boeing universe, Plant II. Even at a snail's pace of two aircraft per month, C-5 would require a new final-assembly bay with a hook height of 65 feet. Destruction of Annexes A, B, C, and D, plus the South Warehouse, would force relocation of parts fabrication to somewhere—maybe to a greenfield in Auburn?

Furthermore, Wilson's desire was to banish the 737 (both engineering and final assembly) to Wichita. Meanwhile, with Commercial Airplanes still in infancy, John Yeasting and his entourage at Renton were hostile toward any disruption of their Puget Sound "critical mass."

It took every bit of Allen's diplomatic skills, intuition, and autocratic tendencies to keep the entire team appeased, productive, and moving forward.

By 1967, matters had sorted themselves out. NASA work was handled at Kent. Models 707 and 727 assembly stayed at Renton. Plant II teamed with the new Thompson site (14-01 building) to build the initial batches of 737s. Lockheed won the C-5 contract, clearing the way for 747 and an entirely new factory at Everett. SST would remain at Developmental Center for the remainder of its existence, and a new parts plant would grace the flatlands south of Auburn. Wichita existed to build parts for Commercial and perform Air Force sustainment (KC-135, B-52, and other new projects).

T. A. Wilson won the presidency of Boeing but lost a few battles on his upward climb to claim the big chair. Model 737 and all other commercial critical mass needed by Boeing Commercial remained in Seattle, and the 747 never went to Livermore, California, or any other distant city.

A 737 certification celebration event is underway on December 15, 1967. To shelter everything from the seasonal rain, the test fleet has also been gathered into building 3-390, then known as the B-52 hangar.

737 Woes

Early troubles with the 737 were many. A damaging spat quickly arose among the airlines, the pilot unions, and the FAA regarding how many flight crew members were needed. Boeing was caught in the middle, and the dispute was hurting 737 sales.

The airline unions lobbied for a third crew member called a "flight engineer"—but there was no useful role for a flight engineer aboard the 737. Railroads called it "featherbedding" when unions insisted on firemen aboard diesel locomotives. The unions argued safety, with the need for a third set of eyes to scan the "crowded skies." The DC-9 was operated by only a pilot and copilot. There was no seat for a flight engineer.

As is evidenced in his working papers, Bill Allen gathered, studied, and retained every scrap of intelligence on this troublesome issue; however, he could address the situation only via surrogates. Boeing pilots worked in collaboration with their airline peers and the FAA. Evaluation of the facts and data eventually disclosed that the third person in the cockpit was a distraction to safe flight. The dispute was ultimately resolved, but not before it had seriously eroded sales.

Even Boeing insiders used such words as "dumpy" and "football" to describe the shape of the newest family member. Flight testing revealed that the stubby body yielded air turbulence (drag) on the aft fuselage. Tufts were attached to help visualize the problem. Small pieces of curved metal called "vortex generators" were attached here and there, as needed, to break up the airflow.

Gerhard Holtje was not at all happy with the Lufthansa initial fleet of 737-100s. They fell far short not only of his expectations, but also the promises of the Boeing marketing department. The 737-100 was quickly phased out in favor of the 737-200, with better engines and many other improvements, but sales were sputtering.

The 737 production nearly died from a dearth of new orders in 1973. Fortunately, an Air Force contract arrived for nineteen airframes designated T-43. Their mission was training Air Force navigators. It was not until the advent of the 737-300, -400, and -500, starting in 1981, that the model 737 delivered on its true promise.

Bill Allen mustered every bit of his aviation business acumen earned over a lifetime to launch the Queen of the Skies. *Time* magazine once put Allen on the cover and cited three main attributes: "He knew when to gamble. He trusted his designers. He forged a team." Yes, thousands of Boeing employees internalized each of Allen's goals as their own. After the recent string of similar undertakings (B-47, Dash 80, 727, SST, and 737), each of them gutsy, internalizing overwhelming challenge was in the corporate DNA. Thus, the company undertook a course that, despite a few bumps along the way, yielded a half century of ongoing orders, long after Bill Allen's retirement as president in 1968. Allen stayed on as chairman of the board and filled in for T. Wilson when Wilson suffered a heart attack at age forty-nine in 1970.

John O. Yeasting, a vicious competitor, visits the Renton flight line. Yeasting created chaos within the Facilities Department by too frequently lowballing the annual business plan, thus depriving Operations of budget, manufacturing resource, laboratories, and office space.

CHAPTER 13
The Yardstick

My office was in the Overmeyer Building, a converted warehouse on the east side of the Renton complex. The railroad, with tracks inlaid on the surface streets of downtown Renton, continues to transport 737 fuselages on their cross-country sojourn from Wichita to Renton. As office space goes, the Overmeyer Building was terrible, and for that I had nobody to blame but myself—because I suggested renting it.

Eight months before, in June 1965, the Commercial Airplane Division was adding nearly a thousand engineering and office workers per month—with no sign of slowing. This avalanche of new hires was not anticipated in time to have expanded office space ready and waiting. The Facilities planning group was hard pressed to find room for the new people.

John O. Yeasting created this mess by lowballing the Renton sales forecast (707 and 727) for 1965 as submitted into the business plan in mid-1964. This strategy gave rise to emergent and unplanned facilities expenses needed to accommodate the surge of new hires.

A new facility, the Kent Space Center, was rising on the rich farmland surrounding the bucolic bedroom community; however, its office space was earmarked for Aerospace Group (working on missiles, rockets, and NASA spacecraft). The site's claim to fame was the lunar rover, a moon buggy conceived at Huntsville. They were used by astronauts aboard the later Apollo missions to motor themselves about the lunar surface in search of interesting rocks and memorable photographs.

The Overmeyer Building was then under construction. I grabbed Don Davis, and together we headed to the warehouse site and walked into the construction shack, where the foreman, talking on the phone, was encountered. A stack of blueprints was on his table. When the call ended, Don asked the foreman, "When will you be finished?"

"Within six weeks this place will have a roof, we'll be done, and it will be ready for rental" was the reply. After a bit more dialogue, the foreman surrendered a rain-streaked blueprint and off we went.

Back at our office, the blueprint was handed to Johnny Johnson, the fastest layout person on staff. I asked him to lay out each bay on standard gridded boards, and specified space allocations and needed utilities (e.g., toilets) for four hundred men and women. Also specified were offices and meeting rooms. Authority from corporate headquarters was requested to sign a lease agreement for immediate occupancy upon completion of the warehouse building. The Overmeyer Building contained 120,000 square feet, as compared to a modern Costco warehouse store at 140,000 square feet.

All of it would be converted to office space. The noise level was terrible because the air-handling fans were warehouse grade and noisy. Furthermore, the acoustics, consisting of walls fabricated of concrete blocks, allowed phone and face-to-face conversations to echo about in the huge open bay. Wires for electrical outlets and telephones dangled from the ceiling—which was 32 feet overhead. The desks were precisely lined up in neat rows that would make a drill sergeant proud.

Despite these challenges, the morale within our group was excellent. People were excited to be part of a winning team. Because of the new jetliners, Boeing was accepted by the public, praised by the media, and rewarded at the New York Stock Exchange. Everyone sensed our company was about to win the commercial airplane war that had raged since the end of World War II.

The location outside the main-factory fence line made parking easy for visiting construction contractors and my own people. Puget Sound runs roughly 173 miles from the state capital in Olympia to the Canadian border at Blaine. Within that corridor, the Boeing construction projects spanned the 55 road miles (depending on route) between Auburn on the south and Everett on the north.

The new interstate highways began to open up in the decade after the 1962 Seattle World's Fair. Our home office at the Renton Overmeyer Building was at a convenient central location, which allowed our team members to efficiently fan out by automobile and oversee construction at the various sites.

Terms were invented in the mid-1960s that have since fallen out of the lexicon. I was a practitioner of using scale models depicting the various Seattle-area Boeing sites, to show the current and potential future arrangements. We would design an ideal aircraft plant and use it as a "yardstick" to measure any proposed new construction or factory modification. The concept was fully developed by me in 1964.

Shortly after we moved in, Don Davis thought up the idea of a planning room, when he said, "John, you ought to have a 'depth study room' where you can spread out the scale models and plaster the walls with project schedule charts and other data. It'll be the ideal place to display the yardstick."

Depth study rooms were all the rage at Boeing back then. It was a place where a team would gather to study a vexing business problem in depth. The room allowed for quick reviews by upper management at any time, permitting an iterative set of inputs as the study progressed. Walk-around reviews could be quick, as little as five minutes. For a sit-down session, a review could last up to an hour.

"That's a great idea," I replied. "I'm tired of having the displays hauled about to whatever conference room happens to be vacant." We partitioned off an empty corner area measuring 30 by 60 feet, with walls standing 16 feet high. At 1,800 square feet, the room had floor space equivalent to a typical suburban rambler.

A sign was placed on the door that stated in bold letters "LIMITED ACCESS." Underneath that sign were the words "AUTHORIZED PERSONNEL ONLY." Words such as "confidential," "secret," and "top secret" have legal and military connotations. Although most of us had government security clearances because of our work on military projects, the information in the room would be proprietary to future Boeing commercial endeavors; therefore, the room was secured with a lock, and access authority was bestowed upon my secretary, Judy Church. She was the gatekeeper who verified and maintained a log of all visitors.

As soon as the room was ready, I had one 60-foot wall posted with all the 24-by-36-inch flip charts from the long-range plan (or yardstick) that was reviewed with all the departments over the past two years. My message was delivered to every manager who would listen, from corporate headquarters on down. As documented in the forty-year plan of 1963, the crux of my argument was that we must be prepared for growth.

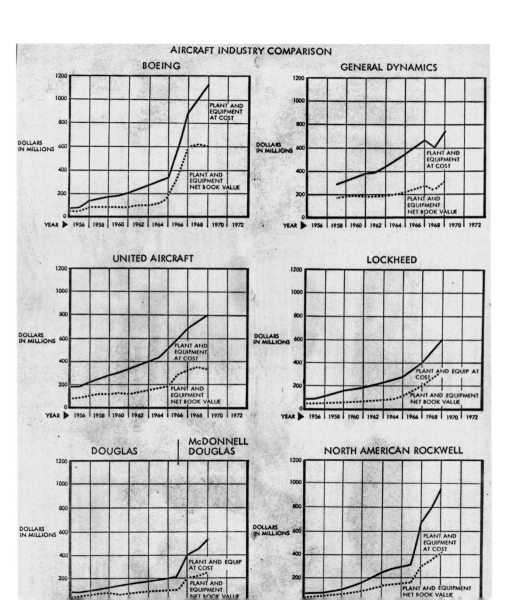

AIRCRAFT INDUSTRY COMPARISON

This conclusion was startling. The marketplace for prime transportation equipment such as aircraft grows five to ten times larger every forty years, which is much faster than overall gross domestic product. The message was a wake-up call to action. My consistent message was "We produce hundreds of airplanes per year at this time. In forty years we will be producing thousands, as long as we hold 70 percent market share."

The next section of the yardstick plan involved the relationship of annual revenue (sales) to space utilized. It was assembled using annual reports of the Big Four of aircraft building: Boeing, Douglas, Lockheed, and North American. All except Douglas produced about $100 in annual sales revenue per square foot of space occupied. Douglas appeared less efficient because they produced only $75 per square foot. Boeing Commercial Airplanes division was on par with the top companies. For the past five years, we'd produced about $500 million in sales each year from 5 million square feet—or $100 in revenue per square foot.[1]

The solid relationship of revenue per square foot was a powerful tool for long-range facilities planning. In a gross sense, it allowed prediction of the demand for space the instant a sales forecast was announced for a new or proposed airplane program. The only data needed were delivery rate and price per unit. The gross demand for space could immediately be estimated without waiting for the various departments to figure out, review, and submit their detailed requirements some months later.

These charts were posted on the wall:

- For every $100 million in sales growth, 1 million more square feet are needed.
- Another Renton-sized plant is needed when demand doubles.
- In forty years, at least five (or possibly ten) plants the size of Renton will be required.
- Alternatively, two plants five times the size of Renton will be needed.

The next section of the long-range plan was titled "Balance":

- Land balance: One-third of the land is devoted to buildings; one-third of the land is devoted to flight line, internal roads, and preflight (not counting runway or taxiway); one-third of the land is devoted to employee parking. (A car parking space equals an employee's working space.)
- Buildings will contain square footage 1.4 times greater than the land area they cover (via use of multiple floors).
- Building balance: 15% is final assembly, 15% is major assembly, 20% is fabrication, 20% is office, 5% is laboratories, and 25% is storage and warehouses. (These values

At forty years out, the question was laughable to them, but not to me. Accountants assign a forty-year life to an industrial structure, and many last much longer than that. In order to design an ideal (or yardstick) factory, we needed dimensions of aircraft forty years hence. For the previous fifty years, every model that went into production was obsolete within five years. The model 707 had then been carrying passengers for six years. Everybody was convinced it would be superseded by model 2707, a supersonic transport (SST), by the time of the next national census in 1970. Why? Because the Boeing internal business plan said so.

After many frustrating bouts with the aircraft preliminary designers, I was handed off to Dick Fitzsimons, the guy who handles nuisance requests. I got nothing from him. One of the few persons in the engineering department who gave me any serious time was department leader Maynard Pennell—an accomplished aircraft designer with 707 (and others) on his résumé. He said, "Just put us on a curve"— and, that's exactly what I did.[2]

After pondering the matter, I prepared hand-drawn graphs depicting the wingspans of Boeing production airplanes. It showed linear growth despite the fact that wing loadings had doubled, tripled, and quadrupled from the mid-1930s to the mid-1960s. Wings had become more efficient as engines became more powerful. The chart indicated that a 300-foot-wide final-assembly bay, like we were using at Renton, would remain viable until the year 2000.

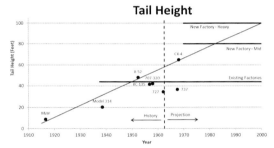

Tail heights were also growing at a linear rate. Existing facilities were designed for aircraft with tail heights under 40 feet. The Boeing military group competed for the C-5A contract. It would have had a tail height of 65 feet. The linear projection indicated a tail height of 75 feet by 1990 and 90 feet after 2000. Conclusion: our yardstick ideal aircraft factory should have crane hook height of 100 feet.

Gross takeoff weights had not grown in linear fashion. Instead, they had grown exponentially, roughly doubling every ten years. The B-17 was a 50,000-pound

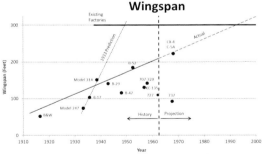

Lacking long-term guidance from the aircraft designers, these three sketches (reconstructed) extrapolated historical trends needed to define future factory requirements. Wingspan dictates main factory door width, weight helps define crane lifting capacity, and tail height is needed to determine ceiling height, crane hook height, and vertical dimensions for the factory main doors.

aircraft. The B-29 tipped the scales at 100,000 pounds, the B-52 was at 488,000 pounds, and the 1960s-vintage CX-4 preliminary design was in the 800,000-pound class. The 747 was in our sights at the same 800,000 pounds.

The study determined an ideal (yardstick) aircraft factory of the future should have 50-ton cranes, 100 feet overhead and in bays 300 feet wide. Not one aircraft designer came forward to challenge these predictions. All indicated agreement, and the list included Wells, Pennell, Steiner, Martin, Withington, and other Boeing luminaries.

The final section of the yardstick plan had two parts: flow and expansion. Flow meant the flow of ideas from laboratories to engineering to mockup to the factory and to the flight line. Furthermore, groups should be as close to each other as possible. Flow also meant the flow of parts from suppliers to fabrication to subassembly to major assembly to final assembly and to the delivery center.

Since everything comes together in final assembly, the shortest flow tends to center on the final-assembly bays. Ideally (but not practically), all the thousands of designers and aircraft workers that it takes to put together an airplane should work in or near final assembly, so the workers can see what they are accomplishing.

Unfortunately, every existing Boeing final assembly had been hemmed in by support buildings, making expansion of the plant virtually impossible without moving to a new location. An ideal yardstick factory should have logical flow for ideas and parts, while preserving an avenue of expansion for additional final-assembly space as business increases.

On the opposite wall of the planning room was the current business plan, the sales forecasts, and the current and projected capital budgets.

Spread out on low tables were aerial photos of every Boeing plant in the Seattle area, with scale models of the buildings placed on the photos. Six plants then existed:

- Original Plant I was on Harbor Island. It was obsolete and abandoned in 1970.
- Plant II, on the north end of Boeing Field, was aging but still functional.
- The Developmental Center (abbreviated DC), at the south end of Boeing Field, was consigned to SST and then later to various military programs.
- Renton Plant
- Kent Space Center: just built
- Auburn Fabrication Plant: under construction

The aerial photographs and building models were at a scale of an inch equals 100 feet. The 10,007-foot main runway at Boeing Field, with plants on each end, took a table 12 feet long to depict. Renton Airport has a short runway (5,382 feet), and its model was 6 feet long. Older buildings had black roofs. Newer buildings had green roofs. Buildings under construction had red roofs.

Upon entry, the planning room gave the initial impression of a room full of tiny model railroads; however, there were no toy trains—just aerial photographs of parking lots full of automobiles, runways, aircraft parking ramps, and balsa wood models of various buildings. Once properly oriented, a Boeing manager could take a simulated flight and view all the sites, the buildings, and construction underway. Any proposed new buildings could be depicted along with a realistic view of them when completed.

A scale model of the Everett factory (dated March 1966) shows it fully expanded, to an extent that has yet to be achieved. The factory, as modeled, was depicted consistently on every site considered. Psychologically, this made the factory a "constant," and the only variable was the site. *John Andrew collection*

The planning room was all set up for a leisurely but deliberate approach to long-range facilities planning, ready to measure every potential expansion against the yardstick, the ideal aircraft plant of the future. That leisurely approach lasted for two days.

A youthful Ernest E. "Tex" Boullioun has mastered the art of flip chart creation and handles the pointer with the skill of a seasoned samurai warrior. Boullioun, a smooth-talking gambler, is on a career trajectory that will land him long tenure as president of the Boeing Commercial Airplane Company.

CHAPTER 14
Where to Build It?

As the days on the 1965 calendar came and went, two invaluable data points for the 747 soon emerged: preliminary configuration and a target price. Configuration and maximum production rate would dictate factory size and arrangement. Renton was already bursting with business. Suddenly, the handwriting was on the wall. A new site with a new factory was needed quickly! But where?

The successful NASA space program demonstrated to T. A. Wilson and others at Boeing the viability of distributed operations. I had already studied three locations in western Washington State as potential 747 final-assembly sites. Aerial photographs and layouts were made for each of them. All were displayed in the site-planning room. The first site was on the east side of McChord Field, south of Tacoma. Another was on a small private airfield south of Puyallup, called Thun Field. And a third site was at the north end of Paine Field, on undeveloped land within the city of Everett.

Headquarters dusted off an Austin Company study they'd commissioned a few months earlier. The screening of fifty cities yielded a recommendation for three: Chicago, Denver, and Livermore, California. Headquarters staff took this flawed study as gospel and were determined to send 747 to one of those cities.

In late October 1965, John Bixby of Corporate Facilities wanted to draft me for an extended on-site study of the Livermore site. There was a meeting among Don Davis, Erle Barnes, and me in Barnes's office. An aerial photograph of a barren site near an airfield with no infrastructure was reviewed. I said, "Don't make me do it. A study like that should have been started three years ago, when those idiots in headquarters thought Commercial Airplanes had no future, and bought the farmland in Kent without a runway. The 747 will have four thousand engineers in less than a year, and they'll all live in Seattle. Nobody will go to Livermore. This study is an absolute waste of time."

This aerial view dated June 1966 shows the north end of the primary Paine Field runway, the factory construction site to the right, Puget Sound ahead, abundant forest, and the curving 450-foot deep ravine that will host a railroad spur.

Erle Barnes sat in stunned silence for an instant and then said, "I'll refuse Bixby's request. We need you here."

Don Davis retorted, "I think we ought to play ball with headquarters and offer to study sites outside the Seattle area. Otherwise, they will think we're biased and insubordinate."

"That's a good idea," I said. "We'll study Wichita, Moses Lake, and San Diego. It's inevitable that someone will insist we look at those places, because Boeing runs the Wichita plant, we have flight operations at Moses Lake, and everybody asks about San Diego because Convair has an empty aircraft plant on the bay. That'll be an easy one to dispense with—because it's too small."

"Then pick another site in the San Diego area," said Davis. "We don't want to look uncooperative."

"Okay," said Barnes. "I'll tell Bixby to ask the Aerospace Division to study Livermore. I'll tell him that we'll study six sites: Wichita, Moses Lake, San Diego, and three in the Seattle area. That should satisfy him and get him off our backs."

By late November 1965, headquarters insisted that 737 go to Wichita. Within a few days, Boeing president Bill Allen intervened when he directed that 737 manufacturing be fitted into Plant II and a new factory be built on the Thompson tract. The new year of 1966 arrived

I was summoned to corporate headquarters on a Saturday morning for a covert meeting with "Tex" Boullioun and T. A. Wilson regarding purchase of the Everett site. From 1936 to 2001, Boeing headquarters resided in this modest art deco structure in the gritty industrial area of South Seattle.

with the assignment of Don Davis to join with T. A. Wilson on the SST program, then the biggest and most important Boeing project underway.

In late January 1966, my phone rang. It was Tex Boullioun, the number two man at Commercial Division. He asked me to quickly prepare a comparison of the three Seattle-area sites and to accompany him to a very private meeting with Boeing president William M. "Bill" Allen. "Bring one of your assistants with you. Have him give the presentation. There will be only three of us with Mr. Allen. Nobody at headquarters wants to overwhelm or press him. I have strict orders from T. Wilson, who has just been appointed executive vice president. He won't even be attending. The meeting place is the boardroom, with only four people: you, me, your assistant, and Bill Allen."

"I'll have Gil Jay, my long-range planning assistant, prepare the presentation. He's familiar with everything. He's unexcitable. He'll be low key and neutral," I replied.

Even the *Wall Street Journal* agreed Boeing had the dumpiest and most spartan corporate headquarters building[1] of any billion-dollar enterprise on the planet. A symbol of Boeing frugality, the 2-24 building, was a little, three-story, art deco–inspired product of the 1930s. Union Pacific Railroad switching locomotives passed within a stone's throw of the main entrance. It was surrounded on the other three sides by industrial buildings. Only a few executive-assigned automobiles could fit into the basement parking garage.

Unlike the engineering building behind, it had not been retrofitted for earthquake resistance. Building 2-24 was hastily torn down in the 1990s before any civic-minded preservationists came forward to nominate it as a national historic site. The corporate executives retreated into the old engineering building behind, the art deco facade was re-created on that building, and very few Seattle residents ever noticed the change.

We quietly entered the boardroom at the appointed hour. Jay set up an easel and placed his set of flip charts on it. As usual, Allen gentlemanly arrived five minutes late, allowing us time to get comfortable with the surroundings. Like a sacred place, the darkened room reeked of aviation history. Separate large portraits of Allen and William E. "Bill" Boeing hung on the dark wood-paneled walls. The visage of the founder peered down upon this pivotal proceeding—the results of which would influence the economy and lives of millions of people for the next century—and maybe beyond.

In this and all my other encounters with Bill Allen, I never witnessed a single instance of a disparaging remark about anybody. In addition, Bill Allen remained interested and came to my assistance during subsequent assignments to a greater extent than any other senior executive; however, as the decade of the 1970s progressed, small hints of approaching dementia were revealed to me. In any case, Mr. Allen always personified the attributes of a true "gentleman."

Jay reviewed the salient aspects of each site: size, cost to buy, highway access, freeway access, distance from existing Boeing sites (especially the emerging Auburn parts fabrication plant), rail access, site conditions, utility availability, community infrastructure, schools, degree-granting institutions nearby, and site preparation costs. Jay deadpanned through the whole thing, showing intelligent interest but no favoritism. He pointed out obvious problems and how they might be solved. Jay's final chart was a comparison of all factors, with check marks showing the best in each category.

The winner, based on objective facts, was quite obviously McChord Field. Existing facilities would remain at their current locations on the west side of the primary north–south runway. There is plenty of precedent for an airplane factory and military base sharing the

CONTENTS

FACILITIES CONSTRUCTION SCHEDULE
(SITE 'N')

The 747 factory site selection deck consisted of over a hundred sheets. The second sheet was contents. Site "N" was the code for Everett, and "Z" was McChord. Also shown is the estimate for construction of a new plant at Everett. *John Andrew collection*

same concrete runway. Boeing Wichita and McConnell Air Force Base both utilize the same airfield and have joint agreements for mutual-aid fire protection.

McChord and Paine Fields had much in common. Each was created in the late 1930s as Depression-era public works projects on donated land intended to deliver a municipal airport, both were named after World War I aviators, both were commandeered by the military during World War II, and both were serving in a defensive role as home for jet interceptors performing the North American Air Defense (NORAD) mission. The runways at each location were of like size and suitable for very large aircraft.

Several privately owned tracts on the northeast airfield perimeter at McChord were of interest. The plan was to purchase various private holdings into a plant site. Boeing had the political clout of Senators Warren Magnuson and Henry "Scoop" Jackson; it would likely be deemed in the national best interest to grant airfield access and operational support.

A Northern Pacific Railroad line bisected McChord, and the nearby freeways were excellent. Interstate 5 ran north to south and State Route 512 was proposed to run east to west. In addition, the Boeing Fabrication Division was nearby at Auburn.

Airfields constructed during World War II normally had a triangle of runways roughly a mile in length. The early jet airplanes (both military and commercial) had anemic thrust, and expensive extensions to one of the runways was dictated. The new standard for runway construction was sturdy concrete pavement 2 miles in length and 150 feet wide. This work was accomplished at major airports and military bases at great public expense. Thun Field, established for only small, private aircraft, required a complete runway rebuild and mile-long extension to handle 800,000-pound aircraft.

Meanwhile at Everett, a new spur would be needed from the main line of the Great Northern Railway, which ran along the shoreline of Puget Sound between Everett and Seattle. Two deep ravines bisected the property and seriously complicated factory construction. Furthermore, aircraft do not taxi well on hills. The plant must be close to level with the runway. Therefore, all of us had been certain that McChord Field would be selected when we entered the boardroom. The facts were inescapable, but it was 100 percent Bill Allen's decision to make. Savoring our excellent performance, we waited in silence for him to speak. I confidently glanced up for a brief instant at the painted portrait of Bill Boeing.

Bill Allen then uttered, "Gentlemen, I agree with your recommendation. Paine Field in Everett is the best site." I sat in stunned silence as he continued: "Three years ago I gave a plant to Kent. Last year I gave a plant to Auburn. They're both south. A lot of good people live in the north end. I think it's time I give a plant to them."

I was speechless, but only for an instant. Tex looked at me as I stared back at him and managed to force a nod in agreement. We had a decision. I knew I could build the best aircraft factory in the world anywhere. It was only a factor of money. Boullioun said, "Thanks, Bill." We all shook Allen's hand and departed the boardroom.

In the hallway, out of earshot of Bill Allen, Tex said, "Christ, John, do you really think you can make it up that hill with a railroad?"

"Of course," I replied. "If we can't make it up the hill in one shot, we'll do it with a switchback, or a cog railway. In the worst case, we'll drag everything up with cables and a hoist. We can make the site work. We got what was most needed—a decision."

Boullioun smiled, relaxed, and said, "Congratulations, John, you finally have your new aircraft plant."

There was no time for celebration. I arrived back at my office in the Overmeyer Building and found a note to return an urgent phone call to Boeing Public Relations. I thought they might be asking about the meeting with Mr. Allen. Instead he asked, "I'd like to bring a reporter from the *Seattle Times* into your planning room to see the models. He'd like to snap some photos." I said, "It's okay with me, if it's okay with you. You guys are charged with talking to the press. Just tell me what you want to take pictures of and what you want me to say."

"It'll be sometime early next week," he said, "probably Monday. I'll give you a call before we come."

I immediately called John Bixby at corporate. He sounded relaxed when he said, "Congratulations, John. I heard you got your new plant."

"Thanks, Bix," I replied. "But that's not what I'm calling about. Boeing Public Relations wants to bring a *Times* reporter into my planning room to see the models. What can I say about Everett?"

"My God!" shouted Bixby. "Don't tell them about anything! Don't show them anything! Our agent hasn't talked to the owner. The price will go up if they know we're the buyer. Cover the Everett model. Cover the McChord and Thun models. Keep those models under canvas. We want to keep everybody thinking we're going south, not north. I'm talking about the Boeing Public Relations people. They've seen the models and know of the sites. Keep them guessing. Don't say a word about a new site or a decision."

"Can I show them the existing sites?" I asked.

"You have no restrictions—unless Public Relations offers some" was the reply.

The front page of the Sunday *Seattle Times* dated February 6, 1966, featured a color image of me and temporary worker Carole Haugen posed with the Renton site facilities planning model. I quickly came to rue this photograph because it caused me grief at home and at work. *John Andrew collection*

The next Monday I received a call from Public Relations. They were on their way. On arrival, I unlocked the planning room and ushered in a trio of visitors, including a Boeing Public Relations representative, a *Times* real estate reporter, and an award-winning *Seattle Times* staff photographer—Richard S. Heyza.

We talked briefly about the expansions going on at every Boeing plant. The reporter took notes. When he was finished, he asked the photographer, "What's your best shot?"

"I like the Renton plant with the lake. The buildings have a lot of color. But I need a girl to jazz things up," said Heyza.

"Can you bring in your secretary?" asked the reporter.

"Not today. She's on vacation," I replied.

"I need a girl in the picture," insisted the photographer.

"Why don't you pick one," I said. "About fifteen women are working here. Look out in the bay." Upon opening the door, the photographer's eyes locked onto a young female in a red dress with dark-reddish-auburn hair piled high on her head.

"Who is that woman?" he said.

"I have no idea," I replied. "I've never seen her before."

I walked to the woman and said, "If you don't mind, would you come into the planning room. A newspaper photographer would like to take your picture. By the way, I've never met you. My name is John Andrew. How long have you worked here?"

"I'd love to have my picture taken. My name is Carole Haugen. I'm from Kelly Services and here for only for a couple days," she said.

The photographer took a completely staged picture of me showing Carole the Renton scale model. I never saw eighteen-year-old Carole again.

"We might run an article in next Sunday's paper. I'm the real estate reporter. Everyone is interested in the Boeing expansion. Real estate should boom with all the new people moving in. Look for the photograph in the real estate section, if it makes it by the editor," said the reporter.

Nothing was said to anyone by me about the potential article. I trekked to the neighborhood drugstore on Sunday morning to buy a copy of the *Seattle Times*. I was floored to see my picture centered on the front page, above the fold, and in color. Color photographs in the newspaper were rare and expensive in 1966. Color was most often limited to only the comics section. Three papers were purchased—one for Nancy, one for my mother, and a spare.

Nancy took one look at the picture and threw the newspaper down. "You get everything, and I get to take care of kids. Look at the glorious work you do, the beautiful secretaries, while I'm stuck at home," she lamented. Our youngest was in kindergarten. Nancy had come through the hardest part of raising preschool kids. She now had free time but was becoming more and more depressed.

My secretary was also angry with me when she returned on Monday morning. I felt alone with my responsibilities at work and isolated while at home.

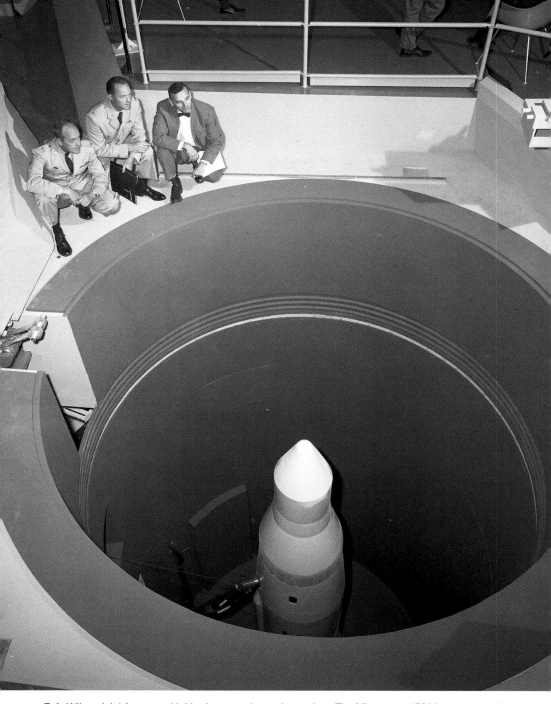

T. A. Wilson (*right*) poses with his signature doomsday project. The Minuteman ICBM was secure in its underground silo and was further protected by a reinforced concrete lid (removed for this image).

CHAPTER 15
2,000 Acres

A jungle of second-growth forest needed to be cleared and leveled at the Everett site. Western Washington was covered in huge old-growth fir trees when the initial waves of European settlers arrived. Trees near dockside were the first to fall. The wood was either consumed locally or exported by sloop to California. Starting in 1881, the arrival of railroads enabled economical harvesting of more-remote trees. Nothing was replanted. The clear-cut stump-lands became overgrown with alder and other low-value trees. The 2,000 acres at Everett was one small example; however, this wooded bluff above the chilly waters at Mukilteo was destined to be transformed into something extraordinary.

The reason Bill Allen selected the Snohomish County location for the 747 factory remains unclear. The site was never ranked above fifth place by the Boeing site selection board. The working papers of Bill Allen are silent on the matter; however, the files make it clear that Allen was close with both Washington senators on a wide range of matters. They were the powerful and respected team of Henry "Scoop" Jackson (1912–1983) and Warren G. Magnuson (1905–1989)—who, in the "other" Washington, were known for their close ties and perpetual support for the company. Lifelong Everett resident Scoop Jackson may have advocated placing a major plant in his lifetime hometown. Also, either senator could have foreseen and warned of complications at McChord. An escalating war in Vietnam was increasing the operating tempo. Disruptive war protests were growing in number, size, and frequency. Bill Allen already knew that Secretary of Defense McNamara was not a friend and unlikely to provide any assistance when the inevitable issues arose in Pierce County.

Bill Allen was oblivious to the fact that he had just approved construction of a building that would dwarf the current "world's largest building" by a factor of two. I'd calculated the volume three months before and was not about to tell anyone in fear that some faceless corporate insurance department bureaucrat would blow the whistle and yell "fire risk."

"Mr. Incredible" was a decal created to adorn the hard hats worn by 747 assembly mechanics working in the unfinished Everett factory. The visage of a fictional Paul Bunyan was in reference to the recently cleared forest.

But the clincher for Senator Scoop Jackson was obtaining a huge plant for his hometown. In a town dependent on lumber and wood pulp, the city fathers in Everett were genuinely grateful to receive a manufacturing plant. All the stops were pulled out to get new roads quickly built (especially the Casino Road off-ramp from I-5), utilities provided, permits flowing, and schools prepared for the influx of youngsters. A $3 million municipal cash infusion from Boeing combined with the promise of thousands of good-paying local jobs and expanding tax rolls put the local officials into a state of civic euphoria.

Archival memos from others make it clear Bill Allen was determined to get the 747 built. If knowledge is power, then Bill Allen was keeping it to himself. Subordinates were uninformed regarding important status items. Yeasting's most fearsome qualm was a shortfall of 2,900 engineers if all three programs (737, 747, and SST) moved forward. Wilson advocated launching the 747 to blunt competitors from first claiming the market for outsized airliners. In any case, T. Wilson, was about to cement his position as number two and heir apparent by being elected to the board of directors.

Launching the 747: Board Meeting February 28, 1966

The pivotal board-of-directors meeting got underway at 10:30 a.m. Already in his sixty-sixth year, it was evident that Bill Allen had been pondering mortality and thinking about succession planning. Lesser executives were expected to depart at the then legally mandated retirement age of sixty-five. There were few exceptions, although an occasional "consulting contract" was arranged. Lacking scandal or premature passing, the normal transition plan starts with a short list of well-qualified successors. Age fifty-five (or less) combined with good health provides the new president tenure of at least a decade.

To interested observers, it appeared that three individuals were in the running to replace Bill Allen as Boeing president. They were rocket scientist George Stoner, project planner T. A. Wilson, and Transport Division president John O. Yeasting. On the basis of capability and age, many observers thought Stoner had the edge. Stoner subsequently passed away from a lung ailment at the young age of fifty-three. Age and health conspired against Yeasting. In the end, it was T. A. Wilson who won the promotion.

Decades earlier, company founder William E. Boeing established his inner circle of Phil Johnson, Claire Egtvedt, and Bill Allen. Now, many years later in 1966, their collective tenure was winding up. Egtvedt was entering his seventy-fourth year, and Allen would celebrate his sixty-sixth birthday. Bill Allen was about to sacrifice the elderly (but docile) Claire Egtvedt to vacate a seat on the board for T. A. Wilson. Allen spoke to the elephant in the room when he stated that directors past the age of seventy-two should opt for emeritus status. Egtvedt took the hint and decided not to stand for renomination. T. A. Wilson was then elected to fill that vacated seat. Thereafter, when Claire Egtvedt attended a Boeing board-of-directors meeting, his nonvoting presence was annotated on the minutes as "director emeritus."

A catered lunch was scheduled from 12:25 to 1:55 p.m. Chief Financial Officer Hal Haynes utilized the time to present financial data and forecasts for the years 1966 to 1969. The meeting resumed deep within Renton's mockup building. The topic was model 747, with

John O. Yeasting as lead presenter. Mr. Yeasting was supplemented by A. K. Little, discussing market analysis; Bob Regan talked about factory schedules, manpower, and make-or-buy approach; Dick Welch addressed finance and cost considerations; and Carl E. Dillon reported on facilities requirements. The board then reassembled in Yeasting's second-floor conference room in the adjacent BCA headquarters (building 10-60).

Funding the corporation was next on the agenda. It was obvious to all that a voracious appetite for cash would accompany a 747-sized developmental program. The proposed solution was to hire the investment bankers of First Boston Corporation, aided by associate underwriters Drexel, Harriman, Ripley Securities Corporation. A motion was made to increase the number of authorized shares of stock from ten to thirty million, with the intention of incrementally selling the new equity at a price of roughly $53 per share. The motion was approved without dissent.

747 Milestones:	
February 28, 1966	Approval by board of directors
February 9, 1969	First flight of RA001
December 13, 1969	First 747-100 delivered to Pan Am
December 30, 1969	Type certificate awarded by FAA

The 747 project dwarfed the 737 effort (which was sanctioned by the board of directors thirteen months earlier); however, the process to achieve consensus on 747 was much crisper. After mulling the matter, the board of directors resolved the following: Management, in its discretion, was authorized to enter into contracts for design, manufacture, and sale of model 747 in freighter and passenger versions. Management was further authorized to order long-lead-time parts and acquire plant and equipment to do the job. The project could be halted if fifty orders were not achieved by August 1, 1966. Meanwhile, the initial order from Pan American (twenty-five aircraft) would soon be augmented with separate commitments from TWA, Lufthansa, and Air France.

An internal and external pronouncement (called a Management Information Bulletin or MIB) dated July 25, 1966, was confirmation to everybody the project was a "go." The wraps were finally off the massive undertaking that was already well underway. The MIB asserted that the major construction project at Everett had been undertaken on "speculation." Pan American's role as kickoff customer with an order for twenty-five of the world's first twin-aisle airliners was confirmed, meaning the expectations of Juan Trippe would influence the design. The inflation clause written into the contract yielded a delivery price closer to $25 million.

Financing for models 737 and 747 would come from $130 million in "convertible subordinated debentures" (long-term unsecured debt that can be converted to stock), bank borrowing, and internally generated funds. Those internally generated funds largely relied on down payments on new orders and subsequent progress payments, which were stipulated by the board to be 50 percent of sales price. The plan was to achieve breakeven with two hundred 747 deliveries by December 1972, and sustained profits with delivery of the four hundredth model 747 in December 1975.

With the board of director's resolution now public, the marching orders were in place. Every group within Boeing set about to perform their own critical role. Each would be essential to overall success. Engineering and product development were in full swing. Tools and tooling were designed and fabricated. Contracts for outside production were let. Work, on a scale and urgency not seen since World War II, was gearing up nationwide at vendors both big and small. Staffing within Flight Test was increasing as planning got underway. Those big, new turbofan engines from Pratt & Whitney topped the list of "flight critical" purchased components. Every JT9D power plant had to perform flawlessly for the 747 to be a success.

Regarding the factory space at Everett, Bill Allen was fully aware of the overall dimensions, along with everyone else in the management chain of command who had already signed off on the plan; however, nobody realized what putting an entire aircraft factory under one roof, and then doubling the headroom, did to volume. The exact location of this building would be an engineering decision, which was my next task, with the Austin Company as our consultant. I had decided to keep my mouth shut until structural steel was on firm order. Otherwise, I'd be forced to build multiple buildings and lose the efficiency of "one-roof manufacturing."

Most of this tract was unsurveyed raw acreage. The owner, as shown on Snohomish County property maps, was Modern Home Builders. Modern Home Builders was a DBA (doing business as) of a private enterprise called Diversified Industry & Timber Company (or DITCO). The site, although wild and very rural, was inside the city limits of Everett, 5 miles away. It was already zoned "heavy industry"—which belied the home-building appellation.

I had driven by the property once, on a windy, blustery day in November 1965. During that only drive-by, I rejected the site as impractical. Visible from the country road that ran for a mile and a half along the south edge of the property was unmarketable second-growth scrub trees and the locked gates of the timber company. The road curved at the end of the runway, dipped into a valley, and climbed to the top of a hill on the other side of the runway. From that vantage point, I could see that the land broke sharply to the north and was cut deep by ravines that steeply descended some 500 feet down to sea level at Puget Sound.

I continued driving another quarter mile west, beyond the property, and turned north on a highway that descended the hill to the ferry dock at the small town of Mukilteo. I parked at the dock and walked beside the railroad track that ran along the shoreline for a look up at the steep wooded hills and ravines. A railroad would have to climb a very steep grade.[1] I could not recommend such a rugged, inaccessible site for a major aircraft factory. Nevertheless, it was apparent that idyllic Mukilteo, with a quaint ferryboat connection to Whidbey Island, would be a scenic and wonderful place to live.

The US Geological Survey map, with 20-foot contour lines (which sold for twenty-five cents), confirmed the steepness. The steep ravines limited the amount of space on top that was level with the runway. Using the crude information that could be derived from the government map, the Austin Company investigated the amount of the earthwork required and provided a rough cost estimate, which was input into the trade studies comparing the various sites.

Within an hour of Allen's decision, I was back at my Renton office and on the phone with Cy Prideaux, regional vice president for the Austin Company. "The decision has been made," I said. "The plant will go to Everett. We need to find a place for the main factory building somewhere on DITCO's 2,000 acres. I need an engineering study recommending where it should be."

"It's a challenging site," he replied. Prideaux was being diplomatic. The words "terrible" or "ridiculous" would have been more appropriate.

"I'm also surprised by the choice," I said. "All logic dictated the factory should go to McChord Field south of Tacoma. But Allen didn't seem to be swayed by logic. He simply said he wanted to put the new factory north of Seattle. He said that a lot of good people live in the north end and that it was time that Boeing also went north. He lives on the north end, you know."

"Does he understand the dual problems of the terrain and railroad?" was the reply.

I explained, "He saw the cost estimates and the extra $10 million. He was looking right at the number when he said, 'Gentlemen, I agree with your recommendation. Paine Field in Everett is the best site.' That statement floored all of us. We purposely hadn't made a recommendation, just ranked the sites by a combination of factors, all pointing south. So, he picked north—because 'good people live on the north end.' There's no time to fight the decision on logical grounds. The schedule can't wait. We're going to Everett—where good people live—period."

I didn't tell Prideaux that I'd made a commitment two months before to build the complete plant for $160 million, which was now etched in stone. Now I was already down $10 million before breaking ground. The internal commitment was my problem, not Prideaux's. His job was to design and build what Boeing asked for. It was my job to do the asking and to keep costs within program commitments that I'd already made. Most of my contingency was gone. Bill Allen had just spent it.

This small acreage was sitting in the middle of what was to become 747 final assembly. It was purchased separately from the main tract. *John Andrew collection*

"We need access to the site," said Prideaux. "Can I send surveyors and engineers to the property?"

"No," I replied instantly, "Our agent hasn't approached the property owners. I have strict orders that there will be no activity at the site, no walk-ons, no drive-bys, no flyovers, nothing—nothing until the property is nailed down by purchase option. That's the responsibility of corporate offices. I have no idea when they'll be able to do it."

"That could take weeks or months," Prideaux replied. "Today is the twenty-seventh of January. The schedule you've asked for requires the pouring of footings for the main building starting on July 1."

"The schedule can't slide—regardless of how much time headquarters takes to buy the property," I said. "Keep the project moving. Firm up the long-lead-time items like steel and high voltage transformers. By the way, what's the status of the structural steel order?"

"Both Bethlehem and US Steel have reserved capacity to roll the heavy 'H' columns and to deliver the first steel in August, as soon as the concrete in the first footings has cured. US Steel has the best price at $290 per ton when erected by their own subsidiary, American Bridge." Cy concluded, "We must firm up our order within two weeks—or lose our place in the rolling mill."

"Don't wait two weeks. Place the order today." I said, then looked at my watch to see it was after 3:00 p.m. in the Pacific time zone. Pittsburgh time was three hours later. "If no one's working late at US Steel," I continued, "Place the order first thing tomorrow morning."

Desperate to get onto the Everett property to accomplish soil tests and site survey, Jim Laws radio-phoned me and said, "The gate is locked. Who has the key?" I replied, "My god! You have a bulldozer. You don't need a key!" *John Andrew collection*

"I hate to do this without knowing the site conditions and testing the bearing pressure of the soil," said Prideaux. "If we have soil that compacts well, we can redesign the big trusses and take advantage of the negative bending over the columns. Right now, we're assuming poor soil like the lakefront in Renton, where pile foundations and pile caps might subside differentially. We've remained conservative in Renton by using simple trusses with positive bending, where stress doesn't change much if there's differential settlement."

"Stay conservative at Everett," I said. "Use the Renton design. The Renton and Everett buildings have equal span, headroom, and crane capacities. If headquarters can't strike a deal on the Everett property, the steel will go somewhere else—maybe to the lakefront in Renton. That's our last-ditch option if the deal to purchase the new site falls apart."

I changed the subject and continued, "What is needed immediately is the study recommending where on DITCO's 2,000 acres it's feasible to put the main plant. If there's more than one location, show us all of them. You know the layout that we want for the big building that must be completed first. Find a location on those 2,000 acres where the first footings of bay number 1 and bay number 2 can be poured on July 1."

"How soon do you need the study?" asked Prideaux. "One week from today," I replied. "Without permission to get on the site, all we have to base our engineering on is the twenty-five-cent USGS map," said Prideaux. "The contours are 20 vertical feet apart. We don't know how accurate they are."

"Let's assume the government guys who did the field surveys and map making many years ago were pretty good engineers," I said. "I authorize you to base your studies on that map. Enlarge the thing photographically and do a straight-line interpolation between contours, if you need to."

I knew that Prideaux was writing notes, or that his office assistant was silently on the line taking down all my instructions in shorthand. Austin was working by the hour. Boeing would get a bill for everything I requested—with my instructions duly noted. I'd be responsible if things went wrong, not Austin.

"I'll assign this to Charlie Wing," replied Prideaux. He's the vice president of our Midwest Region in Chicago. We've brought him to Seattle to run design and construction of the new plant. He'll report to me and will exclusively devote his time to the Everett plant. He'll bring onboard a design engineer and a construction manager in the next week or two. They'll set up shop in our old district office in Seattle. That way, the Everett plant will get the undivided attention of an experienced Austin district-level team and not get mixed into the other work we are doing for you in the south end."

"I'll be glad to meet him," I said. Prideaux was acting like the infusion of more talent was his idea. Three months before, when I was reporting to Don Davis, we told Prideaux that Austin had to bring in another experienced management team to design and build the new plant. I was glad this was finally happening, just in time to get the new people familiar with the project as it got underway.

Early the next week, I got on the phone with John Bixby, corporate director of facilities. Bixby would be the closest person at headquarters regarding property acquisition. It's urgent that we get on the site," I said. "When will this deal be closed?"

"Nothing's happened yet," replied Bixby. "Elmer Sill [Boeing's real estate agent] wants to know how much acreage to buy. He works directly with Bill Allen. Allen said he didn't know."

I was shocked, almost flabbergasted. "I thought Allen authorized the purchase of the whole 2,000 acres last week. We showed him an estimated price—$2.6 million."

"After the meeting with you guys," said Bixby, "Allen got with Sill. Sill said he could save money if we didn't buy the whole thing."

"Damn it, Bix, you know as well as me that DITCO will sell all of it or half for the same price. I've heard they're broke. They badly need two million bucks. What's more, that land's not worth more than a thousand dollars an acre anyway—maybe less. It's so blooming rugged that it's been sitting there for fifty years and there's been no buyer. Two million dollars buys 2,000 acres of second-growth forest land anywhere in the Seattle area. I threw an extra $600,000 into the estimate because there's at least one other owner within the property, and four or five others who have 10-acre tracts on the perimeter. I wish Sill reported to me. If he did, he'd be buying the whole thing for less than two million dollars."

"Sill's got Allen wrapped around his finger," said John Bixby. "Allen won't deal with us or anyone else when it comes to buying property."

"You and I know something else," I added with passion. "From a long-range standpoint, we ought to control as much land as possible surrounding our aircraft plants. We ran out of land at Plant I thirty years ago, at Plant II twenty years ago, and at Renton ten years ago. Now we have a chance to buy a big chunk of property next to a runway. Someday we'll wish we bought every acre available when it was dirt cheap. We'll have twenty thousand workers there three years from now. Think of what acreage will be worth then. We're shortsighted if we don't buy it all."

"Land speculation is not our game," replied Bixby. "We're in the aircraft business, John, not the real estate business."

"That's what I'm talking about, Bix, the aircraft business for our kids and grandkids" was my retort.

My world was one of market forecasts, trends, demographics, human factors, and critical mass. I'd played my part by keeping the 737 in Seattle by leveraging critical mass. Now, I was about to achieve another goal, building the yardstick factory of the future. I realized the site was difficult—but it had a future. Ample land was about the only advantage of the Everett site. I hoped that a two-bit real estate agent wouldn't screw it up.

"How do we get this deal back on track?" I asked Bixby. "I think you'd better be prepared to come back to headquarters and explain exactly what is needed. Allen won't be pushed, and it's tough to get a meeting onto his crowded calendar," said Bixby. "I'll see what I can do."

"Austin is now looking into the amount of land needed at Everett. I hope they say all 2,000 acres," I said, concluding that discussion.

At the end of the week, I drove to the Austin office for a meeting with Cy Prideaux and Charlie Wing to review their study on plant location. They brought two of Austin's most senior executives to the meeting. Al Waidelich, senior vice president from Cleveland, had flown in. Wally Engstrom, the semiretired vice president of the Seattle district, was called on to attend. I was glad the old-timers were invited. Bill Allen trusted these two men more than me, or any other Boeing person, on the topic of plant construction or major expansion.

Prideaux began the meeting. He used construction industry jargon. A "cut" is the bulldozing, scraping, or grading of land to make it level. The excavated dirt is then pushed into a low point, making it "fill."

"John, the name of the game is 'cut.' The only place where we can begin to pour footings on July 1 is on land that has been cleared of trees and then 'cut.' We can't pour foundations on land that's been filled, because we don't have enough time to spread, roll, and compact the fill properly. Filling and then compacting can't possibly be completed until the end of summer. By then, we must have foundations poured, and the columns up for bays 1 and 2. We'll be hanging trusses in those bays in September. Bays 3 and 4 can wait until the filling and compacting is finished. They come later in the year. By then, they can be built on fill dirt."

"I understand what you are telling me," I said. "Where can you make the cut for bays 1 and 2?"

"Only in two places," replied Prideaux. "One is on the west side of the property, on the ridge between Japanese Gulch and Powder Mill Gulch. The other is on the much-larger ridge between Powder Mill Gulch and Merrill & Ring Creek way over on the east side of the property."

Prideaux spread plans on a table. Austin had enlarged the twenty-five-cent Geological Survey map and, by interpolating between the 20-foot contour lines, had taken a slice through the property at runway level. All land above runway level would be cut down. All land below runway level would be filled.

I could see that the ridge between the two gulches had the smaller cut area. Prideaux laid a transparent tracing of the big building on the cut area and said, "We can fit bays 1 and 2 here on the cut. Bays 3 and 4 and future extensions will grow to the east. There's not enough room for the factory to grow to the west. The clear zone for the runway approach is in the way."

I looked at the overlay and said, "This is a mirror image of what we ought to be building. The engineering department will be in an office complex on the east. They should be near the airplane mockups. The mockups need to be near the wire and blanket shops, major assembly comes next, and final assembly—last. Factory flow is okay, but the intellectual flow is all screwed up. The engineers will have to walk a half mile to check work in the mockup shop and the wire shop. The building should grow to the west and not to the east. How does the cut on the other ridge look?"

"No problem there," said Prideaux. "We can cut an area that will contain the building, its expansions, and almost all of the supporting structures, including the office complex. Of course, the paint hangar and the field aircraft parking stalls will go on the 160 acres across the road, next to the runway. The airfield facilities will be the same regardless of where the main factory is located."

"What's the difference in cost?" I asked. "Not very much," replied Prideaux.

"But we can't be sure until we have access to the site. When will that be?"

"I don't know," I said. "Headquarters is waiting to see where the plant can go. Now I can tell them. Formalize what you've showed me. Meanwhile, begin detailed building design. Start work on the railroad design also. Buy the rails and ties. You should have 100,000 tons of steel coming. That will fill at least twenty freight trains, each a mile long. Don't unload two thousand freight carloads of steel in Everett. Unload the steel on-site—where it will be needed."

Two working days later, the next Monday, Austin delivered the bound copies of their location study to my office. I reviewed the plan with my boss, Erle Barnes, and asked him for ideas to get Bill Allen to review the plan and get moving on land acquisition.

By now, Barnes had five thousand people in his organization. By taking charge of facilities planning, I was doing exactly what he wanted. Barnes was turning out to be a better manager than expected. He allowed me to range freely in order to do my work. He never expressed qualms when I spoke directly to his management. "Why don't you ask Tex Boullioun to help," said Barnes. "He was with you when Allen made the decision to put the plant in Everett. Boullioun may be able to break things free because he's a sidekick to T. Wilson."

I immediately made an appointment to see Tex. He commented on the *Seattle Times* photograph. I told him it got me into trouble both at home and at work. I switched topics by explaining the real estate acquisition delay to Tex and showed him Austin's analysis on building placement. "I'll call T. Wilson and tell him he needs to look at this data," said Tex.

The telephone rang later that same day. It was Tex. He said, "Here's the deal. Bill Allen made the decision to go to Everett. Allen has now delegated to Wilson the decision of how much land to buy. Wilson will make that decision on Saturday. Meet me in his office at 10:00 a.m. Bring Austin's report. Don't bring anybody else. The meeting will be private—just among the three of us."

Colleagues from this era describe T. Wilson as extremely bright, capable, visionary, brutally honest, and quick to grasp new concepts. They also recall an endearing storyteller who loved jokes regarding coworkers, while remaining extremely loyal to trusted members of his entourage.

Maybe it was security guard Dan Carroll who was kind enough to wave me through the gate. A Boeing badge and car pass authorized vehicle entry. Everybody else was expected to enter via a pedestrian gate.

Each department set about preparing for the first Boeing wide-body jetliner. The flight line shopping list included 747-sized fire trucks, towing equipment, step trucks, jacks, and aero-stands.

On the morning of Saturday, February 12, 1966, I displayed my badge and parking pass to gain access to Plant II and parked beside the small, thirty-year-old corporate headquarters building. The structure had a lobby and executive dining room on the first floor and private offices on the two floors above. It had the ambiance of a place where thoughtful people weighed options before making important business decisions. The hallways were islands of quiet, shielded from adjacent airfield and factory noises by poured-in-place concrete walls. The thick carpet was spotless and dark wood paneling prevailed.

Thus, when I stepped from the elevator onto the third-floor hallway, I expected to be greeted by the usual dead silence. Instead, I was surprised to hear voices coming from T. Wilson's open office doorway. I realized both men were there ahead of me. Was I late? My wristwatch said I was five minutes early.

The tone was not loud, strident, or boisterous. Nor was it low key and confidential. Instead, the conversation was coming from two men who seemed to know one another well and were engaged in friendly relaxed conversation—probably about past adventures. Without an office assistant because it was Saturday, I realized the door was left open for me.

Wilson, aged forty-five, and Boullioun, forty-eight, were the apparent heirs to the highest positions in the Boeing Company. The pair achieved the military-industrial version of stardom by leading the Minuteman program, where thousands of workers in many locations collaborated to deliver to the Air Force a thousand nuclear-tipped ballistic missiles individually buried deep into separate, widely spaced underground silos strung out all along the northern tier of the United States. Each missile stood ready to launch instantly upon an authenticated order from the US president.

The perceived missile gap with the Soviet Union had been eliminated. It never existed. The incoming John Kennedy administration was surprised to find out about Minuteman and the advanced state of the United States nuclear deterrent (a triad consisting of bombers, submarines, and ICBMs). Boeing was already working on ways to make the Minuteman more lethal, by installing three warheads atop each of them.

With election to the board of directors and promotion to executive vice president, February 1966 was an eventful month for T. Wilson. It was becoming increasingly obvious to all that T. Wilson was on the short list to replace Bill Allen—when that time came. Abiding by the recent decisions of Bill Allen had suddenly put me and T. Wilson on the same page regarding plant construction at Everett. We differed only on details.

Starting in October 1965, Tex Boullioun arrived at Commercial Airplanes headquarters in a double box (shared leadership) with John Yeasting. Everyone, including me, quickly learned the quirky spelling of his last name. I found Tex to be affable, easy to work with, shrewd, and quick to decide. He had a reputation as a gambler. Company lore has it that the nickname was bestowed shortly after he was hired in 1940, when he bet a month's wage on a Texas sporting team. When faced with a decision between equal courses of action, he was known to flip a coin rather than hesitate. Tex later enjoyed long tenure as the president of Boeing Commercial Airplanes. Customers liked making deals with the globetrotting master salesman because he could negotiate quickly without excessive home office coordination.

To me, Wilson seemed the exact opposite. He was quarrelsome, quick to take issue, and eager to criticize. His penny-pinching ways extended everywhere.

In his early years at Boeing, T. A. Wilson helped organize the engineering union. SPEEA was originally an acronym meaning Seattle Professional Engineering Employees Association, later redefined as Society of Professional Engineers Employed in Aerospace. After promotion to management, it was said he expressed qualms about his role in forming the collective-bargaining unit. Nevertheless, Wilson was probably the best program manager at Boeing, or anywhere else. If there was a job to do, he was a pusher and demander and would raise his voice (or more) if ever a schedule milestone or cost target was missed. His friends called him "T"—which he preferred to his given first name of Thornton.

As I entered the office, Wilson caught sight of me but continued talking to Boullioun; however, his tone changed as he said, "Like I was saying, Tex, you've got to help me shut down that goddamn 'hobby shop' at Renton."

I knew what he was talking about. Both men were from the military side of Boeing. For years they had made profits that were mostly eaten up at Boeing Commercial. Boeing Commercial had never made a profit because every year a new model or major improvement had been made in the quest to stay ahead of the competition.

To Wilson, Renton was a hobby shop that did nothing but produce new models or variants of models. The past dozen years yielded the exact same number of new models or variants—but never at a profit or an indication of black ink forthcoming in the future.

Everyone knew that Wilson disliked Jack Steiner, the brilliant aerodynamicist and chief salesman of new models at Commercial. Steiner seemed oblivious to most everything if he could continue to design and sell new airplanes.

I also knew that Wilson considered me to be a card-carrying member of the "hobby shop," as the chief proponent for facilities expansion. I would sell the need for facilities expansions as hard as Steiner sold new airplane designs. Wilson turned to me and dryly said, "Congratulations, Andrew. I saw your picture in the paper last Sunday. I hope you bought an extra copy and sent it to your mother."

"Yeah, I sent one to my mother immediately," I replied. "She'll appreciate it, but not everybody did. I got two 'poison pen' letters this week."

"Welcome to the club, Andrew; I've got a drawer full of them." Wilson opened his top left desk drawer and patted a fat stack of paper. "When this fills up, I'll ash-can the works and start over."

Wilson looked me directly in the eye and continued in his squeaky voice. "Andrew, don't worry about people liking you, just make 'em respect you." Immediately ceasing any further small talk, Wilson shifted gears: "Show me what you need at Paine Field."

I spread the Austin studies on the conference table, explained the cut-and-fill issues, and said, "These are the only two possibilities. If we use the west location, the flow of parts in the factory will be fine, but the flow of ideas from the engineering complex will be backward. I can't put a price on that, but the long walks will be inconvenient, and interchanges between engineering and manufacturing will be less frequent."

I continued: "If we build on the east location, we can orient all functions properly and save a lot of walking. We'll also have more property for future expansion."

Wilson responded, "As far as the engineers are concerned, let the bastards walk. It'll do 'em some good. They'll live longer."

Then Wilson asked, "How many acres does the east location take?"

"Two thousand," I replied.

"How many acres does the west location take?" asked T.

"Seven hundred sixty" was my response.

T: "How many acres have you got in Renton?"

Me: "Three hundred twenty."

T: "Renton's the biggest aircraft plant in the world, isn't it?"

Me: "Yes, it's bigger than Douglas at Long Beach, North American at Inglewood, or Lockheed at Marietta."

T shifted into autocratic mode. The bad cop was emerging. "Seven hundred sixty acres is all you need at Everett. It's all you're going to get. Make it work!"

I decided to take one last stab at 2,000: "I think we ought to control property around our site. I'm dead certain we can get the whole property for the same price as the frontage we're buying. I've been told that DITCO (Diversified Industry & Timber Company) is broke. They need two million bucks. That's the price for all or part. We ought to get it all and sell any excess at a profit. When we move in, land values will go up."

"Damn it, Andrew, we're in the airplane business, not the real estate business! I will get you 760 acres and that is all" were the last words spoken.

Boullioun said not a word. He just watched the show and smiled.

I left the meeting to stop and check up on other construction. I reflected on the eventful morning while driving back to Renton for a brief Saturday office visit. With the help of Tex to arrange the much-needed meeting, we had obtained most of what was needed. Good project managers are "here and now" people. Because Wilson was the best there was at project management, I was confident the logjam at corporate was broken and the land would be promptly purchased.

Product line managers are another breed. They need to take a longer view, beyond the individual project, and do what's best for their product line. Chief executives have both project and product line managers reporting to them. Chief executives need a still-longer horizon to make the best longer-range decisions.

I concluded that T. A. Wilson had just flunked his first test as chief executive.

CHAPTER 16
Mud, Sand, and Dirt

T. Wilson's decision to purchase only 760 of the 2,000 acres available at Everett was disappointing and shortsighted. It reaffirmed my other experiences with headquarters bureaucrats when they most often reduced whatever was requested. Wilson was no different. When given a choice, they predictably went for the smallest (or cheapest) option. I was not presenting 2,000 acres as a straw man in the hope of getting 760.

Although Tex Boullioun indicated support before the meeting, he offered none when face to face with Wilson. Boullioun was a gambler who knew when to bet, bluff, or fold. He chose to fold. I knew this decision was final. There would be no further appeals. My disappointment was tempered by a feeling of relief, bordering on elation. Wilson made a quick

Grading the Everett site utilized the same equipment and crews that were building the nation's interstate highway system in 1966. Here, two massive Caterpillar D-9 tractors team up to push a scraper. *John Andrew collection*

In the interest of safety and comfort not only for crew members but also older travelers, the iconic 747 spiral staircase—with roots on the model 314 Clipper of 1939—gave way to a conventional staircase.

This staged mockup photo shows the spiral staircase and a crew of models selected and attired in accordance with the norms of 1967.

decision by not asking for more study and additional alternatives. When he said, "I will get you 760 acres," it was assurance that Elmer Sill would soon consummate the purchase.

Schedule was extremely critical, and that was always Wilson's strongest suit. An expedited program was critical to recoup the outlay of cash necessary for nonrecurring costs stemming from designing a revolutionary new airplane, new factory construction, and certification expenses. The first 747 needed to roll out of a massive, nonexistent factory in 2.5 years on a piece of land that was yet to be purchased. Land acquisition was now the most critical item on the 747's schedule.

Various project management tools were in the Boeing arsenal, and the semantics made their way into our everyday lexicon. Sometimes the most-important events line up to create a "critical path." At other times, the pacing item was referred to as "the long pole in the tent."

My spirits were further buoyed because Wilson had passed the "Rorschach test." The ink blot in question was the blackened outline of the 747 factory. We had worked long and hard to achieve that victory. It was not by accident.

Six months before, in September 1965, Earl Bowden, our manufacturing planner, was making his first try at fitting the 747 into what we called our "yardstick," or theoretical ideal aircraft factory. At that early stage, the 747 was depicted to be a fat, double-decked airplane with a peak production rate of 8.5 aircraft per month, or a hundred deliveries per year.

Computer-aided design systems have eliminated the need to construct and (in this case) attach cockpit instrument wiring into a full-sized 747 Class III mockup.

"The program takes about one-third of the ultimate factory," said Bowden. "There are no problems; the industrial engineers are pleased with the layout. So is the factory superintendent."

"Draw a heavy line around what you need," I said. "We'll call that 'Phase 1' of the ultimate factory."

Bowden's layouts showed detail inside the factory, detail that was too fine to show on the alternate site plans that were being prepared by Gil Jay, the site planner. At the scale that Jay was using, most buildings were depicted as small rectangles, as were the outdoor airfield preflight parking stalls. The main factory building, even in its ultimate size, was small when compared to the length of a 2-mile runway. Not being able to show ultimate detail, Jay simply blackened in the portion of the ultimate building used by Bowden's 747 layout.

Another planner, Bob Richardson, saw what Jay had done and said, "Hey, that looks like a Dungeness crab that's lost one of its big claws." Richardson was known for his wild imagination, especially when it came to fishing—or crabbing. He'd grown up in Port Angeles on the Straits of Juan de Fuca, 100 miles northwest of Seattle. "Once in a while," he continued, "I've pulled up a pot and found a crab that looked like that."

I glanced at the silhouette blackened by Jay. It had a strange shape because the facility for wing cleaning, sealing, and painting, a hazardous activity, was joined to the main factory by an enclosed 100-foot airlock instead of being housed in a separate building. The airlock allowed the overhead crane to move wings and other parts in and out of the sealing area without transfer to wheeled dollies for towing to separate buildings.

An integrated crane system was one of the huge advantages of one-roof manufacturing. However, in Richardson's fertile imagination, the sealing area was the claw, the airlock was the arm, and the main factory was the body of a one-armed Dungeness crab.

"There is a resemblance, Rich," I said, "but I see something else. What I see in Jay's ink blot is the 747 being manufactured in Phase 1 of our ultimate factory."

The four of us shared a laugh. Richardson went on his way.

I was struck by the thought that the same ink blot meant different things to different people. It reminded me that Rorschach's test indicated personality differences when people interpreted the same ink blot differently. I wondered if the concept could be used in reverse—to make different people see a silhouette yet think of the same thing.

I spoke to Bowden and Jay and said, "We must imprint on the mind of every person who comes into our planning room that this ink blot is the 747 factory at a new site. No matter where the new site is—Chicago, Denver, Livermore, San Diego, or any of the new sites around Seattle. We want to keep management's attention on where the new plant will be, and not on what it will be. We've spent two years to get this far. I don't want the yardstick factory of the future torn apart during the site location arguments between Boeing Commercial and Boeing headquarters. The building must survive. Its ability to expand must survive. This ink blot must be imprinted on the mind of every person who reviews our studies, so when they see this shape, they think only of the 747 at a new site and not a Dungeness crab or anything else."

For the next six months, arguments reached heated levels between headquarters staff under Wilson, who wanted to build the 747 in a distant city and send the 737 to Wichita. It was the Commercial Division under John Yeasting that insisted the division not be torn apart—but remain near Seattle. During the many heated meetings and studies that transpired during the argument, one thing remained constant: whenever a new site was depicted, the outline of the factory upon it was identical.

Wilson had visited the planning room several times. When shown alternative locations at Everett, the positioning of offices and warehouses varied; however, the ink blot of the factory was constant. He never questioned the content of that ink blot. T. A. Wilson passed the Rorschach test.

As I made the short walk from the headquarters building on that fateful Saturday morning to my powder-blue crew-cab pickup truck parked in front of the historic Plant II hangar doors, where B-17s emerged during World War II and Cold War B-52s followed a decade later, I could hear in the distance the crisp, steady hammer of a diesel pile driver. I loved that sound. Every hit was a controlled explosion of diesel that drove a pile deeper into the ground. I knew the same explosion caused the heavy steel hammerhead to rebound upward, only to fall again with another gulp of diesel and another hit. The sound gave me a sense of pride. Old Charlie Thompson's property would no longer stand vacant.

The Thompson tract was a few hundred feet south of Plant II, almost within shouting distance. In less than two minutes, my pickup truck was entering an open construction gate. I drove in a short gravel pad and parked at the Boeing portable construction office, which was in a trailer. Beside it was the Austin Company's construction office in another trailer. I knocked at the Boeing office. Getting no response, I opened the door and walked in. Nobody was there. It was Saturday, almost noon. Unlimited overtime was approved for this critical job, which was to have a new final-assembly building ready for the 737 by July 1, 1966. I wondered, Where was the site engineer?

I knocked on the Austin trailer, walked in, and found it also empty. A blueprint with a construction schedule was on the wall. I saw red marks but did not take the time to determine if they indicated ahead of schedule or behind. I decided to walk to the loudly hammering pile driver to find out.

Charlie Thompson's former 16 acres looked like a sea of mud. The pile driver was working near the Duwamish waterway at the far end of the property. The waterway was created many years before my watch. The history books tell us it was dredged over a multiyear span starting in 1913. Engineers working for the City of Seattle wished to eliminate seasonal flooding while reclaiming wetlands by straightening out the meandering Duwamish River. The channel is known as the Green River south of Tukwila.

I looked down at my polished Cordovan wingtips and cuffs of my dark-gray slacks. A blue blazer, white shirt, and maroon tie, and a tan London Fog raincoat to shield me from the persistent raw February mist, completed my outfit. I was dressed for the solemn corporate halls of ivy, and not the quarter mile of mud separating me from the pile driver.

I opened the back door of my crew cab and pulled out a pair of knee-high, five-buckle overshoes, which slid easily over my wing tips and buckled over the cuffs and ankles of my slacks. A red-and-black Mackinaw coat replaced the blazer and London Fog overcoat. A white hard hat covered my otherwise bare head. I set out across the mud.

The Austin Company had a rigid pecking order when it came to hard hats. At the apex were hard hats painted gleaming gold. They were worn by Austin partners and vice presidents. Superintendents wore hard hats painted shiny, chrome-like silver, making them look like army soldiers in an elite honor guard. Foremen wore any colors of their own choosing—except shiny gold or chrome.

A month before, Cy Prideaux had presented me with one of their gleaming gold hard hats. He said, "You're the owner's top man. We all work for you. Please wear this gold hard hat whenever you visit an Austin construction site. Everyone will know you're the boss."

"Thanks, Cy," I replied. "I'll wear the standard white hard hat like all the Boeing guys. If anyone needs to know I'm boss, they'll know it damn quick. Otherwise, I'd rather be anonymous."

I was anonymous while slogging across the muddy flat. A cluster of five men stood on the other side of the pile driver. Each stared intently at the pile being driven while occasionally glancing at their wristwatches. The Boeing site engineer was unknown to me except by his surname of "Thompson"—which was ironically appropriate for the Thompson site. I barely knew his boss, Al Williamson, who was the construction manager for several nearby projects, including a new 737 paint hangar that would replace one of the old B-29 hangars on the north end of Boeing Field, and the installation of two large automatic wing riveters in the old B-17 factory at Plant II. Williamson was a recent transfer from the Minuteman project at Ellsworth Air Force Base, Rapid City, South Dakota.

Williamson reported to Bayne Lamb, my overall construction manager. Yes, Bayne was still on my team. My qualms about him turned out to be totally unfounded. Bayne Lamb was extremely loyal to me and hard working. The experience, energy, and aptitude he brought to the job more than compensated for the lack of a college degree.

I joined the cluster of men standing within the ear-splitting din of the pile driver. By 1966, the steam-powered pile drivers of the colorful olden days of dock and railroad construction were mostly obsolete and gone to scrap. The steel pile was well into the ground. The hammer, which spit a large puff of blue smoke with every stroke, was almost at eye level. White lines a foot apart on the vertical driving tower indicated progress.

I knew the men were counting the strokes between each white line and timing the minutes to sink a pile. These were friction piles, steel tubes 110 feet long that would never find solid bottom. They would develop their strength by the friction of the pile against the soil. The number of strokes to sink 1 foot was the measure of resistance. When resistance reached the prescribed level, the tube would be cut and filled with concrete.

The Duwamish waterway presented a unique challenge. The tides of the Pacific Ocean surged upward and downward at least twice a day. The change in water level was enough to move the concrete seawalls restraining soggy earth, and thus affect the delicate jigs and assembly tools bolted into the factory floor, which, in turn, secured the bigger aircraft parts during mating. Additional concrete mitigated the problem; however, precision instruments could still measure the minute movements, which derived from the gravitational tug of the moon and sun.

The work was familiar to me. Ten years before, when I was a young construction site engineer for Boeing, I had counted hits of the hammer, driving piles for the 10-50 building in Renton. Lake Washington, while 30 miles in length, was too small to generate measurable tides; however, lake levels varied as much as 3 feet, depending on seasonal rainfall.

Just being next to that loud, authoritative machine was reassuring. My disappointment when leaving Wilson's office had temporarily vanished. I felt more at home ankle deep in construction mud than I had less than half an hour ago in the halls of corporate headquarters.

Suddenly the racket stopped. The pile had reached its design strength. Williamson recognized me and introduced me to Thompson and to the Austin general foreman. "How's the job going?" I asked.

"We're just getting started," replied Williamson. "The structural steel will begin arriving in two weeks. By that time, we'll have half the piles driven and enough concrete caps poured to begin steel erection near the river."

"I appreciate you guys working Saturday," I said. "I know the schedule is nearly impossible, but this building is vital to the 737."

"We're slamming down piles tomorrow too," said Williamson.

I slogged back to my pickup truck, noticing the small surveyor's flags above the mud. These flags defined the column lines I had penciled onto a sketch pad late at night while sitting at my kitchen table a mere two months ago. The proposed new building on Charlie Thompson's vacant tract saved 737 final assembly from going to Wichita. More importantly, it preserved Boeing Commercial's critical mass in Seattle.

T. A. Wilson was on the opposite side of that issue. He had lost a skirmish with John Yeasting. Prior Boeing presidents took up residence in a north-end elite gated community of stately brownstone-clad homes called the Highlands. In a demonstration of personal frugality, the Wilson family remained in a modest wood-framed rambler in Normandy Park, a suburb south of Seattle.

Wilson eschewed a limousine and bodyguard by driving himself to work daily. His business travel was in coach class on scheduled airliners. The commute forced him to drive by a building that he detested. The 737 program was growing roots extending 110 feet into the rich alluvial muck. It would henceforth take more than a corporate bureaucrat to yank that program out and transplant it somewhere else.

Crossing swords with a future CEO would not help my career, but I didn't give a damn. Unlike many aerospace jobs, which are not portable, I was an established and competent civil engineer with skills badly needed elsewhere. In a hot economy fueled by the Vietnam War and a space race to the moon, I could find a new job anywhere—in an instant.

Fully at comfort within the military-industrial complex, T. Wilson was clinging to his core competency as a fading Cold Warrior. He was manifesting ignorance by making short-sighted mistakes about not only land acquisition but also the critical mass needed to seize and hold on to the future of Boeing—the growing commercial airliner market. His propensity to fragment the operation by sending vital pieces hither and yon were destructive. Fortunately, circumstances and others were keeping his more dangerous instincts in check.

At another company, I might have been fired by a T. Wilson; however, Boeing had a tolerant culture that even encouraged the degree of nonconformity that was necessary to constantly probe for defects in critical product systems that must be brought to light. A culture that ostracizes the whistleblower will send an unacceptable message to all—hide problems, because the messenger will be shot. The consequences of suppressing or ignoring dissent might someday allow a fatal flaw into airliner operations. Technically competent nonconformance at Boeing was tolerated, even if not celebrated.

On the way back to the Overmeyer Building, I drove to the lakeshore in front of the main Renton plant. I loved that beautiful setting on the shore of Lake Washington, with Mercer Island across the water a mere mile away. Within the huge gray doors of the flying-boat factory were the production lines for models 707 and 727 jet transports. Production rates for both were rising and would soon outstrip the capacity of the beautiful waterfront factory; however, the purpose of my visit was not to enjoy the scenery, but to check out activity on the lake.

I was relieved to see a large hydraulic dredge anchored 300 feet offshore. A 12-inch pipeline supported by floats snaked its way from the dredge to shore, where it climbed up and over a 12-foot-high dike. From where I was standing, I could not see over the dike, but I knew it enclosed a 20-acre plot of land that was being prepared as the location for a new final-assembly building for models 707 and 727. The expansion would yield two new assembly buildings that already had numbers: 4-81 and 4-82. The new buildings were of massive proportions and twice the height of the adjacent buildings. Solid foundations were mandatory, but the 20-acre parcel was unstable swampland that needed to be filled with 11 feet of over-burden to compress the swamp. After the soggy bottomland had been compressed, the overburden would be removed to fill 20 additional swampy acres. The lakefront parcel was recently purchased from Puget Sound Power and Light, a regional utility provider.

A month before, when I took over the job of director of facilities planning and construction, I reversed the decision of the Austin Company to use dry fill from the hills south of Renton. There had been a meeting between me, Bayne Lamb, and Cy Prideaux of Austin Construction.

Prideaux led off: "In a month, we will begin placing a preload of fill material on the 20 acres that will underlie the 4-81/4-82 buildings. That land is low-lying swampy lakeshore. We will first bring the area up to grade and then add an extra 11 feet of fill as preload to compress and squeeze out the water from the swamp. After the preload material has sat for thirty days, the swampland will be stabilized and will provide an unyielding subbase for your factory floor. The building structure, of course, will be supported by composite pilings bedded into a firm layer of glacial gravel 65 feet below floor level.

Prideaux continued: "Beginning a month from now, we will need to bring a thousand truckloads of fill material from the hills south of Renton, through the city, and through the plant to the lakeshore. We will need to develop a plan with you and the city to accomplish this with a minimum of disruption."

"How many days will it take to bring in a thousand truckloads?" I asked.

"Oh, I'm sorry," said Prideaux. "I meant one thousand truckloads per day for thirty days."

"That'll be a terrible disruption," I protested. "The roads are already clogged. Can't we pump sand from the lake? That's the way the old-timers did it in 1941. I've seen the pictures."

"Hydraulic fill will take too much time," said Prideaux. "Hydraulic fill is sloppy. It'll add sixty days to the schedule; that's sixty extra days to drain out the water and firm up before we can remove the preload and start construction."

"We simply can't afford to have a thousand dump trucks a day disrupting plant opera-tions," I replied. "I'll take full responsibility for directing the use of hydraulic fill from the lake bottom."

"We'll need to get permits from the US Army Corps of Engineers," said Prideaux. "They control navigable inland waters. How far out in the lake should we go?"

Over the past year, we had worked well with Prideaux. I was mildly irritated that he would ask me a geotechnical question that was within his own purview. Either he or his engineers should tell me the answer, but I instead shifted gears by offering background from my own experience. "Ten years ago, I personally drew a map from soundings taken of the bottom of Lake Washington in front of the Renton factory. The map was complete with boring samples taken from the bottom of the lake," I explained.

"We were exploring the use of hydraulic fill for the construction of the 10-50 building. Although the option was declined, I learned a lot about the lake bottom. There's an

80-foot-deep hole starting about 200 feet in front of the factory. That's where they sucked out fill for the factory in 1941. Don't count on getting fill from there. Ask for a permit farther out and wider."

Now, I was back in the driver's seat of my sky-blue pickup truck where it sat on the lakefront aircraft parking ramp. A glance across the water showed that the big dredge was anchored, the pipeline was in place, and a 12-foot temporary dike had been built to hold 11 feet of muck for sixty days until it drained and firmed. I worried that the 20-acre pond would never dry out—thus seriously delaying construction of the much-needed 4-81/4-82 final-assembly hangars.

Like Tex Boullioun, I was taking a calculated gamble. The person who countermanded the best advice of the Austin Company was me. The fault would be mine, and mine alone, if things went wrong. I drove to the office and found a note from Cy Prideaux to call him at home. He answered and said, "John, I wanted to tell you the dredging will begin tomorrow, on Sunday. I can't be there, and there is no need for you either. Let's get together on Tuesday to see how pumping lake bottom muck is progressing."

"That's fine with me," I replied. "Also, I have news for you regarding Everett. Wilson made the decision this morning to place the 747 factory on a 760-acre tract on the west side. He rejected putting the plant on the eastern 2,000 acres. We still can't get on the property because it has yet to be purchased; however, the engineers can now focus on the final layout for placement of buildings, parking, roads, and utilities. Let's add earthmoving at Everett to the agenda for Tuesday."

When the sun arose on Sunday, I could not resist checking on the dredging. Our new residence was only fifteen minutes away from the Overmeyer Building. When I returned to the dike overlook, nothing was happening. Then a stream of clear water gushed from the pipe. The water's color quickly changed to light gray and then to dark gray before turning black. The dredge pipe was only a foot above the ground. It was supported by hollow skids that would float above the rising black muck. I knew it would take a long time for enough muck to be pumped to raise the level and float the pipe.

I went to my office satisfied that pumping had begun and hoping to limit Sunday work to a couple of hours before returning home. After an hour at my desk, Jim House came charging in. Jim House was a thirty-three-year-old senior planning supervisor who specialized in laboratory planning and budgeting. He was brilliant in this role, and furthermore, I could depend on him to be at work most any time of the day or night. I knew a secret. As a divorced alcoholic with a penchant for brilliance, he worked those extremely long hours to keep himself from drinking.

Jim was agitated. "John, I was out at the dredge site. Everything was okay until the pipe clogged up. They have ceased pumping!" My heart sank. A screwup on the hydraulic fill was the last thing we needed.

I grabbed my white hard hat and jumped into my crew-cab pickup truck. Fortunately, I was dressed for a construction site with steel-toed boots and work jeans, with the intent to keep up on those weekend household chores. The red-and-black Mackinaw coat would keep me warm. Jim grabbed his own hard hat and joined me in the crew cab as we raced through the construction gate and skidded to a halt on the muddy parking pad at George Fulton's construction shack.

We scrambled our way along a series of wobbly planks (called duck boards) that scaled the dike, and made our way to the end of the pipe—where two laborers were standing around by leaning on their shovels. George Fulton was watching with a skeptical eye.

Fulton, a man in his fifties, was a soldier of fortune and veteran of large construction projects around the world in various management capacities. He claimed to own a beautiful home in Connecticut where his adult daughter took care of his invalid wife. He lived sparingly, sending most of his paycheck home. Fulton, like Jim House, seemed to use work and long hours as a palliative.

"Hand shovels won't do the job," said Fulton in a slightly Scottish accent. "They need a bulldozer."

"I've sent for a D-6," said the Austin foreman. "I've never seen finer beach sand. That's the best fill in the world. You can walk on it right now." I stepped over to the mound of sand at the end of the pipe, where the laborers had given up shoveling. My steel-toed boots left only small imprints in wet black sand that reminded me of the beaches on the Pacific coast where we dug razor clams at low tide.

A snorting D-6 Caterpillar bulldozer soon trundled onto the scene. Like a mechanical dinosaur, it climbed the dike before dropping into the basin on its slow but determined clattering march to the sand pile. The foreman signaled the dredge to resume pumping. The dozer cleared the pile at the outlet and spread the growing field of black sand as it spewed from the end of the pipe.

"We'll be pumping around the clock until this berm is filled," said the foreman. "We won't have to wait for sixty days for this to drain and firm up. It's already almost as hard as concrete."

Yes! My own gamble had paid off! The 80-foot-deep hole in front of the 1940 Renton seaplane factory was the clue that excellent sand was plentiful on the nearby bottom of Lake Washington.

It was a more than memorable weekend. T. A. Wilson made the needed decision on Everett land acquisition, piles were being driven at the Thompson site, we picked up sixty days of schedule time at Renton because fine beach sand—instead of watery muck—was spewing from the 12-inch dredge pipe, and a thousand truckloads per day were not disrupting the roadways of Renton.

So much for mud and sand. It was the dirt of Everett I was looking forward to hearing about on Tuesday. There were 5 million yards of dirt to be moved in the three short months of summer. If Cy Prideaux's plan did not pass muster, he would hear of mine . . .

Moving Dirt at Everett

On April 1, 1966, I prepared a presentation titled "New Site Plan of Action and Status" for review with Erle Barnes.

"I agree, the rolling of steel needs to begin," said Barnes. "Show this to Reagan and Dillon. Get them onboard. Go to Boullioun. Then go to headquarters."

After a meeting with Tex Boullioun and T. Wilson, I prepared an authorization letter for Boullioun's concurrence dated April 15, 1966—which he signed. This letter was authority for Austin Construction to proceed immediately with long-lead items, to begin spending money at Boeing's risk—especially the huge steel bid from American Bridge, the construction arm of US Steel Corporation.

Despite T. Wilson's "decision," land for a 747 factory had yet to be acquired. Headquarters kept delaying the purchase of acreage at any new site. It was now April. The McChord properties, the forest at Everett, and Thun Field each remained in play. The steel structure still had to be adaptable to the lakefront at Renton, the only place we had property, and the time to negotiate a few more acres from Puget Sound Power and Light.

I reminded Cy Prideaux for the second time in two months, "We have permission to negotiate with an earthmoving contractor. Whom do you plan to negotiate with?"

"I can't say this minute," replied Cy. "Come to my office in two days. I'll have a proposal for you."

I headed for Prideaux's office first thing on Monday morning. I knew Austin Company was extremely busy that weekend. The first 300-foot truss for the 4-81 building was being raised on Tuesday, April 19. Austin decided to put it together on the ground and raise it in one piece, with four giant cranes and a fifth heavy construction crane to rack the receiving-tower structure the last quarter inch, if need be. It had attributes of not only a delicate engineering challenge but also a precision construction task.

Cy's secretary saw me enter the building. By the time I reached his office, he seemed to be dismissing a meeting. I recognized Ray Rowan, vice president in charge of construction. I knew Ray had been an ironworker who had walked the beams erecting steel on Chicago skyscrapers. I assumed the group had been going over final plans and engineering for the critical truss raising the following day. I also recognized Dennis Koskinen, Austin's head structural engineer. It was not surprising to see him. The erection of a steel structure requires analysis as challenging as design.

While the previous meeting participants filed out, Cy beckoned me in. He motioned for me to sit down at his conference table as he wrote notes and gathered the loose papers. Then he extracted a thin folder from his desk-drawer file. He stood across the conference room table and began to lay papers in front of me.

Before I glanced at the papers, he said, "We propose to engage a consortium of Seattle-area dump truck companies. The subcontract will be with a joint venture called 'Anderson Earthmoving.'"

Startled, I reacted: "I never heard of Anderson. Does he own one dump truck or ten? Is he still driving a dump truck?"

"I realize you've never heard of Anderson, but you will recognize the other dump truck companies," replied Prideaux.

I was aghast at the idea. Pushing papers aside, I said, "I don't think there's enough equipment in the Puget Sound region to accomplish what we need to do in the time remaining to do it," and added, "The least dirt needing moving at Everett is 5 million yards. That's 500,000 dump truck loads at 10 yards per load. All the local guys are finishing interstate projects—I-5, I-90, and I-405."

Prideaux's plan was woefully inadequate. Anger welled within me. I did not want to argue or raise my voice. We had too many other projects in the works. Teamwork was essential.

I held my temper and said, "I need to think about this for a few hours before I can authorize you to proceed. I will have an answer at 3:00 p.m. tomorrow after you guys raise the first truss at Renton. I hope the damn thing won't collapse. We have twenty-two to raise at Renton and sixty-two more at the new site."

I left Prideaux's office extremely irritated. I wanted to scream. All the new sites remained viable. We did not own land at any of them. Everett was the most difficult site. We had to protect schedule there. The other sites were easier. At McChord we could begin on level ground. The same was true at Thun Field.

Ten years before, I had worked for the biggest dirt mover then on the planet, the Morrison-Knudsen Company from Boise, Idaho. They were still big in dirt moving but fully employed with huge military contracts tied to the Vietnam War. The biggest earthmoving projects in history involved earthen dams—mostly in the middle of America. With the national commitment to interstate highways, Peter Kiewit Sons of Omaha, Nebraska, was now the leading dirt mover.

Another contractor we used was Sound Construction, in partnership with the Leo Daly design firm. They were working on a project to build three paint hangars and an office building in Renton. I was very happy with the attitude of Phil Carlson, president of Sound. He was on par with Cy Prideaux when problems had to be resolved and fixed.

I phoned Carlson. "Hey, Phil, you guys were bought by Peter Kiewit last year, were you not? How's that deal going?"

"Yeah, I report to them. The home office doesn't interfere at all. They don't know much about harbors, docks, or local industries like paper mills and Boeing work. They're mostly dirt movers from Omaha. That's their forte," reported Carlson.

"Boeing may have a quick dirt-moving subcontract this summer. I don't know if it will happen. I'm trying to get an idea about available capacity to move dirt, clearing, grading, ripping, and scraping. Would you call your home office and see what they have available on short notice?" I asked.

"Make sure you tell them the assignment is remote. There are 760 timbered acres to clear. Five million yards of earth to move. Those are round numbers. The time frame is limited to two or three summertime months. We will need equipment with operators and management to work at the direction of a general contractor. If your home office has a problem working with Austin, let me know," I explained.

Carlson returned my call at midafternoon. "Kiewit has a highway spread, loaded on a train of flat cars sitting on a siding in South Dakota, waiting for the next assignment. They have another highway spread coming off a job in a month. Each spread can clear timber and move dirt. They go anywhere to build freeways."

By noon on April 19, 1966, the first truss on the 4-81 building was raised successfully.

I joined with the Austin executives and invited them to lunch in the Renton executive dining room. I used the Boeing executive dining room for most of my luncheons with senior engineering and construction company management. That way, the meal was on Boeing. They were my guests, not the other way around. I never wanted to be their guest, not at noon, not at night, and not on weekend fishing trips. The ambiance of a Boeing dining room gave me a chance to explain Boeing policy on gifts and favors by demonstrating strict adherence.

Only Prideaux could attend. That was good because it was an opportunity to lay out my approach to dirt moving in private. I gestured toward the nearby offices of John Yeasting and Tex Boullioun and concluded by saying, "Site preparation at Everett is on the critical path for the 747. If we fail to make it, the only answer I can give those guys and Bill Allen is that we hired the biggest dirt mover in the world, and he failed. What other answer can I give?"

Prideaux looked relieved. He was off the hook.

Milestone: May 1966. After weeks of secret negotiations, 760 acres of forest within the city of Everett were purchased for the 747 plant. Construction on the first building began on June 20, 1966.

Boeing hiring continued at a prodigious pace. Peak employment in 1966 of 136,918 was exceeded in 1967 when the head count hit 148,493.

The first 747 claws its way into the damp wintertime air on February 9, 1969. The excitement is palpable. Consistent with the Wright brothers' first flight in 1903, bystanders clamber for the best view of a history-making event.

CHAPTER 17
Building Factory at Everett

The Boeing Company was embarked on the largest facilities expansion program in its history—mostly driven by launching the world's first wide-body airliner. The entire 747 project was a convoluted sequence of separate but interdependent events, which, in hindsight, overlap into a blur. Since the product was of unprecedented size, dollars were measured in millions, workers were counted in thousands, and the schedule matched the urgency of warfare.

The scenario was further complicated by the simultaneous need to acquire land; define and build factories—plus other ancillary site improvements; design, build, and certify the airplane; and acquire the human resources necessary to accomplish all of this. The Everett program management team was incrementally being assembled. Recognizing the futility of the Turbine Division, Mal Stamper freed himself for a bigger assignment by selling it to Caterpillar Company—thereby creating a stepping-stone to become vice president in charge

Train crews, two locomotives, and two cabooses were certified for service on Jet Spur, now the steepest conventional rail line in North America. Trains are short and the locomotive is always on the downhill end of the train.

of the emerging 747 Division, an assignment that yielded for Mal a bigger paycheck and a secure place in the annals of aviation history. His capable team of subordinates came to include such people as Bruce Gissing (procurement), Wil Loeken (finance), Bayne Lamb (facilities), Joe Sutter (engineering), and others too numerous to mention. Many of them (including Mal) were later rewarded with even-bigger assignments at Boeing.

During the summer of 1966, land clearing and massive earthmoving were accomplished. Like at early Civil War battles, some nearby residents arrived on sunny weekend days with picnic baskets to observe the dusty transformation of forest into factory. Summer turned to autumn, and at a latitude north of Duluth, Minnesota, autumns in the Northwest become winterish by the dark days of November. Many forms of bad news were endured during that season.

Labor unions for the construction companies (on projects separate from Austin) went on strike. Powerful floodlights were brought in for around-the-clock illumination. The winter weather in the autumn of 1966 was terrible. With a half century of vegetation freshly scraped away, constant rain predictably yielded a soggy worksite. Somebody suggested paving over the mud with asphalt. The temporary pavement brought great relief. Trenches were cut into the asphalt for the needed water, sewer, telephone, and power lines.

Railcars to transport oversized 747 parts were custom built and covered to protect the delicate aluminum skins from vandals throwing rocks, or other trackside hazards.

Jet Spur

The rail line up the heavily wooded ravine was called "Jet Spur" by the railroad. Building new railway lines was rare by 1966, and this one was destined for the record book as the steepest conventional rail line in America. My stipulations included heavy rail, heavy ballast, and 40-foot oversized (marine) clearances above the rail and side to side (in case there was ever a need to move outsized barge parts up the hill). Great Northern (GN) would be the exclusive operator, and sole ownership was held by Boeing to preclude other rail traffic.

Clearing of trees commenced in June 1966, and grading followed. Rails were in place by October. An easement had been established in World War II for a pipeline to deliver fuel to Paine Field either from rail cars spotted on a sidetrack or barges tied to a pier 450 feet below. Existing technology allowed for transportation of either aviation gas or jet fuel via the same pipe.

Building the line proved to be a challenge despite the use of modern bulldozers and earthmoving equipment. Bayne Lamb said his phone rang one night at 3:00 a.m. It was reported that 30,000 cubic yards of waterlogged dirt slid from above onto the railroad line being built into the ravine below. The volume of the slide may have been exaggerated, and in any case, there was plenty of earthmoving equipment on hand to clear it; however, Bill Allen himself was alarmed by rising cost of the spur and signed a letter to Charlie Wing of the Austin Company, complaining of rail line costs. Charlie dutifully responded in writing without reminding Allen that he was solely responsible for picking the wrong site.

My father was director of safety at GN headquarters in Minneapolis. We chatted on the phone. "I want to see your railroad," he said. "It's been the talk of our executive suite in St. Paul. At 5.6 percent it'll be the steepest grade on our line; it'll be tested in a couple of days."

"Are you coming out to witness the test?" I asked.

"Yes. I'll be in Seattle aboard the *Empire Builder* the day after tomorrow. I'll talk to Mr. Shober at the King Street Station. He's the Cascade Division superintendent. You can be my guest, if you want."

"Yes, I'd like to ride that train if possible. But I've already been told nobody from Boeing, Austin, or the roadbed subcontractor will be allowed on the test train. It's a Great Northern operation only."

"That's why you'll be my guest as my son, just like the old days."

I picked Dad up as the first light of dawn filtered through the overcast sky. At Mukilteo, the test train had pulled through the switch and sat idling on the jet spur. At the caboose, Dad introduced me to Cascade Division superintendent Shober, system motive-power superintendent Marsden, air brake supervisor Whitney, and division roadmaster Solga.

"How does it look?" asked Dad.

"Two of our newest road switchers have been qualified for this run," said Marsden. "That's one of them. Nothing else will be allowed to push short trains of cars up this steep grade. The engine will always be on the downhill end. It's the heaviest and has the most-powerful brakes."

Mr. Reichert, a senior railroad civil engineer, took Dad aside and said, "The spur has been built to main-line standards using 120-pound rail and heavy oak ties. The first curve is tight for a main line, but at 10 miles per hour it's no problem." He continued, "There's no super-grading, or tilt to the curves, like the main line needs for higher speeds. That's the proper way to build a steep spur. Drainage and erosion control have been taken care of. They've left nothing undone."

We climbed aboard. The other railroaders rode inside the modern steel caboose. Dad and I stood on the rear platform. The backward ride up the hill was done in about ten minutes. Jim Laws was surprised to see me at the top of the hill. The ride down took longer. First the dynamic locomotive braking was engaged. Diesel locomotives can engage traction motors as generators and direct the electricity to overhead electric grids for dissipation as heat. Locomotive brakes were next engaged. Finally, train brakes (the brakes on every car) were activated. Each of the three forms of downgrade train control proved more than adequate.

The parts for the 747 came from many companies and were subject to rebidding over the decades. The design of fuselage sections needed to be broken down into pieces small enough to fit into specially designed railroad cars. Some had slots in the floor to allow oversized parts to dangle below floor level but above the railhead. Those cars were normally provided with removable covers intended to shield the contents from errant rocks thrown by trackside vandals. Every car consigned to Boeing Everett needed to be pushed up the twisting 3.3-mile steep hill. Devices called "derails" are installed at the top of the hill to put an errant railcar on the ground rather than careening downgrade.

The railroad tracks extended into the factory, so the overhead cranes could first remove any protective canopies before grasping the assemblies themselves. Some years later, an old steam locomotive turntable was acquired by Boeing from an abandoned midwestern roundhouse. It was installed at the top of the hill so railcars could be turned (if needed) before entering the factory for unloading.

Office Space

The facilities requirements list at Everett included the factory, the paint hangar, the flight line, employee parking, cafeterias, and offices to house the white-collar workforce. Adequate office space for the facilities department was carved from the area above a heating plant called the boiler house; however, there was an increasing need for proper office buildings to welcome to Everett new arrivals of every ilk. They included 747 general manager Mal Stamper and entourage, Joe Sutter and the engineering team, plus early-arriving finance and contracts people. On November 13, 2019, while researching this book at the Boeing Archive, an employee question arrived:

Question: "Many of the walls in the 40-81 building [at Everett] have huge steel plates built into them. These plates are about 3 inches thick and extend floor to ceiling. Our Tooling Group is curious about their purpose. This building will be razed in the next few months."

John Andrew's answer: "The heavy steel doors in the first office building at Everett were there to provide nuclear-fallout protection for all occupants. Boeing headquarters levied that requirement on its various divisions in about the year 1960. At that time some homeowners were digging fallout shelters in their backyards.

"When headquarters decided to establish a space center in Kent, Washington (designed in 1963), they decided to standardize the design of office buildings. They chose a "campus" format, with each office building having 140,000 square feet on two floors each measuring 70,000 square feet. Each floor had a central core that contained long hallways to toilets, conference rooms, stairwells, and maintenance facilities. The second story, with a thick poured-concrete floor, was stacked atop the first floor. Farther above was a penthouse containing heavy electrical vaults with duplicate heavy transformers, and all heating and air-conditioning equipment with blowers distributing both chilled and heated air to multiple zones within the building.

"Fallout experts of that day determined that the bulk of heavy stuff stacked above the first floor was enough for fallout protection vertically. However, the general office bays had continuous window walls that looked out on beautiful gardens (at Kent) for all employees to enjoy. Double panes of insulated glass provide almost no radiation protection. The only radiation glass in those days was several inches of lead glass used at Hanford and in nuclear power plants, but totally impractical for office windows. Boeing instead required heavy steel sliding doors to be installed on slightly inclined tracks hidden within the wall at every door from the central core into the windowed bays of the first floor.

"All 1,200 employees in each building would be instructed to gather in the long hallways of the first floor. The heavy steel doors would then be closed by wardens who could trigger the closure by gravity, without need for muscle or electric power. Enough food, water, and galvanized garbage cans for waste were stored in the central core for about one week of shelter until radiation with a short half-life had lowered enough for people to risk evacuation.

"This concept was obsolete the day it was adopted. The world had long progressed from the atomic age of Hiroshima in 1945 to the thermonuclear age introduced in 1953. Kilotons had grown to megatons. Anyone who could read the newspaper realized that by 1962, a massive Soviet missile warhead, bursting in the air above central Puget Sound, could kill almost everyone from Bellingham to Olympia. Nevertheless, Boeing headquarters insisted on fallout protection. The long utility and pedestrian tunnels under the main plant at Everett were required for fire escape, so fallout protection was automatic and free in the factory.

"I did not have time to challenge the 'campus' approach when laying out the Everett plant in January 1966. The first office building had to be built in less than a year. I simply hired the same engineer who designed the new Kent Space Center, and told them to place one module in Everett. It was the only example of that design at Everett.

"The next year, Joe Sutter was presented with a 140,000-square-foot air-conditioned office building for him and his project engineers—completely carpeted, fully compliant with fallout protection, without the steel doors, at half the cost of the standard design. Boeing offices for the rank and file had never previously been carpeted; however, reduced pricing now made it cost effective. In addition to a psychological boost, the soft surface cut down on the noise level, thus allowing creative workers to better concentrate on whatever important task was at hand.

"Similar structures were built later without any of the other useless fallout protection, at even less cost. I told the corporate headquarters staff to make the chief executive tell me to spend useless money. They did not go to him. They knew they would lose that argument.

"For about five years it was my job to question obsolete rules and regulations on behalf of Boeing Commercial; however, there was no time to debate the merits of steel doors in the spring of 1966. By 1968, the fallout nonsense had been eliminated, unless it was part of fire protection or evacuation codes and thereby free of extra cost. I'm glad the new generation is curious about those doors. They never did make sense."

The "Incredibles" Arrive

Finally, the walls and roof of the main building began to take shape. Sitting on a high bluff and overlooking open water, a windstorm blew in and removed a large part of the newly installed roof. Manufacturing operations moved into the new Everett factory as soon as possible. Workers were told to wear long johns and rain gear because big gaps remained in the walls and roof. Reminiscent of model 314 outdoor construction, work on the 747 mockup began with wind and rain swirling around these new pioneers. They wore construction hard hats bearing a Paul Bunyan cartoon inscribed with "Incredibles." They were soon followed by the tooling people. Experienced workers were drawn from Seattle and Renton plants. Some former B-52 workers opted to relocate from the tornado-prone flatlands of Wichita, Kansas, to the serene wooded hills of Snohomish County.

They brought with them a common set of manufacturing techniques. Unlike the SST, the 747 design leveraged existing technology. It was merely bigger than every other Boeing aircraft that preceded it. Consistent with previous models and the long-standing methodology advocated by Oliver West, each 747 body section bore a standardized number. The center wing was body section 11. The cockpit and nose were body section 41—and so it went. Each body section consisted of many thousands of fasteners binding together a menagerie of mutually interdependent parts. The primary metal was aluminum, but titanium, composites, and steel also made their way into the 747 airframe. The parts came from a plethora of suppliers, ranging from other Fortune 100 companies to small family-owned machine shops. The initial 747 production run was fabricated mostly from parts of US origin.

During this time, Boeing commercial jets were normally half fabricated in-house, with the other half being purchased equipment. Engines were the most expensive component.

The offshore placement of major outside production contracts came in later decades. Foreign parts procurement to secure offshore sales was called offsets. Japan later became a big player, with supply chain names including Mitsubishi, Fuji, and Kawasaki Heavy Industries. Japan Airlines (JAL) was to become the biggest 747 operator, with All Nippon Airlines (ANA) also a valued Boeing customer.

The top of the wing was skinned with a tapered solid-aluminum panel over 2 inches thick where it joined the fuselage. When asked about this, an engineer explained that the lift necessary to keep 800,000 pounds airborne is generated by the vacuum on the top of the wing, and the 747 wing was thickest at its inboard end. Anything less would peel open, he explained.

Jack Waddell, 747 Project Pilot

Seasoned and affable test pilot Jack Waddell was appointed project test pilot for the 747 program. A tall fellow with a bald pate and perpetual smile on his face, Jack went beyond the traditional role of overseeing cockpit design and flight-handling characteristics. Even as Joe Sutter and his talented crew of engineers set about to firm up every bit of the structure, plus mechanical, electrical, propulsion, and hydraulic systems, Jack was reaching out to the pilots at committed airlines and other operators likely to become customers. The worldwide demand for 707 and 727 aircraft was impressive, but international sales would be even more vital to the sustained success of model 747.

Two things were done when airline pilots expressed concerns about the ability to steer the 747 around existing airfields. A test truck with an elevated cockpit simulator was fabricated and tested in October 1967 (in a seasonal jack-o'-lantern motif). Second, the aft pair of main-body landing gear pivot opposite the nose gear, thus enabling sharper taxi turns.

It was only a decade prior when the major airports of the world were forced to rebuild themselves to handle 707 and DC-8 sized aircraft. At great expense, runways and taxiways were widened, lengthened, and strengthened to handle the heavy jets. Taxpayers and airport commissioners had no appetite for a repeat. Bottom-line requirement: the 747 must operate from existing commercial airports without rebuilding them.

The airlines were expected to purchase and provide their own larger tow tractors, airstairs, and other ground-handling equipment; however, at roughly three stories above the tarmac, some pilots were alarmed at taxiing the behemoth from such a lofty perch. So, in 1967, Jack Waddell had a truck modified to carry a simulated 747 cockpit high above the flight line. Various airline pilots were invited to take control, with Waddell observing. No problems were encountered; therefore, another "concern" was addressed and stricken from the list. Other airport officials were worried about jammed-up parking lots, delays in customs, and baggage claim snarls. These issues also ultimately worked themselves out.

Jack stated the need for a control tower for use by an Everett-based Boeing radio operator. Such a facility had long existed atop the 3-390 building (B-52 hangar) in Seattle. Budget was committed to build a similar structure atop the roof of the 747 factory, where it remains in service to this day.

The first 747 flight found Boeing pilot Jack Waddell at the controls. The flight test mechanics had their own ratings of the various test pilots. The 747 was designed to be simple to fly. Waddell was considered excellent at smooth talk, charm, and marketing rhetoric, but rather average as a pilot—or (in their view) perfectly matched to demonstrate the easy-to-fly attributes of the 747. Rumor has it that Waddell pocketed for himself a cash bonus big enough to buy a retirement ranch in Montana.

When it came time to paint the first 747, the following was stipulated: The paint scheme was white with accent marks of red. The bare metal below the exit doors was polished. The name "Boeing 747" appears high and forward on each side of the fuselage. The aircraft was named "City of Everett," and that was painted lower on the forward fuselage, but nobody called it "City of Everett." When on the ground, it was always referred to by its manufacturing (also called "drawing tab") designator: RA001 (pronounced "R-A-One"). This moniker was painted on the nose landing-gear doors. Whenever in motion or aloft, radio call sign "Boeing-four-seven-zero-heavy" was utilized for communications between pilots and air traffic control. It was derived from the registration number "N7470" painted on the empennage ("N747" had previously been randomly applied to a small business jet once owned by Union Pacific Railroad). The word "EXPERIMENTAL" was stenciled above the forward cabin doors. This was a reminder to all that the airplane was not certified for commercial use.

Finally, the names of the flight crew who first took RA001 aloft were later inscribed below the cockpit windows. They are Jack Waddell, pilot in command; Brien Wygle, copilot (and vice president of Flight Operations); and Jesse Wallick, flight engineer.

The general goal when building military aircraft is to make them all identical. This simplifies manufacturing; however, commercial airplanes of various types, and destined for various airlines, most often travel the assembly line adjacent to each other. Various 747 options over the years include freighters (without passenger windows), nose loaders, side loaders, and a short version called the 747SP. Fuel capacity varied by configuration, but 47,000 gallons (US) of standard-grade kerosene (Jet-A) was typical.

RA001 bears that same designation in retirement at Seattle's Museum of Flight. It was "borrowed" back from the museum in the 1990s to test out the powerful jet engines that propel the model 777 twin-engine wide-body aircraft.

The early 747s, in general, had fewer problems than the smaller 737. An exception was the initial batch of JT9D engines. As first delivered from Pratt & Whitney, their performance proved to be unreliable and inconsistent. One engine locked up with such force while running on the ground that the engine pylon was bent. Surging (sometimes emitting a "bang" like an automobile backfire) was but one of the vexing problems. Late engine delivery and rework yielded a bevy of 747s parked outside the Everett factory bearing chunks of concrete hung from their engine struts (some cynics sarcastically called the concrete "solid state" engines). The deadweight kept the wing spars properly stressed while simultaneously reducing the risk of an errant windstorm upsetting the otherwise empty airframes.

The relationship with Pratt soured. The rules of "Industrial Age chivalry" chafed as distrust between buyer and seller mounted; however, the partnership continued out of necessity because without engines, there was no airplane. Technical improvements were made, engine performance became more consistent, and the situation crept back toward normalcy in time for the 747 to enter service. Henceforth, Boeing vowed that future aircraft designs would offer engines from multiple sources. There would be dialogue with engine builders Rolls-Royce, General Electric, and anybody else who came forward.

Many "first" aircraft never enter airline service because of the extreme rigors deliberately inflicted by flight testing. As compared to their peers, they get rough treatment, are subjected to greater stresses, and often carry extra weight or special modifications. For instance, RA001 was equipped with a bailout chute with an entrance on the upper deck and exit on the bottom of the fuselage.

Engineering and manufacturing improvement come rapidly as the assembly process speeds up. The long-accepted concept of building subsequent airplanes quicker and better is called "learning curve."

A three-day cycle yields seven airplanes per month. This has been the maximum 747 production rate for half a century. In fact, maximum rate has seldom been achieved because the demand for the twin-aisle jumbo jet has always been less than the single-aisle Renton-built airplanes. The assembly rate for 747 has often been a single airplane per month—yet,

Two substantial construction cranes working in tandem are required to hang the massive doors, which were later reflected in my rearview mirror. Note the wetness on the concrete floor remaining from the persistent winter rain.

lacking an industry peer for many decades (until the Airbus A380), the "Queen of the Skies" was sold without discount, thus contributing to the profits essential to keep Boeing solvent and new models in the developmental pipeline.

The records of "Scoop" Jackson are housed at the University of Washington Library Special Collections unit. The files imply a paternal interest by Senator Jackson as his office grapples with forgotten issues that now appear trivial. Lacking incoming Soviet bombers to battle, the Air Force instead took aim at their new neighbor settling in at the other end of the 2-mile runway. An aide was assigned to inventory items of dispute and keep the senator updated. Issues included the following:

- operational concerns regarding sharing the airfield with 747-sized aircraft
- damage to airport surfaces by very heavy aircraft on an airfield intended for small, fighter-sized aircraft
- a new road (Airport Way) needed to get quickly built across land occupied by the base's earth-covered munitions storage igloos
- In a strange arrangement, the Airport Commission sold electricity to the base. A disputed $25,000 annual surcharge on the base electric bill was for "rent."

Jackson's staff apparently tended to Air Force concerns while keeping them invisible to Boeing. Meanwhile, the airport commission and city officials kept the flow of municipal permits and requisite plant infrastructure (roads, schools, and utilities) moving forward at breakneck speed. Maybe Bill Allen was truly clairvoyant and had selected the "best" site after all—as measured by supportive people rather than uncooperative topography and lack of adequate surface streets.

Investment Tax Credits (ITC)

Investment tax credits are monetary incentives conceived in Congress to influence the behavior of corporations who pay federal taxes. Subject to judicial review, it is the Internal Revenue Service that interprets and enforces such regulations. Like the Facilities Department at Boeing, the Finance Department is broken down into many subfunctions. They include cost accountants, estimators, pricing, internal auditors, financial accountants, and taxation specialists—who are frequently CPAs or lawyers (or both).

The topic at hand was "Investment Tax Credit" (or ITC), and factory machinery qualified for this tax provision. Boeing factories contain overhead cranes, elevators, and the industrial-sized mechanisms to open and close the massive hangar doors. The finance people sought me out to help determine what percentage of factory cost would qualify for ITC. They were inclined to go with 30 percent. I countered, "100 percent"—which resonated to most accountants as beyond the intent of ITC.

"The foundation provides needed structural stability, the walls hold up the cranes and elevator shafts, and the roof is needed to keep the circuit breakers and electric motors dry," I asserted.

The tax people are aggressive when going after every feasible tax break; however, the potential for fines, censure, or some form of criminal fraud invokes caution if there is any risk of overstepping professional norms.

On this day, I made the daily drive to Everett and headed to my shared executive suite with Bayne Lamb for an 8:30 a.m. encounter with visitors. The appraisers were from Chicago, a team of independent professionals with the initials MAI on their business cards, meaning each was a certified member of the Appraisal Institute. They were led by a vice president from the American Appraisal Company, hired by Boeing controller Vic Knudsen to render a decision on whether the factory was a building or a machine.

Boeing seldom goes to the mat over mundane accounting matters, but if the issue involves significant dollars or precedent, they strive to be fully girded for battle with the highest caliber of professional opinion. Up to $6 million was at stake. Boeing would get a mere $2 million of tax credits if they counted only the moving parts of the machinery, but if the whole building qualified as a machine, Boeing would qualify for $8 million—a $6 million swing.

When they filed into the conference room first thing that morning, escorted by several Boeing accountants, I knew they were prepared for a technical analysis about the structure and the crane system. Instead, I broadsided them with a high-level board-of-directors style presentation—the same flip charts I'd used five years before.

A 747 indoors only looks small because the factory was designed for aircraft twice as large. Hangar doors, nearly the size of a football field, are adorned with oversized schedules. RA001 appears eager to leave its nest. This jumbo-sized historic artifact is now displayed at Seattle's Museum of Flight.

The factory assembly rate of seven 747 aircraft per month has never been exceeded during the first fifty years of 747 production. Lack of a competing peer airliner for several decades ensured the 747 was profitable—even in low-rate production.

My presentation began with the sixty-year history of aircraft size and weight, from the Wright Brothers in 1903 to the proposed 747 in 1965, and it showed projections forty years into the future, to the year 2000—thus spanning a century. Then the world commercial aircraft market was shown—beginning in the 1920s, to the prop-driven airliners of the 1950s, to the jet age of the 1960s, with long-range projections showing more growth extending through 1999.

Merging the two forecasts called for a factory of great physical size and strength to build huge aircraft—and a lot of factory space to satisfy a market clamoring for so many of the winged giants. I showed how the factory was a de facto huge machine that avoided the disorderly conglomeration of structures plaguing every other aircraft plant in the world—including Boeing operations elsewhere. My parting words to the appraisers were "This factory is a machine, a machine where twenty thousand workers gather to assemble the world's largest airliner."

"Take 'em into the catwalks first," I told Jim Laws, our construction engineer. Then as the group was leaving the conference room, I smiled and commented to the newcomers, "Don't be concerned; it's safe. There are elevators in several places, and the weather's quite nice up there."

Catwalks were the best place to get a bird's-eye view, and we had 2 miles of them spun in giant webs 90 feet above the production lines. What they would not see is HVAC (heating, ventilation, and air-conditioning) equipment. Puget Sound enjoys a mild climate. During winter, the big factory doors are kept closed, and the heat generated by lights, machinery, and people is adequate to maintain a shirtsleeve working environment. During summer, the big doors are cracked open and cooling breezes coming off the chilly waters of Puget Sound keep the work spaces comfortable.

I knew the MAI appraisers would spend the next month poring over design drawings and cost allocations, and I wanted to get them started in the right direction with enthusiasm for building airplanes.

Tie a Ribbon around It

Resurrecting my own enthusiasm, even for an hour, had been exhausting. My smoothness and patience had been used up, and my back ached when I walked into Bayne Lamb's office a few minutes later. "What's this I hear about a holdup on the perimeter road?" I asked. "The weather's getting better and we're ready to go."

"There's no budget for it," said Lamb, as he reached for a paper on his desk. "I've just signed this facility request. It'll go into the next capital budget."

"That'll delay it for a year," I protested. "And the way things are going, headquarters is rejecting everything. Hell, it might even wait for five years. There'll be a thousand workers in the new Interiors Building on the north side, and they'll have to walk almost a mile in mud, rain, and wind. A perimeter road lets them park in the construction yard that we paved two years ago. That place needs a road to provide employee access."

Bayne Lamb was director of facilities at the Everett branch. He was fast building an organization of about a thousand people to maintain the plant, run its massive crane system, sweep the floors, empty the wastebaskets, and do everything else necessary to keep the lights on and the plant running. His thousand people were about 5 percent of the total transferred or hired to build the 747. The total site workforce was over twenty thousand, roughly divided into fourteen thousand aircraft mechanics and other hourly craft people plus six thousand engineers and other while-collar salaried workers. In addition, many services were provided by contractors. Their employees ranged from cafeteria workers and telephone installers to photocopy machine servicemen.

I had been director of facilities planning and construction for the entire Commercial Airplane Division. Lamb reported to me three years earlier, and I convinced 747 project general manager Malcolm Stamper that Lamb was the right person for the job. The choice had worked well, and for the past three years we worked as a team under the general proposition that Andrew builds it, Lamb fills it. Lamb worked full time at Everett. I spent mornings there and the remainder of each day overseeing planning and construction at the other three Commercial Airplanes factories. Now, with construction completed at Everett, I had turned the keys over to Lamb.

"Good god, Lamb," I continued "Anyone with any sense should know that a plant needs a road around it. It was in the capital budget three years ago because I wrote the damn budget. It wasn't shown on the drawings because we had no idea where the land clearing and earthwork would end. Now we know."

"Yeah, I know that," said Lamb. "But the accountants didn't know it when they capitalized all new construction and set up the depreciation accounts two months ago. The window of opportunity closed. Now it must be a new capital request because the cost estimate is $90,000, and headquarters approves all items above $10,000. We'll have to defer the road and put it in the next capital budget."

"Go ahead and put it in the budget," I retorted. "The road will be there when the bean counters at headquarters review the capital budget six months from now. We're tearing out two temporary rail spurs and ripping up the asphalt in the construction roads. Just allocate that material to the perimeter road. A capital budget number is not needed for a reallocation. In fact, I'm going to tell the guys to issue a change order today for the perimeter road."

"Damn it, John, you know you can't do that!" protested Lamb. "If you relocate the same road it's an expense charge, but if you build a completely different road, it's a new capital budget item. A perimeter roadway out around the plant, outside the security fence line, looks like a brand-new road to me, and it will look like that to headquarters, and to everyone else."

"Just keep quiet," I said. "If anyone asks questions, just say, 'Ask John Andrew'; I'll plead an engineer's ignorance of the finer nuances of accounting policy."

"That'll make my life easier," said Lamb. He knew that Mal Stamper would complain every day he saw interiors workers walking almost a mile in rain and wind, and that would be every day from September to May. I also knew Lamb was in a vise, trapped between corporate bureaucracy and a boss who didn't care. Breaking rules had been my job for three years. That's why the completed 747 assembly plant sat there properly designed, ahead of schedule, and under budget.

I stepped into my former Everett office and summoned Earl Bowden, the on-site facilities construction planning manager. Earl was an expert in factory production, workflow, and plant layout and was one of my stalwarts. He'd laid out the first 747 factory plan when it was still a double-deck airplane in 1965, when he struggled to fit it into Renton.

When the site was committed to Everett in January 1966, Bowden had established the production lines for the single-deck version. That's when the 747 and our hypothetical "factory of the future" suddenly coalesced. The "yardstick" was perfectly suited for assembly of subsequent wide-body aircraft (767, 777, and 787), when they ultimately arrived.

"Get the damn perimeter road going today," I told Bowden. "Issue a change order to the Austin Company. Tell them to use existing railroad ballast and recycled asphalt. Make sure they do it that way, and make sure that every invoice mentions relocating and recycling."

"It'll probably cost less than $90,000 doing it that way," said Earl with a laugh. "Everything's mobilized. The scrapers, dozers, loaders, and trucks remain on the site and are ready to go."

When Earl left my office, it was almost 11:00 a.m. At age thirty-seven, I felt like an elderly grandfather. The lingering effects of adult-onset polio, marital woes, rearing children by myself, and a decade of constant workplace stress combined to take their toll on my emaciated body. Three hours at Everett had worn me out. My back was killing me. God, it hurt. In the privacy of my office, I cinched a second leather belt a notch tighter. Hidden by my suit, and cinched as tight as possible, it helped me endure pain, stand straight, and walk past two hundred people sitting outside my office, and then limp downstairs without drawing attention. I struggled when climbing into my crew-cab pickup truck. It had been so much easier at 6:45 that morning.

747-200B MAKE OR BUY

AERONCA
AUBURN
BOEING, CANADA/WINNIPEG*
BOEING, PORTLAND
CLEVELAND PNEUMATIC
EVERETT
FUJI, JAPAN**
HAWKER de HAVILLAND, AUSTRALIA**
HEATH TECHNA
KAWASAKI, JAPAN**
MITSUBISHI, JAPAN**
NORTHROP
PRATT & WHITNEY
GENERAL ELECTRIC
ROLLS ROYCE
ROCKWELL INTERNATIONAL
ROHR INDUSTRIES
WICHITA
BRITISH AEROSPACE/EVERETT
SHORT BROS & HARLAND
SIERRACIN
PPG INDUSTRIES
TRIPLEX (PRIME)
VERTOL
VOUGHT SYSTEMS
WICHITA

*WING/BODY FAIRING AT NORTHROP PRIOR
TO C/L 702
**WING FLIGHT CONTROLS AT FAIRCHILD
PRIOR TO C/L 702   June, 1986

Engineers were working on the next bundle of enhancements (dubbed 747-200) even as the earliest versions (designated 747-100) were being built, flight tested, certified, and delivered. The improvements delivered longer range, greater passenger comfort, less airport noise, more engine options, and better fuel efficiency. An updated "make or buy" chart helps visualize the source of major components.

CHAPTER 18
The Rearview Mirror

I rested my right arm over the back of the front seat, thereby taking weight off my lower back, waved at the smartly uniformed Boeing security guard wearing a revolver on his hip, drove out the gate, and headed south from the 747 assembly plant.

I'd done enough at Everett that morning. There were other tasks waiting at my new job. My biggest obligation on that day was family. I would get home early, bake a casserole, and attend an important family evening event—the annual February Blue & Gold Cub Scout banquet for our young son, Jim.

After driving for a mile, I glanced at the large, rectangular rearview mirror bolted to the driver's door. The mirror perfectly framed the building with its three main doors, each the length of a football field. The vision was so jarring that I pulled to the shoulder of the road and stopped.

My work on the plans began in 1962, when I was asked to develop concepts for "Plant X," a hypothetical aircraft factory of the future. "Design it for forty years, to the year 2000 and beyond," I'd been told. By 1963, I had scale models of a dream factory. During the following year, executives from every corner of Boeing, as well as hundreds of lower-level managers, visited the planning room and shared their own thoughts and dreams while making suggestions.

Under the visionary guidance of Erle Barnes, the plant was designed for a mythical airplane of 2 million pounds, with 250-foot wingspan and a tail rising 80 feet. No such aircraft has ever been built. Nor did anyone think such a factory, with everything under one roof, would ever be built—but it was fun to dream. Then, in December 1965, when the 747 suddenly came along, I was told to order steel, build the thing, and build it fast. The 747 would easily fit into a factory designed for an airplane over twice as large—an airplane that Boeing has yet to build. But the trends were pointing that way.

Now, in February 1969, with the first 747 flying and production starting to roll, everyone in the world thought the new factory was custom built for only the 747. Over twenty thousand "Incredibles" moved in and claimed the place as their own.

Everything about the Boeing Everett complex is "big." The assembly bays were built large enough to host an airplane larger than the 747. So far, Boeing has never needed that capability. Meanwhile, the area covered by the main factory building roof is over 100 acres. There is an underground theater plus long and straight utility tunnels beneath the factory floor, which provide recreational running space with neither vehicular traffic nor inclement weather. This undated (ca. 1973) archival description was written by the Everett Facilities Department:

The Everett facility represents an aerospace capability unmatched in the world today. In the original planning of the site, a master plan was developed which allows an orderly growth of the facility to more than twice its original size. In the initial construction, all major utilities (electrical, communication, sewers, gas, water, and fire protection) were sized and installed for the ultimate site development. The main source of process and comfort heat for the site is furnished by one electric fired boiler and three multiple fuel fired boilers, each capable of being fired on natural gas, oil, or jet fuel. The electrical system was designed with dual feeders from the main substation to the building substations to assure [sic] continued operation in the event of a feeder failure. The fire and domestic water systems are installed in a loop system with sectional valves in case of a pipe failure.

The plant is laid out with production flow in mind, with the support functions adjacent and surrounding the assembly bays. A typical assembly bay provides a clear span area 300' wide by 1,000' long by 87' high. The south face of the bay has a 300' wide by 81' high door system. The area is equipped with below grade trench systems that provide a full complement of utilities including power, plant air, water, and vacuum. The bay has automatic fire sprinklers, ADT alarm system, and a lighting system that provides 100-foot candles at working levels. Adjacent to the open bay area are 50' wide support towers that provide building structural integrity. These towers are multifloored and provide area for personnel services, offices, stores, and electrical/mechanical building system.

The entire main assembly building totaling 2.5 million square feet is covered by nineteen thirty-four-ton cab type hoists capable of traveling to any point in the building on thirty-three underslung bridges which are interconnected by transfer bridges between building bays. Auxiliary floor mounted bridges are positioned over all sub and major assembly tools. All movement of assemblies is computer programmed. Conveyor systems move miscellaneous materials internally within shops. The entire plant is programmed for the least amount of handling to provide production efficiency.

The buildings at the Everett site are designed to be energy efficient with full insulation, low energy lighting systems, flexible lighting controls and energy efficient mechanical systems.

The electrical and water supply to the site is fed from two sources to assure [sic] uninterrupted operation of the site. Natural gas is the only utility that is from a single source, however, we have ample supply of oil and propane to maintain operations for a period of thirty days. Utility service costs at the Everett site are equal to or lower than anywhere else in the nation. The site has full data communications with other Boeing sites by microwave to preclude the loss of information in the event of a telephone line interruption. The site is adjacent to the Snohomish County airport (Paine Field) and is also served by the [BNSF] railroad and major interstate highways.

I realized that I'd made my last big push at Everett. The plant was complete, being accurately appraised, and the ribbon around the package would be a proper perimeter road. I occupied not only a front row seat but also a unique position to advocate for enduring choices regarding property, plant, and equipment. The obligation and duty of the last seven years was finally discharged. Like a home builder, it was time for the new occupants to settle in, and it was best for me to vacate the premises.

Editors from the *Guinness Book of World Records* took note, and their next edition posted a new record for building volume: 210 million cubic feet, eclipsing by nearly twice the old record holder, NASA's Vertical Assembly Building in Florida, built four years prior for Saturn V moon rocket assembly. I knew that someday the Everett buildings would grow even larger. My mirrors reflected only its first phase. Second and third phases of logical growth would make it as much as three times larger, because it was planned for expansion into the twenty-first century.

A wide-angle shot was needed to see the entire building, so I looked in my right mirror and burned that image into my memory also. I observed the building's west wing, the extension for fuel tank sealing with the Boeing radio control tower perched on top, the new paint hangar, and the second 747 (destined for Pan American World Airways) parked in a fueling position, being readied for flight.

Its older sibling, the first 747 (RA001), had lifted off for the first time twelve days earlier—on February 9, 1969. The first flight was a complete success, and the new age of commercial aviation was underway. Other big airplanes followed, but none of them have ever inspired the awe of the 747 in its infancy.

Ecstatic first-flight observers included (*left to right*) chairman of the board Bill Allen, director of facilities Bayne Lamb, chief engineer Joe Sutter, an unknown person, and division vice president Mal Stamper (*with binoculars*).

These three smiling men are (*left to right*) Malcolm Stamper, T. A. Wilson, and Ernest "Tex" Boullioun. Handpicked in the waning years of William M. "Bill" Allen's twenty-three-year reign, they became Boeing's executive leadership upon Allen's retirement in 1968.

The freighter version of the 747 debuted with a swing-up nose (like a C-5A Galaxy), yielding a gaping maw able to ingest and expel tons of cargo. Note Jack Waddell's control tower atop the hangar.

How fitting it was to see the factory building in my rearview. After the images were burned deep into my soul, I just closed my eyes and sat there for several minutes parked on the shoulder of Airport Way. The better part of my career is in that building, and now it's behind me. The view was due north along Everett's Airport Way, which, if extended, would run directly into the building. The big doors seemed to be looking back at me with eyes of innocence, like an animal that has no concept of what it's done wrong.

Soon those big factory doors would disgorge a new jumbo jet every three working days. The physical plant, my former responsibility, was doing its job and performing flawlessly. Less than three years before, in May 1966, when we broke ground, my budget was $110 million for the main factory building and another $45 million for offices, warehouses, hangars, and flight test aircraft parking stalls. By 1969, I was about the only person on the 747 Program, or the Commercial Airplane Division, of the Boeing Company—for that matter—who had any money left in his budget. I had $5 million left over, and we had built the biggest building in the world in record time, ahead of schedule.

Malcolm Stamper, the vice president in charge of the 747 program, quite publicly took credit for the underrun because he included the plant budget as part of the overall project cost. It gave him an island of fiscal sanity in an otherwise sea of red ink. Accountants assigned to 747 were internally admitting to a $2.0 billion loss on the first two hundred aircraft, and I knew that project-cost accountants close to the situation privately estimated it might go as high as $2.6 billion.

For me, as a thirty-seven-year-old civil engineer at the time, the delivery of the biggest building in the world ahead of schedule and under budget was a major achievement and matter of personal pride. But all I saw personally in the mirrors was a seductive monster that mesmerized me over the past seven years.

Life's Challenges

My back hurt, and my life was a wreck. My assignment at Commercial Airplanes was complete, and it was time to get back to normalcy. My lifetime path ahead held both challenge and reward, but it would never take me back to the excitement of commercial airplanes. The new assignment was working for another of the great men of Boeing—Richard "Dick" Taylor—as director of facilities for Military Airplane Systems Division.

In 1972, I became president of Boeing Environmental Products Company, which pioneered zero-discharge water treatment worldwide under the name Resources Conservation Company. In 1984, Boeing sold the subsidiary to what is now Trans Ocean, and then I sold the subsidiary to Haliburton Company in 1991.

Pan American was the kickoff customer for both the 707 and 747. Lacking domestic feeder flights, the once-pathfinding airline found itself hobbled with only unprofitable international routes and did not survive airline deregulation.

Epilogue

John Andrew retired in 1991, or thirty-five years after hiring. Mr. Andrew states that his greatest lifetime accomplishment was rapid construction of the Thompson site (14-01 building) because it thwarted the move of 737 to Wichita—thus preserving BCA "critical mass" in Seattle. Second was the great factory complex at Everett, and third was the Renton factories (numbered 4-81 and 4-82) with the innovation of doors on both ends.

The appraisal arrived in due course. The Appraisal Institute decided that the Boeing Everett 747 factory was 85 percent machine; therefore, the Boeing tax accountants claimed the preponderance of factory cost as a tax credit.

Following the lead of Pan American, other airlines committed to take delivery of 747s. Unlike the late 1950s, this time there was no direct or immediate competition. In a counter-intuitive move, Trippe encouraged sale of 747 aircraft to various foreign-flag carriers, including Alitalia, Air France, British Airways, Japan Airlines, and Lufthansa. This would ensure that the Pan Am wide-body fleet would not be locked out of strategic international airports over contrived barriers: allegations the 747 was too big, too noisy, or otherwise too disruptive.

Bad financial news began emerging after the first flight of the 747 in February 1969. Airline traffic, as measured in revenue seat miles, suffered a downturn by coming in well under growth expectations. Domestic airlines such as American, Braniff, Continental, Delta, and Eastern ordered 747s but found them oversized for domestic routes. The demand for new 747s was further depressed when these were offered for resale.

At the same time, inflationary pressures on fuel and labor caused airline-operating costs to soar. Profits nosedived as airlines encountered financial turbulence. Orders for new airliners

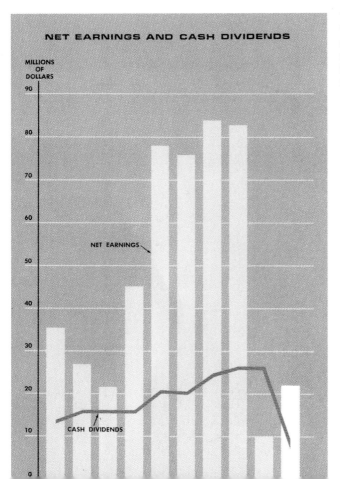

This chart from the Boeing 1970 Annual Report shows the drastic reduction in profits and dividends, thus triggering the draconian layoffs of that era.

Why Was the Boeing SST Never Built?

The Boeing Supersonic Transport (SST—model 2707) was defunded in the US Senate on March 24, 1971, at the hands of Wisconsin's William Proxmire. Neither competing Russian nor European SSTs ever achieved commercial success. *Courtesy of Wisconsin State Historical Society, WHS 58409*

At least one US senator was outside Bill Allen's circle of political friends. William Proxmire from the distant state of Wisconsin was a crusading maverick whose "golden fleece" awards lampooned wasteful government spending. Proxmire led the political crusade focused on elimination of federal funding for the supersonic transport (SST).

Milestone: The decisive US Senate Supersonic Transport (SST) vote came on March 24, 1971, effectively killing the project.

After years of study, the SST was abandoned in the mockup stage—before the design was finalized. The concerns were economic (i.e., too expensive) and environmental (sonic boom combined with excessive fuel consumption, yielding air pollution at all altitudes). Residents of Washington State, unhappy with a political defeat, staged a boycott of Wisconsin dairy products—but it was to no avail.

William E. Boeing and his handpicked cadre (P. G. Johnson, Egtvedt, and Bill Allen) nurtured and grew the company for its first fifty-two years from 1916 to 1968. The brilliant product choices of Bill Allen (including models 737 and 747) laid the foundation for another fifty years of prosperity benefiting all stakeholders—including shareholders, employees, customers, government, and air travelers worldwide.

Hard Times in Seattle

Seattle folklore is rife with tales of the huge layoffs at Boeing. Tough times spread throughout the community when home values tumbled. Stories abounded of displaced aerospace engineers eking out a living by driving a taxicab, house keys surrendered at the mortgage company front desk, or the iconic billboard that said, "Will the last person leaving Seattle—Turn out the lights." It was a close call. Disaster, in the form of a Boeing bankruptcy, was narrowly averted. Unlike Lockheed, General Motors, or Chrysler, no federal bailout was needed.

As springtime follows winter, the air traffic slump ultimately subsided. Airline volumes both for freight and passengers resumed their normal upward climb. The "critical mass" consisting of massive new buildings, a seasoned workforce, advanced equipment, and a loyal worldwide customer base were all locked into place. Inevitably, new airliner orders arrived along with fresh military business, some of which relied on commercial airframes.

Career opportunities at Boeing continue to evolve over the span of a century—but only for those willing to embrace change. Wood and fabric were initially replaced by metal. Some metal parts were later superseded by composite parts baked in an autoclave. Jet engines displaced piston power. Straight wings were phased out with the advent of swept wings. Ever smaller (but more-powerful) computers crept into the shops and offices. Advanced electronics first made their way into the cockpit and then into airborne entertainment systems, as computer chips were embedded into each passenger seat back.

In a company prone to nepotism, a mill-town family-friendly tradition lingers. With the passage of the decades, many sons and daughters joined their parents at Boeing. In some instances, three generations of the same family were simultaneously in the workplace—and then, as the years passed, the youngsters wished their elders a happy retirement when it was time for toolboxes to be closed for the last time.

As measured by gross weight and seating capacity, the Boeing family of jetliners was bounded for over a half century by two enduring bookends—the 747, as "Queen of the Skies," held the high end, while the workaday 737 remained the "Baby Boeing," even as other models, sized between the two icons, came and went.

Their shared vision of a giant luxury airliner has been achieved. Bill Allen prepares to warmly greet Juan Trippe (*unseen*) at the World Press Tour on December 2, 1969. Marketing events are carefully scripted; however, the emotions evoked were profoundly genuine.

Maps

Maps depict the buildings as they were in 1984. Site maps help employees navigate to meeting rooms and other workplace locations. Utilizing a consistent numbering scheme, every Boeing building (whether owned or leased) has clearly labeled floors, columns, and doors.

Puget Sound Region

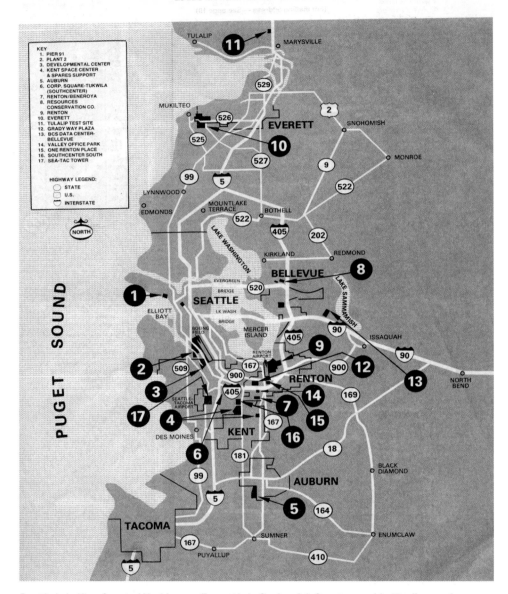

Seattle is in King County, Washington. Everett is in Snohomish County, roughly 40 miles north. Tacoma, about 40 miles south of Seattle, is in Pierce County.

Plant 2

7755 East Marginal Way So., Seattle, Wa. 98108

(For mailing address — See page 19)

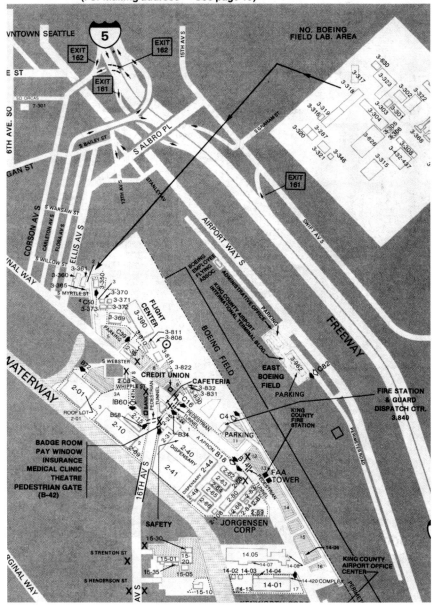

Seattle

Renton

8th & Logan Ave. No., Renton, Wa. 98055

(For mailing address — See page 19)

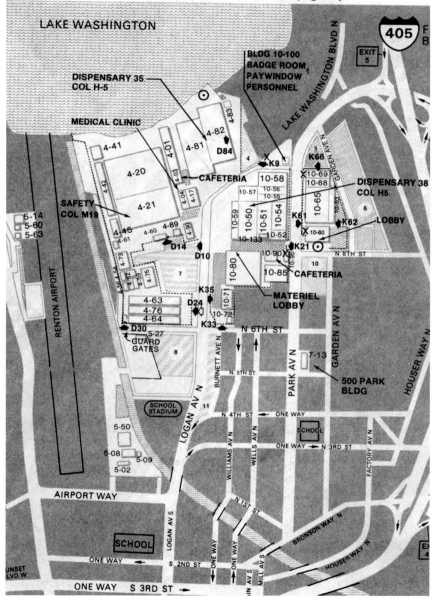

Renton

Everett

3003 West Casino Road, Everett, Wa. 98203

(For mailing address — See page 19)

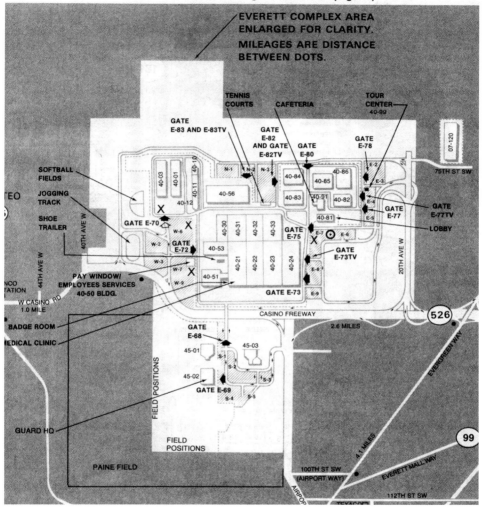

Everett

Endnotes

Chapter 2

1. Out of military necessity and patriotism, a surge of women joined the industrial workforce during World War II. Many departed to tend to their young families during the postwar baby boom. Those who remained paved the way for the generations of women who followed them into the factory, offices, and the executive suites.
2. By the mid-1980s, most of the "Greatest Generation" was at retirement age.
3. William Allen was appointed partner in the law firm of Todd, Holman, Sprague & Allen in 1939. That firm evolved into Perkins Coie, which continues to serve Boeing and currently employs a thousand lawyers.
4. This enduring quote of Mr. Boeing was regularly reiterated for decades at employee training sessions: "I've tried to make the men around me feel, as I do, that we are embarked as pioneers upon a new science and industry in which our problems are so new and unusual that it behooves no one to dismiss any novel idea with the statement that 'It can't be done.' Our job is to keep everlastingly at research and experiment, to adapt our laboratories to production as soon as practicable, and to let no improvement in flying and flying equipment pass us by."

Chapter 5

1. The Dash 80 served as a flight test workhorse until its retirement from daily service in 1969. Its service history spanned fifteen years, 1,691 flights, and 2,350 hours aloft. It now reposes at the Smithsonian's Udvar-Hazy Center at Dulles Airport as one of the dozen most-significant airplanes of all time.
2. The 1967 Boeing Annual Report (p. 7) states a top cruising speed of 620 mph for the turbofan-equipped model 720B.
3. The sole XB-15 spent the war as a transport. By 1945, it had earned the name of "Gramps." Worn out, it finally broke down for the last time while in the Panama Canal Zone, where it was scrapped in place.
4. Only one Sea Ranger was completed and test flown, thus earning for it the informal name of "Lone Ranger."

Chapter 7

1. An antitrust pall still pervaded Boeing in the wake of the Air Mail Act of 1934 and the breakup of the company, but Boeing leadership persisted in their quest for ever more market share.

2. What did the future hold for the Austin Company? The partnership was purchased by National Gypsum, a firm financially wounded by asbestos litigation. The Austin Company is now a small shadow of its former self, surviving as a subsidiary of Kajima USA.

Chapter 10

1. In 2020, the 14-01 building at the Thompson site hosts installation of military mission equipment in Navy P-8 Poseidon aircraft. The 737-inspired airframe performs maritime surveillance missions.
2. Commercial operations at Wichita were divested to Spirit AeroSystems in 2006. The BNSF railroad continues to deliver Spirit-built 737 fuselages to Renton.
3. Gordon Link quietly disappeared from corporate offices after this meeting.
4. The only things that a model 737 of 1967 has in common with a modern 737 are pedigree, general configuration, and model number. Several major upgrades have yielded the modern 737, a workhorse that handles the routes and payloads formerly the domain of model 707 or 727.

Chapter 12

1. The story of Tex Johnston barrel-rolling the Dash 80 was adapted from Robert J. Sterling, *Legend & Legacy: The Story of Boeing and Its People* (New York: St. Martin's, 1992).

Chapter 13

1. Two factors prevent making the revenue-per-square-foot computations today: annual reports no longer offer the simple and reliable data. In addition, inflation (difficult to predict) skews the purchasing power of a dollar.
2. Well, nobody gets every forecast correct. Who could anticipate that models 737 and 747 (with major overhauls and engineering upgrades) would stay in production for over fifty years?

Chapter 14

1. Boeing World Headquarters was relocated from Seattle and opened in Chicago on September 9, 2001. The Boeing offices occupy the upper floors of a thirty-six-story building on Canal Street. The boardroom portrait of company founder William E. Boeing was left behind.

Chapter 15

1. Japanese people segregated themselves by establishing their own secluded settlement in the gulch. The most credible account is that the expatriates (ca. 1900) performed acceptance inspection on custom-milled woodwork being exported to Japan from the Port of Everett.

Sources

Allen, William. Working papers residing in Boeing Historical Archives.

Boeing Annual Reports, 1967 and 1970.

Boeing Logbook. Created by the Boeing Company to commemorate its 75th anniversary on July 15, 1991.

Cook, William H. *The Road to the 707*. Bellevue, WA: TYC, 1991.

Fredrickson, John. *Boeing*. Mt. Pleasant, SC: Arcadia, 2016.

Fredrickson, John. *North American Aviation in the Jet Age*. Atglen, PA: Schiffer, 2019.

Jackson, Henry "Scoop" (US senator). Working papers residing in University of Washington Library (Special Collections).

Mansfield, Harold. *Vision*: *A Saga of the Sky*. 2nd ed. New York: Madison, 1986. Originally published in 1956 (New York: Duell, Sloan, and Pearce).

Serling, Robert J. *Legend & Legacy*: *The Story of Boeing and Its People*. New York: St. Martin's, 1992.

Sutter, Joseph. *747*: *Creating the World's First Jumbo Jet*. New York: HarperCollins, 2007.

Index